HUMOR IN THE

AMERICAN PULPIT

HUMOR IN THE

AMERICAN PULPIT

FROM GEORGE WHITEFIELD THROUGH HENRY WARD BEECHER

BY

DOUG ADAMS

A prominent divine of another denomination, meaning to be slightly sarcastic, once said to my old friend, Mr. Cartwright: "How is it that you have no doctors of divinity in your denomination?"

"Our divinity is not sick and don't need doctoring," said the sturdy backwoodsman.

THE SHARING COMPANY
AUSTIN, TEXAS

This book is dedicated with thanks
to my doctoral committee who have
maintained a full sense of humor
through years of higher education:

Harland Hogue
Jane Dillenberger
John Dillenberger
John Bachman
Wayne Rood

Our appreciation is extended to publishers for permis-
sion (received or requested) to reprint the materials:
Discerning the Signs of the Times, c. Harper and Row;
Encyclopedia of Black Folklore and Humor, c. Jonathan
David Publishers;   Folk Laughter on the American
Frontier, c. The Macmillan Company; Modern Revivalism,
c. Ronald Press; New Mexico Village Arts, c. University
of New Mexico Press, The Pulpit Treasury, c. Prentice
Hall; "Research Human Interest & Humorous Stories," c.
The Christian Century; The Teachers of Drew, c. Drew
University; The Word on the Brazos, c. University of
Texas Press.

The cover illustration (from the author's personal
collection) is   "Our National Bird As It Appeared
When Handed To James Buchanan, March 4, 1857," pen
lithograph, M. A. Woolf, artist; T. W. Strong,
publisher. See pages 145-146 for Henry Ward
Beecher's use of it in preaching.

ISBN 0-941500-10-1

TABLE OF CONTENTS

ix

PREFACE

In the concluding passage to "Humor and Faith," Reinhold
Niebuhr summarized his thought on the relationship of
humor and Christian faith:

> Insofar as the sense of humor is a recognition of
> incongruity, it is more profound than any philoso-
> phy which seeks to devour incongruity in reason.
> But the sense of humour remains healthy only when
> it deals with immediate issues and faces the
> obvious and surface irrationalities. It must move
> toward faith or sink into despair when the ultimate
> issues are raised.
> That is why there is laughter in the vestibule of
> the temple, the echo of laughter in the temple
> itself, but only faith and prayer, and no laughter,
> in the holy of holies. 1

Knowing the Christian worship place as a nave and the
Christian worship as an action of liturgy, we may
question whether Niebuhr's static ground of temple
vestibule and holy of holies was adequate to show forth
dynamic relationships of humor and faith. But Niebuhr
raised this relationship to a level for modern theological inquiry; and his essay of 1946 is properly given
a place in the latest collection of more recent essays
by theologians who inquire further into humor and
faith. 2 I seek to forward this inquiry by studying
the dynamics of humor in the Christian Worship of a
particular historic period: "Humor in the American
Pulpit from George Whitefield through Henry Ward Beecher"

---

1. Reinhold Niebuhr, "Humour and Faith," Discerning the
Signs of the Times, (New York: Harper and Row, 1946),
pp. 130-131.
2. M. Conrad Hyers, ed., Holy Laughter: Essays on
Religion in the Comic Perspective, (New York: Seabury
Press, 1969). Hyer's volume gives an indication of
contemporary theological interest in this relationship.
Among essays by Niebuhr and himself, Hyers includes
selections from works by Nathan Scott, Jr., Samuel H.
Miller, Elton Trueblood, Barry Ulanov, Hugo Rahner, and
Wolfgang Zucker.

1

The methodology of this study provides definition to
the terms. The study is based on the sermons of ninety-
one American preachers who were identified by their
contemporaries as using humor in the pulpit. [3]   Wherever possible the identification of specific sermons
as humorous is based on testimony of these same
contemporaries. In other cases the humor of the material
was identified by smiles and laughter which result
from reading the material and which are in keeping
with the ministers' original intentions. The time frame
from Whitefield through Beecher is chosen to coincide
with the configuration of ministers cited as using
humor in the pulpit.

"Pulpit" in the title of this study indicates that the
humor under consideration is that used by the ministers

---

3. A thorough reading of William Sprague's *Annals of
the American Pulpit* I-IX (New York, Robert Carter and
Brothers, 1857-1865) identifies fifty-five ministers
noted for their use of humor in the pulpit. All of
these were active in preaching between the 1740's and
the 1850's. From other sources this list may be supple-
mented to extend the time period to 1900 and the
number of preachers to ninety-one (cf. appendix one)
A few sermons are extant for nearly all these ministers;
and a large number of sermons are available for some of
the more prominent (e.g. Whitefield, Mayhew, Dwight,
Finney, Parker, Moody, Jones, Beecher). Although
limited in number, verbatim sermon reports most faith-
fully preserve the humor. Single and collected sermons
edited by the ministers or others were often published
for their timeless qualities or as memorials to show
ministers' saintly sides : editorial principles which
in their minds mitigated against inclusion of much
humor. Supplementing these sources with remembrances
of humor used in sermons are memoirs by ministers,
biographical notices by others, and reports in newspapers and religious periodicals. Sprague's *Annals*
are a compendium of several thousand letters written
by close friends of the most prominent preachers who
completed their service to American churches by 1860.

in sermons, prayers, and other moments of worship
services. Study of ministerial humor outside of the
worship service is of interest for this study only
insofar as it helps one to understand the use of humor
in the worship. In worship, many of the ministers did
not use what we would recognize as pulpits. And some
of the ministers who were opposed to liquor or tobacco
used unlikely pulpits. In his San Francisco Street
preaching, William Taylor would speak from the top of
a whiskey barrel; for indoor worship on the frontier,
a tobacco barn or tavern as well as a school house
or court house would be used as a place of worship. [4]
Even in prestigious eastern churches such as Henry
Ward Beecher's Plymouth Church, Brooklyn, there was no
pulpit as we think of one. Beecher used a small
undraped table for his notes, ridiculed the use of
pulpits, and humorously handled his congregation's
attempts to drape his table:

> We had almost extinguished the power of the human
> body by our pulpits....When a church was built
> they made a pulpit that was like the socket of a
> candlestick, and put a man in it; and thus entubbed
> he looked down afar upon his congregation to speak
> to them... as through a speaking trumpet, from
> the second story, to one down below....Some of
> the ladies, honourable and precious, waited upon
> me to know if I would not permit a silk screen to
> be drawn across the front of my table, so that my
> legs and feet need not be seen. My reply to them
> was, "I will, on one condition - that whenever I
> make a pastoral call at your houses you will have
> a green silk bag into which I may put my legs."
> If the legs and feet are tolerable in the parlour,
> or in a social room, why are they not tolerable on
> a platform? It takes a whole man to make a man....

4. William Taylor, Seven Years' Street Preaching in
San Francisco, California (New York: Phillips and Hunt,
1856), p. 40; William Milburn, The Lance, Cross, and
Canoe (New York: N. D. Thompson Publishing Co., 1892)
p. 353.

> You shall no longer, when men are obliged to stand
> disclosed before the whole audience, see ministers
> bent over a desk, like a weary horse crooked over
> a hitching block, and preaching first on one leg,
> and then on the other. 5

Any study of humor should take seriously and humorously
E. B. White's warning against analytically defining forms
of humor -- a process which White likened to the dis-
secting of a frog -- a process in which the subject dies.
A straight forward effort to define the different forms
of humor is in most cases based on an assumption of a
dichotomy of mind and body; for instance, "wit" is
applied to that body of material which a person created
with a mind to achieve some other end (such as to cut
down some person or idea) while "humor" is applied to
that body of material which benignly bubbled up out of
the person's body as an end in itself. While Horace
Bushnell used this philosophical distinction, he noted
that no such distinction is possible until we pass into
the subjective state of the person's mind. 7 Standing
in a faith where the word becomes flesh and in a time
when the structure of intentionality is traced beyond
subjectivity into the tacit dimension of the mind-body-
in-the-world, I find it no longer possible to take the

---

5. Henry Ward Beecher, Lectures and Orations N. D. Hillis,
ed., (New York: Fleming Revell Co., 1913) pp. 140-142.

6. E. B. White, "Some Remarks on Humor," The Second Tree
from the Corner, (New York: Harper, 1954). In his
dissertation, Soren Kierkegaard avoided killing his
subject by writing The Concept of Irony ironically, a
strategy which has intrigued and bewildered his readers
ever since but which was overlooked by his examining
committee which insisted on the removal of his many
obvious humorous remarks as unbecoming a serious
academic work. Cf. Capel,(Bloomington: Indiana
University Press, 1971), p. 11.

7. Horace Bushnell, Work and Play, (New York: Chas.
Scribner, 1864), p. 31f. Even Sigmund Freud's distinc-
tion of wit and humor grows out of a mind-body dichotomy
Cf. "Jokes and the Comic" among others in Robert W.
Corrigan's Comedy: Meaning and Form,(Scranton: Chandler
Publishing Company, 1965).

wit-humor dichotomy seriously. [8]   But the nineteenth century use of terms does reveal an intention in the materials.

If one were to use Bushnell's terminology, he would classify most of what follows in this study as wit; for most of the laughter and smiles evoked by the American pulpit during the period was intended as a means to other ends. While this distinction was observed by others, Bushnell's application of terms was not. Terms such as "humor," "wit," "satire," sarcasm," "ridicule," "irony " were applied in fluid ways by most eighteenth and nineteenth century preachers and their contemporaries; and when any careful distinctions were made, "humor" was used where Bushnell used "wit"; and "levity" was used for "humor." [9]   Delineation of the shifting uses of words ("humor," "wit," "satire," etc.) is of interest in this study only insofar (and it is not far) as such delineation aids understanding how and why any of these forms of humor were used in relation to faith. My use of "humor" in this study follows the prevailing nineteenth century usage and thus includes all of the foregoing forms as they were used intentionally by the preachers. In this study, any labeling of sermons as satirical or ironical is based on the application of these terms by the preachers' contemporaries in their discussions of the sermons.

---

8. From the standpoint of Michael Polanyi's achievement in modern epistemology (Cf. Personal Knowledge: Towards a Post-Critical Philosophy, New York: Harper and Row, 1964; and The Tacit Dimension, Garden City : Doubleday & Co., 1966), one may more easily see why attempts in the field of humor to classify new materials according to agreed upon sets of definitions have given way to reliance on highly skilled personal judgment of those in the field: Robert C. Elliott, "The Definition of Satire," Yearbook of Comparative and General Literature, No. 2B (1962) pp. 19-23.

9. Sprague, Annals, passim.

Whatever they labeled these humorous passages, little
of the humor in the sermons was frivolous. Bushnell's
appreciation for the meaningful play of God and man as
a higher quality of humor than the intentional purposeful work of wit is an appreciation shared by many modern
philosophers and theologians but not by many in his own
age.[10] Purposeful use of humor for a particular end
characterized most of the humor in the eighteenth
and nineteenth century pulpits including Bushnell's
own.[11] The purposefulness of the humor is reflected
in chapter one's discussion of the minister's awareness
and use of humor from the tradition of Christian preaching. Although aware of humor from previous periods, the
ministers used that humor sparingly and used much more
frequently the humor developed by their own contemporaries to deal with the particular forces in the church
and culture that competed with ultimate loyalty to the
coming of God's kingdom as they understood it. And
whether they borrowed humor from their predecessors or
contemporaries in the pulpit, they altered the focus of
the humor so that the point had a purpose in dealing
with what they saw as a competition to God and his
purpose in the world.

Although we may appreciate the meaning of the modern
understanding of God as a God of play (and so heave a
sigh of relief that we need no longer attempt to discern
God's purpose in all contemporary historic events), the

---

10. Bushnell, "Work and Play", Work and Play, passim.
Kierkegaard's appreciation of pointless medieval pulpit
humor would come close to Bushnell's appreciation. (Cf.
The Concept of Irony, p. 270ff.) For a modern appreciation of God as a God of play, consult Alan Watts,
Behold the Spirit: A Study in the Necessity of Mystical
Religion, (New York: Pantheon, 1947), pp. 175-181.
11. Bushnell's method of writing out all sermons and then
reading them as written curtailed introduction of the
spontaneous unintended comments that he would have
called "humor".

purposeful humor of the eighteenth and nineteenth century
American ministers witnesses to their firm belief that
God was preeminently a purposeful God of history (whom
we only imperfectly understand but must struggle to
serve). While God may be seen as both a God of purpose
and play, a recent stress on the latter term in theology
may benefit from a remembrance of the former term to
which the materials in this study testify.

The eighteenth and nineteenth century pulpit humor was
intentionally directed by the minister against those
ideas or persons whom he believed threatened the very
souls of his congregation and the soul of the nation
by attracting people's attention to them and away from
God and his service. The majority of twentieth century
American Christians may see little earth shaking in
issues of using an organ in church worship or believing
this or that doctrine; but for these ministers and many
of their listeners, these issues were serious matters
bearing on the life and death of the soul. The resort
to humor in the pulpit to deal with these issues reveals
the very serious and not frivolous nature of the issues
under discussion.

Humor in the American pulpit was heightened during the
eighteenth and nineteenth centuries by the directions of
preaching which we see in two distinct styles or strategies discussed in chapter two. An evangelistic strategy
with its hortatory style aimed at conversion of those
outside the church was exemplified in preaching through
camp meetings on the frontier and protracted meetings in
the cities. A theological strategy (expressed by Timothy
Dwight at Yale and employed within the churches) attacked
detractors from Christianity. Both strategies attempted
to secure the sovereignty of God at the center of the
people's lives and fight the encroachment of a host of
idolatries exorcised in chapters three through five.
And these directions in preaching affect some awareness
and use of the tradition of pulpit humor as noted in
chapter one.

Chapter one explores these preachers' awareness and use of humor from the tradition of the Christian pulpit: the biblical record, church fathers' sermons, as well as the efforts of their eighteenth and nineteenth century contemporaries in Europe and America. The purpose of the first chapter is both to see the background of the minister's awareness and experience of humor which provided him with source material and to understand his purposefulness in using humor which altered the focus of the borrowed materials. The patterns of shared humor point to professional training and association as well as publications as the context in which the ministers came to sense the appropriateness of using purposeful humor in the pulpit. In chapter one we are not concerned with detailed and systematic discussions of the theological and social context for subjects of humor. That detailed task is reserved to chapters three through five. Chapter one is concerned with tracing the use of common anecdotes and establishing the interrelations of the ministers using humor -- interrelations which encouraged such use in the pulpit and supplied some of the materials used. While the minister's awareness of these historic humorous materials established the propriety of using humor purposefully in the pulpit, it did not provide clearly the particular purposes for such use. The compelling motivations to use humor grew out of the minister's contemporary context examined in chapter two.

Chapter two examines the American preachers' motivations for using humor in the pulpit: the evangelical motivations to attract, control, and convert the people and to open communication on controversial subjects, and the theological motivations to exorcise idolatries and affirm and defend doctrines when logical argument was inconclusive. Chapters three through five delineate the subjects of humor in the pulpit and the theological dimensions of the subjects which had a life within the ongoing idolatries of the day: excesses of political and ecclesiastical power, pretentions of wisdom, and

burgeoning manifestations of wealth.
The framework of these chapters allows not only an
exposition of the humor from the pulpit but also serves
as a ground against which we may see how faith and
humor are interrelated: how awareness of the faith's
traditional humor affects subsequent use of humor, how
that use alters the humor's original intent and expression of faith, how the pattern of use reveals characteristics of different denominations in different geographic areas during different periods, how the contemporary problems are reflected and affected by pulpit
humor, and how faith prompts the concentration of pulpit
humor around particular subjects in the culture.
Studies of American humor include examples of Puritan
elegies and epitaphs; but one would conclude from such
studies that after the seventeenth century the branches
of American Christianity were humorless with the exception of scattered comments by some frontier ministers.
The representation of eighteenth and nineteenth century
American Christianity as humorless is partly the fault
of scholars in the religious field who have neglected
or eliminated the humor in their subjects. This neglect
or elimination may have resulted from the scholar's
concern that their subject and work be taken seriously
or may have resulted from the fact that the humorous
materials are often associated with the concrete and
timely social issues of the periods and that scholars
have often been more concerned with abstract and timeless ideas. [12]

12. Brom Weber, who studied Puritanism with Perry Miller,
indicated an openness to including religious materials
in his excellent Anthology of American Humor, (New York:
Thomas Crowell Co., 1962). The fact that he includes
religious materials only from the seventeenth century
Puritan period accentuates the need for studies of
religious humor in later periods. Existing treatments
of humor in American Christianity of the eighteenth
and nineteenth centuries are devoid of critical approaches
to sources and often lack any footnotes. The best of
these set the religious materials alongside the secular
works of the area or period (e.g. Mody C. Boatright,
Folk Laughter on the American Frontier, New York: The

I hope this study will require a reassessment of the
polemical role of some church worship in American life
and suggest courses of action for contemporary Christians faced with cultural idolatries and theological
impasses analogous to those which eighteenth and nineteenth century preachers handled with humor. In
historiography, this study should make apparent omissions
in past biographies and histories and prompt historians
to represent more fairly the humor of their subjects.
As a result, future anthologies on American humor may
include more Christian materials and result in a more
accurate understanding and appreciation of American
Christianity in its concrete as well as abstract dimensions. And for the field of American studies, I hope
this study will uplift pulpit literature for its proper
attention as a major popular literature of the eighteenth
and nineteenth centuries through which we may see forces
shaping dimensions of the American character.

Those who have studied American humor most thoroughly
have approached the subject through the perspective of
departments of English and American literature. These
scholars will find chapter one most in line with their
concern to trace the life of repeated anecdotes. Chapter
two will be more satisfying to theologians and psychol-
ogists who have sought to understand the motivations for
humor. Chapters three through five will be most satis-

---

12. Cont.
Macmillan Co., 1949); and the least critical amount to
nothing more than jumbled books of anecdotes (e.g. Israel
Harold Weisfeld, The Pulpit Treasury of Wit and Humor,
New York: Prentice Hall, 1950). While biographies of
some of the most humorous American Ministers neglect or
eliminate this aspect of their work (e.g. Charles Akers'
study of Jonathan Mayhew: Called Unto Liberty, Cambridge,
Harvard University Press 1964), a few biographies include
treatment of the humor (e.g. Arthur Eaton's The Famous
Mather Byles, Boston: W. A. Butterfield, 1914). William
G. McLoughlin Jr. is one of the few modern historians to
provide a careful index listing of humor (e.g. Modern
Revivalism: Charles Grandison Finney to Billy Graham,
New York: Ronald Press, 1959).

fying to church historians and others in eighteenth
and nineteenth century American history; for these
chapters most fully place the humor within its historic
context.

In shaping this dissertation so that it speaks to several
different communities of scholars whose fields converge
when one studies humor and faith of the period, I am
indebted to the members of my doctoral committee: Harland
Hogue and John Dillenberger, whose concern for church
history and theology encouraged elaboration of the
motivations and contexts of the humor; and Jane Dillenberger, Wayne Rood, and John Bachman whose extensive
appreciation of art as an end in itself encouraged
exploration of the humorous materials in and of themselves.
My thanks are also extended to several scholars of
nineteenth century religion who responded to my inquiries with helpful suggestions and words of encouragement:
H. Shelton Smith, William McLoughlin, Jr., Edwin Gaustad,
Winthrop Hudson, Robert Handy, Sidney Mead, John Tracy
Ellis, John B. McGloin, Maynard Geiger, and Sidney
Kaplan.

This study of humor spans a period from the Great
Awakening in the 1730's through the American Revolution,
the Second Awakening in the periods of territorial and
economic expansion including the economic depression
of the 1830's and the agitation over slavery during the
Mexican War and the Civil War, and extends through the
period of reconstruction and the Gilded Age to the end
of the nineteenth century. Those studied for their use
of humor in the pulpit include a wide and diverse range
of preachers: George Whitefield in the seaboard colonies
during the Great Awakening; Jonathan Mayhew in Boston of
the pre-revolutionary period; Timothy Dwight at Yale,
black Lemuel Haynes in Vermont, Peter Cartwright in
Illinois, Jacob Gruber in the Middle States, and Lorenzo
Dow in the south during the early period of the Second
Awakening; Baptists Jabez Swan and Jacob Knapp in
protracted meetings throughout the northeast from the

1820's; revivalist Charles Finney moving from New York to
Ohio; Presbyterian missionary Reuben Tinker returning
from the Sandwich Islands to Ohio and then New York in
the 1840's; antagonists such as Unitarian Theodore
Parker and Methodist sailor preacher Edward Taylor in
Boston of the 1840's and 1850's; allies such as Horace
Bushnell and Leonard Bacon in settled Connecticut churches
for five decades from the 1830's. Spanning the Civil
War, we look to Hiram Stimson in New York, Michigan,
Wisconsin, and Kansas; Henry Ward Beecher first in
Indianapolis and then in Brooklyn's fashionable Plymouth
church; William Taylor and Charles Wadsworth in San
Francisco. And we examine also those active to the end
of the century: Samuel Upham at Drew University
Seminary; Dwight L. Moody and Sam Jones touring the
country with extended meetings; Catholic Archbishop
John Ireland and traveling Dominican evangelist Thomas
Nicholas Burke; and blacks from carriers of popular folk
traditions to Oxford educated Episcopalian Alexander
Crummell.[13]   Changing political, intellectual, and
economic conditions in different areas combined with
different denominational backgrounds to lead preachers
to concentrate on different expressions of the idolatries; but the continuing purpose of the humor was to
restore man's attention to God and his service.

---

13. The foregoing sentences give a hint of the preachers'
periods and places to help orient the reader. Most of
these preachers were active for such extended periods
that they defy exclusive classification; for example,
Peter Cartwright, who is often associated with the
Second Awakening, continued preaching from 1802 to 1872
(cf. appendix one for exact periods of preaching for
each minister.)

CHAPTER I

THE AWARENESS AND USE OF HUMOR

FROM THE TRADITION OF CHRISTIAN PREACHING

> A prominent divine of another denomination, meaning
> to be slightly sarcastic, once said to my old friend
> Mr. Cartwright: "How is it that you have no doctors
> of divinity in your denomination?"
> "Our divinity is not sick and don't need doctoring,"
> said the sturdy backwoodsman. 1

A Peter Cartwright anecdote appearing in nineteenth
century Methodist sermons opens our consideration of
ministerial awareness and use of humor from the tradition of Christian preaching. Little of the humor in
ministers' sermons of the eighteenth and nineteenth
centuries may be shown to be borrowed from any source;
but when such borrowing is evident it was largely from
contemporary preachers by Methodists, who altered the
point of the humor to put down those who competed for
the attention which belonged to God alone. The Cartwright anecdote is representative of this tradition and
originated in repartee between ministers -- a channel
which encouraged the spread of pulpit humor. Exploring
the interrelations of ministers noted for using humor,
one comes to appreciate how the purposeful use of humor

---

1. William Henry Milburn, Ten Years of Preacher-Life:
Chapters from an Autobiography, (New York: Derby and
Jackson, 1860), pp. 92-93. The detailed theological and
social context to help the reader fully appreciate this
humor and other humor in this chapter is given in chapters
three through five. The humorous anecdotes are presented
in this chapter as they assist the tracing of the common
materials which indicate ministers' awareness and use of
the tradition of Christian preaching and the ministers'
purposeful use of such materials not simply to gain a
laugh for its own sake but to achieve socially significant
ends. The particular ends are briefly noted with many
of the anecdotes in this chapter, but are elaborated
in subsequent chapters. Revealing purposefulness that
characterizes nearly all the pulpit humor of the period
is the concern of this chapter.

was encouraged primarily through professional training
and association and secondarily through publication.
Pulpit use of humor in or imposed on bible passages also
reflects a purposeful dealing with the particular
problems of the minister's period and place.

Shared Nineteenth Century Humor

The varieties of shared nineteenth century pulpit humor
form the following classes: cutting anecdotes or retorts
used chiefly by Methodist ministers in response to
similar situations of conflict in the worship or community; short humorous expressions of Henry Ward Beecher
expanded by Methodist evangelist Sam Jones; extended
satirical treatments of contemporary ideas; and exempla
used by black and white communities. In determining
purposes, a humorous anecdote or expression should be
considered in its full context wherever possible; for
the same anecdote was used sometimes for opposite ends.
And a witty expression originated by one preacher was
expanded by another with a specific application
unintended by the originator.

Different Context and Meaning

Defending his Methodist denomination which in the early
1800's had few D.D.s, presiding Illinois elder Peter
Cartwright responded to the taunts of a minister who
probably held a D.D. and Calvinist views, "Our divinity
is not sick and don't need doctoring." Cartwright and
his fellow Methodists were deeply concerned to reach and
save as many people as possible; and they bitterly
opposed the highly educated Calvinists whose time was
spent developing and defending doctrines which excluded
rather than included the many and made conversions more
difficult. The comment was apiece with his early
antagonism to formal ministerial training and its trappings, but reflects no attack on college education which

he championed.[2]   In contrast, southerner Lorenzo Dow
used this anecdote against higher education in general
and the Methodist hierarchy in particular which he felt
was setting itself up between the people and God's
service in a later day when D.D.'s were heading the
Methodist Church:

> The Edinburgh Factory bestowed the pompous title of
> "Doctor of Divinity," on the masters of the Indian
> school at Lebanon, who sought for a more convenient
> place as a suitable site. Hence the origin of
> Dartmouth College, with the President there, the
> Rev. Dr. Wheelock!
> A preacher being asked in the solitary days of
> Methodism during the time of their simplicity; --
> Why the Methodists did not have "doctors of
> divinity?" boldly replied, our Divinity is not sick!
> But now matters are reversed and the doctors are
> to be found at the helm of affairs to keep pace
> with other societies, and be like all the nations
> about. 3

By 1842, Cartwright indicated no qualms in becoming a
D.D. himself when Methodist institutions of higher
learning were bestowing the honors.[4]
In his attack on the Methodist church hierarchy and its
growing authority, Dow used another anecdote more

---

2. Cartwright's attitudes to varieties of education will
be fully explored in chapter four. Englishman E. Paxton
Hood, a nineteenth century collector of anecdotes
incorrectly credits this anecdote to Jacob Gruber whom
he calls Kruber. (cf. The Throne of Eloquence: Great
Preachers, Ancient and Modern, New York: Funk and Wagnall
1888, p. 243). Hood cites W. P. Strickland, The Life of
Jacob Gruber, as his source but that book contains no
such anecdote. Milburn's crediting of this anecdote to
Cartwright seems more reliable as he served with
Cartwright in the Illinois Methodist church before becoming chaplain to the United States Congress.

3. Lorenzo Dow, "Omnifarious Law; Ecclesiastical Law,"
The Dealings of God, Man and the Devil exemplified in the
Life and Experience and Travels of Lorenzo Dow, (New
York: Nafis and Cornish, 1849), II pp. 165-166.

4. Tetsuo Miyakawa, Protestants and Pioneers: Individual-
ism and Conformity on the American Frontier, (Chicago
University Press, 1964), p. 96.

commonly used against the Episcopal or Catholic church
claims of apostolic succession. In the common version:

> A Methodist preacher made the following refutation
> of the doctrine of apostolic succession: A traveler
> lost his way in the backwoods country. While
> wondering which path to take, he heard the breaking
> of twigs in the underbrush, and presently there
> emerged an overgrown boy with a rifle on his arm.
> By way of opening conversation, the traveler
> remarked, "That's a good looking gun you have."
> "Yes," replied the youth, "this was Grandpap's gun.
> He carried it through the Revolutionary War."
> Surprised by this statement, the traveler looked at
> the gun more closely. "Why the barrel," he said
> seems shorter than those of the Revolutionary
> period."
> "Yes," said the boy, "Pap had a new barrel put on."
> The traveler continued his examination of the gun.
> "That looks like a new stock," he observed. "Yes,"
> said the boy, "Pap had that put on." "The lock
> can't be very old either," observed the traveler.
> "Pap had that put on too," said the boy.
> "Then you must have a new gun."
> "No," said the boy, "its the same old gun Grandpap
> carried through the Revolutionary War." 5

In Dow's variation the gun became a pocket knife and the
Methodist hierarchy the target:

> But there is a distinction to be made betwixt the
> old economy of primitive Methodists under Wesley,
> following the openings of Providence, 1739 in
> Europe, and 1769 in America; and the new fangledism
> from Rankin, who began the closed doors business,
> 1773, and which Coke and Asbury and Wm. M. have
> improved upon and changed like the Irishman's jack
> knife, which was 29 years old; had it from his
> father, it had worn out five new blades, and three
> new handles and still was the same good old
> knife. 6

A personal anecdote which displayed a minister's wit at
eluding a parishioner's question was transformed by a
different context into an attack on the minister. In
"The Law of God," delivered at the Boston Music Hall,
Unitarian Theodore Parker preached in defense of civil

---

5. Mody C. Boatright, Folk Laughter on the American
Frontier, (New York: The Macmillan Co., 1949),pp. 137-138.

6. Dow, "A Cry from the Wilderness," The Dealings,
p. 127. Wm. M. was William M'Kendree who served as
Methodist bishop after Asbury.

disobedience to the Fugitive Slave Law and ridiculed
those who urged obedience:

> King Darius forbade prayer to any God or man except
> himself. Should the worshippers of Jehovah hold
> back their prayer to the Creator? Daniel was of
> rather a different opinion. A few years ago a
> minister of a "prominent church" in this city was
> told of another minister who had exhorted persons to
> disobey the Fugitive Slave Law, because it was
> contrary to the Law of God and the principles of
> Right. "What do you think of it?" said the
> questioner, who was a woman, to the Dr. of Divinity.
> "Very bad!" replied he, "this minister ought to
> keep the statute, and he should not advise men to
> disobey it." "But," said the good woman, "Daniel,
> we are told, when the law was otherwise, prayed to
> the Lord! Prayed right out loud three times a day,
> with his window wide open! Did he do right or
> wrong? Would not you have done the same?" The
> minister said, "If I had lived in those times, --
> I think I should -- have shut up my window." 7

But some stories would be retold to put down the same

inclinations. Samuel Upham, Methodist Professor of

Practical Theology at Drew University Seminary in the

late eighteen hundreds, used an anecdote of Father

Edward Taylor's to quash the questions of the speculative

student mind:

> One Monday morning at the preachers' meeting a
> young theolog came up to Father Taylor and said: --
> "Father Taylor, science has proven there can be no
> physical resurrection of the human body. There is
> only a limited amount of phosphorous in the earth,
> and it takes a certain amount of it to make a human
> body; at the time of the final resurrection there
> will not be enough phosphorous to make bodies for
> those who have died -- from Adam to now -- let alone
> those who will live and die from now until the
> judgment day; therefore, there can be no physical
> resurrection of the body." Father Taylor replied --
> "Young man, that argument does not worry me in the
> least. The good Book says, 'The dead in Christ
> shall rise first' -- we Christians will be all right;
> you infidels will have to scurry around for your
> own phosphorous." 8

---

7. Theodore Parker, The Law of God and the Statutes of
Men, (Boston: Benj. Mussey and Co., 1854), p. 24.

8. James Richard Joy, ed., The Teachers of Drew,(Madison,
N. J.: Drew University, 1942), p. 95.

Similar Conflict and Humor

Those who disrupted meetings in similar ways prompted
ministers to use similar humor in putting down disrupters
and restoring attention to God's worship. Probably an
acquaintance with other ministers' successful experience
in dealing with disrupters is reflected in some witty
comments. One young man, gayly dressed in a profusely
ruffled shirt, stood up on a camp meeting seat to
overlook the congregation:

> Some of the ministers from the stand requested him
> very politely to descend. But he paid no attention.
> After seeing their failure Mr. Gruber took him in
> hand. In quite a distinct and loud voice he cried:
> "O brethren, let the young man alone; let him enjoy
> himself. Don't you see he wants to show his fine
> ruffled shirt; and after all I dare say it's bor-
> rowed." The young man instantly jumped down and
> made off, saying, with an oath, to a friend, "How
> did he know I had a borrowed shirt on?" 9

Peter Cartwright recounted a similar incident from the
Breckenridge circuit camp meeting:

> There was another circumstance happened at this camp
> meeting that I will substantially relate. It was
> one of our rules of the camp meeting that the men
> would occupy the seats on the one side of the stand,
> and the ladies on the other side, at all hours of
> public worship. But there was a young man, finely
> dressed, with his bosom full of ruffles, that would
> take his seat among the ladies; and if there was
> any excitement in the congregation, he would rise
> to his feet, and stand on the seats prepared for the
> occupancy of the ladies. I reproved him personally
> and sharply, and said, "I mean that young man there,
> standing on the seats of the ladies, with a ruffled
> shirt on." And added, "I doubt not that ruffled
> shirt was borrowed." 10

Evidence is lacking to help us determine who was the
first to use this phrase. Jacob Gruber and Cartwright

---

9. Strickland, The Life of Jacob Gruber, (New York:
Carlton and Porter, 1860), p. 367.

10. William P. Strickland, ed., Autobiography of Peter
Cartwright the Backwoods Preacher, (Cincinnati:Cranston
and Curtis, 1856), pp. 130-131.

were Methodist contemporaries: the former's period of
preaching extended from 1800 to 1850 through Virginia
and the middle states; the latter's from 1802 to 1872
through Kentucky and Illinois. We explore their possible
contacts as fellow Methodists at the end of this chapter
in a general discussion of interrelations of ministers
using humor. Noting that William P. Strickland edited
both Gruber's and Cartwright's works, one may be tempted
to credit his editor's hand for the similarity.
Strickland, who served as assistant editor of The
Christian Advocate and Journal, did introduce other
minister's pulpit humor in these books; but he demonstrated care in crediting the source. [11] The introduction of organs into worship with an increasing
attention to quality of music evoked similar humor from
both preachers who saw such concerns as standing between
man and God. Rev. Dr. Holdrich, corresponding secretary
of the American Bible Society, gave this glimpse of
Gruber's wit:

> Passing a house of worship in which he heard the
> organ, affecting simplicity, he said, "What is dat?"
> "It is the organ," said his companion. "And what is
> de organ for?" "O they are worshipping God in
> singing." "O! And do they have a machine to say
> their prayers too?" [12]

In an exchange with Father Edward Taylor at the 1860
Buffalo General Conference of the Methodist church,
Cartwright expressed similar regard for the organ:

---

11. His biographies were not of the more typical nineteenth century types which described one man's life in
terms of long passages written originally by someone else
about a third party. (e.g. John A. Roche, The Life of
John Price Durbin, New York: Phillips and Hunt, 1889).
In the columns of The Christian Advocate and Journal,
Strickland occasionally shared humor from his research
which was a way some later ministers learned of other's
humor. William B. Sprague, ed., Annals of the American
Pulpit: Methodist,(New York: Robert Carter & Bros.,
1869), VIII, p. 345.
12. Strickland, The Life of Jacob Gruber, p. 364.

> I did not know how a modest man like myself could
> preach, with their old wooden god up there, groaning
> and bellowing like a dying prairie bull, and the
> people turning their faces to the choir and their
> backs upon the minister, leaving him to count his
> fingers; and then when he said, "Let us pray," they
> all turned round and sat down. 13

Similarity of other rejoinders reflects the similarity
of situation with no necessary awareness of other
ministerial humor. Holding a meeting in New York City's
Mulberry Street Church, traveling Baptist evangelist
Jacob Knapp humorously handled a disrupter:

> A young man rose in the presence of a vast congre-
> gation and requested prayers for the devil. Elder
> Knapp quietly remarked, "Brethren, this young man
> has asked you to pray for his father." 14

At the close of an earlier worship service in Rutland,
Vermont, black Congregationalist Lemuel Haynes had
resorted to a similar humorous strategy to deal with two
young disrupters:

> Having agreed together to make trial of their wit,
> one of them said, "Father Haynes, have you heard
> the good news?" "No", said Mr. Haynes, "what is
> it?" "It is great news," said the other, "and if
> true, your business is done." "What is it?" again
> inquired Mr. Haynes. "Why," said the first, "the
> devil is dead!" In a moment, the old gentleman,
> lifting up both his hands, and placing them upon
> the heads of the young men, in a tone of solemnity
> and concern replied, "Poor fatherless children,
> what will become of you?" 15

---

13. Gilbert Haven and Thomas Russell, Life of Father
Taylor, the Sailor Preacher, (Boston: The Boston's Port
& Seaman's Aid Society, 1904), pp. 219-220. This ground
for opposing the organ differed from that of many
Calvinists who opposed the introduction of anything
(including organs) which were not mentioned in Biblical
worship.

14. Jacob Knapp, Autobiography of Elder Jacob Knapp,
(New York: Sheldon & Co., 1868), p. xiv.

15. Letter, The Rev. Timothy Cooley to William Sprague,
January 20, 1848, William B. Sprague, ed., Annals of
the American Pulpit: Trinitarian Congregational, (New
York: Robert Carter and Brothers, 1857), p. 185.

Short witty phrases applied in one specific case were
used in other cases with a change in meaning. After a
sermon was read by a young minister, Jacob Gruber gave
the closing prayer:

> "Lord, bless the man who has read to us today --
> let his heart be as soft as his head, and then he
> will do us some good." 16

Rev. S. Cushing reported that Edward Taylor, Boston
sailor's Methodist preacher, used the phrase for another
end:

> He smote down the anti-Masons, as he thought, by a
> single word: "Lord, make their hearts as soft as
> as their heads." 17

The most humorous expression was directed uniformly
against ministers who cared too much about earthly
rewards. But the reason a man used the phrase varied
according to his own primary concern. Orestes Brownson
gave the phrase its full expression in explaining why
many ministers would not care for "My Creed" he created
during his Unitarian days:

> The orthodox will reject it because it is not
> mysterious, and the priests generally, because it
> will require them to pay as much attention to the
> flock as they have hitherto paid to the fleece. 18

The phrase is associated with Virginia Methodist William
Cravens' attack on ministers who did not speak out
against slavery: "The priests, who taught for hire --
men who cared more about the fleece than the flock." 19

---

16. Sprague, _Annals of the American Pulpit_, VII, p.346.

17. Haven, _Father Taylor_, p. 274.

18. Henry Francis Brownson, _Orestes A. Brownson's Life_,
(Detroit: H. F. Brownson, 1898), I, pp. 25-29. "My
Creed" appeared originally in Brownson's _Gospel
Advocate_,(1829), pp. 199-201.

19. Rev. J. B. Wakely, _The Bold Frontier Preacher_, A
Portraiture of Rev. William Cravens of Virginia, 1766-
1826, (Cincinnati: Hitchcock and Walden, 1869), p. 85.

And the phrase was in circulation among Lutherans as well. [20]

Expansion of Borrowed Phrases

Southern Methodist Sam Jones borrowed humorous phrases from the sermons of Brooklyn Congregationalist Henry Ward Beecher although Jones did not always credit his source or use the material in the same way. Before Jones began to preach, Beecher had put down preoccupation with doctrines: "DOCTRINE is nothing but the skin of Truth set up and stuffed." [21] Beecher recognized that some minds needed to develop ideas in theology; but he would not equate such expression to the faith and held that many could thoroughly appreciate and participate in religion without studying theology just as he could thoroughly enjoy his chicken dinner without taking up the study of ornothology. [22] Sam Jones borrowed and expanded Beecher's phrase but narrowed its meaning to creeds:

---

20. Gotleib Shober, known for his humor in preaching, shows acquaintance with the phrase as do others in Lutheran circles. Gottleib Shober, A Comprehensive Account of the Rise and Progress of the Blessed Reformation of the Christian Church, (Baltimore: Schaeffer and Maund, 1818), p. 208.. William Sprague, ed., Annals of the American Lutheran Pulpit, (New York: Robert Carter & Brothers, 1869), p. 120.

21. Edna Dean Proctor, Life Thoughts, Gathered from the Extemporaneous Discourses of Henry Ward Beecher, (Boston: Phillips, Sampson, & Co., 1859), p. 97. Proctor used her own notes and those of fellow Plymouth Church member Robert Benedict in preparing this collection which is one of the few sources for Beecher's sermons before the Civil War.

22. Beecher, "Prayer," Eleanor Kirk, ed., Beecher As A Humorist, (New York: Fords, Howard, and Hulbert, 1897), p. 145. When Beecher spoke against "doctrine," he and his congregation thought of their antipathy to the narrow New England Calvinism of their childhood -- a Calvinism that in Beecher's own case had caused family anguish because its doctrine of regeneration failed to give any hope to Catherine Beecher that her fiance was not among the damned.

CREED! What is a creed? It is the skin of the
truth dried and stuffed with sand and sawdust.
If I had a creed I would sell it to a museum.
Orthodoxies have ruined the world. My, my! how
a man will fight for his doxie, and then see his
Saviour insulted and never resent it! You must not
step on my creed; if you do you are a goner! 23

While both Beecher's and Jones' evangelical concerns may

be seen in their humorous treatments of divisive theol-

ogies, Jones went further than Beecher in expressing

personal dislike for "theology" which was another code

word for Calvinism and other highly academic approaches

to religion that attracted the attention into a maze and

excluded many from religious experience:

I am no theologian -- never studied theology. I am
not boasting of the fact, but I state it as a fact:
I despise theology and botany, but I do love religion and flowers. There is many a fellow that has
studied theology until he knows theology, but he
doesn't know anything else in the universe. He is
fit for heaven, but not fit for earth. 24

In a passage against eleven o'clock Sunday morning

Christians, Jones explicitly acknowledged his acquaintance

with Beecher's anecdotes:

"Gentleness." Beecher once had a horse brought to
him for a buggy-ride, and he asked, "Is that horse
gentle?" And they answered: "Yes, sir; he is not
afraid of anything in the world, and he will work
anywhere." And Beecher said: "I saw a great big
fine bay horse once that would not work anywhere
except to a light, striped buggy. These Sunday
morning eleven o'clock Christians are striped
buggy fellows. Some of you have not been to church
only at eleven o'clock Sunday morning for years.
That is the dress-parade crowd. These striped fancy
buggy fellows! If you were to hitch them up to a
prayer-meeting they would run away. If you were to
hitch one of them up to family prayers he would kick
the buggy all to pieces. 25

23. Rev. Sam P, Jones, Sermons, Wise & Witty, (New York:
Cheap Publishing Co., 1885), p. 56. (cf. Rev. Sam Jones,
Hot Shots; Sermons and Sayings, Nashville, Tenn. South-
Western Pub. House, 1885 , First Series, p. 147.)

24. Sam P. Jones, "Righteousness and Life -- Sin and
Death," Sermons and Sayings, (Nashville: Southern Methodist Publishing House, 1885), 1st Series, p. 147.

25. Jones, Hot Shots, p. 106 (cf. Jones, Sermons Wise
and Witty, p. 45).

The common problem of nominal Christians whose attention
was fixed so firmly on avoiding evil that they did little
good gave rise to the use of other similar sounding
humor. In his sermon "Law and Liberty", Beecher ridiculed negative Christianity:

> There are a great many people who seem to think that
> religion means not doing wrong. As if a knitting
> machine that never knit any stockings would be con-
> sidered a good one because it never misknit! What is
> a man good for who simply does not do something? 26

Jones uses a similar strategy although a different
imagery:

> Negative goodness is not religion. If negative
> goodness was religion, then one of these lamp posts
> out here would be the best Christian in town; it
> never cursed nor swore, nor drank a drop since it
> was made; it never did anything wrong. 27

The foregoing examples illustrate the difficulty of
determining definite reliance by one minister on another
for humorous material. While the reliance may not be
proven in each case, the similarity of humor points to
some similar situations faced in popular religion across
denominational and geographic lines during the post civil
war period.

Extended Satirical Arguments

In discussing Lyman Beecher's use of humor in the pulpit
John Ross Dix observed, "as with most men of Dr. Beecher's
order of mind, satire and logic are one." 28 For reasons
outlined in chapter two, Yale president Timothy Dwight
increased such use of satire among those ministers who
followed him. When applied to similar issues, the use of

---

26. Henry Ward Beecher, "Law and Liberty," Kirk, Beecher,
p. 46.

27. Sam P. Jones, "Grace and Salvation," Tabernacle
Sermons of Rev. Sam P. Jones, (St. Joseph, Missouri: The
Herald Publishing Company, 1885), p. 53.

28. John Ross Dix, Pulpit Portraits, or Pen-Pictures of
Distinguished American Divines; with Sketches of Congregations and Choirs; and Incidental Notices of Eminent
British Preachers, (Boston: Tappan and Whittemore, 1854),
p. 166.

a common satirical method in argument led to some similar
pulpit humor. Such similar humor does not necessarily
indicate a knowledge or borrowing of others' pulpit humor.
But Baptist John Leland, who predated Dwight's theological turn, used satire in arguments on establishment in
which he was followed so closely by others in their
arguments against toleration that an acquaintance with
his humorous sermons or each other's may be assumed.

While one legislative act to enhance establishment of a
single church and another act to tolerate all churches
may appear to be quite opposite, they are based on the
same assumption if one approaches them from the standpoint of those who oppose any state action in relation
to churches; for from this standpoint the state has
neither the right to establish nor tolerate churches.
The similarity of humor shows the common assumption
underlying establishment and toleration acts. In "A
Blow at the Root. . . A Fashionable Fast-Day Sermon"
delivered at Cheshire, April 9, 1801, Leland ridiculed
an amendment to the law which would have extended support
to established religion by requiring additional teachers
of religion. He suggested the following expansion of the
amendment to clarify its implications:

> Be it enacted by the Senate and House of represent-
> atives in General Court assembled, that the almighty
> God shall qualify and send forth a competency of
> teachers of morality, piety and religion, to supply
> all the towns, parishes, precincts, religious
> societies and bodies politic, within the commonwealth
> of Massachusetts, and on failure thereof shall
> forfeit his moral government over the state. 29

29. John Leland, "A Blow at the Root . . . A Fashionable
Fast-Day Sermon," (April 9, 1801), L. F. Greene, ed.,
The Writings of the Late Elder John Leland, (New York:
Arno Press & the New York Times, 1969). N. Carolina
Presbyterian Henry Pattillo acknowledged another passage
of Leland's extended satire as his source for "An
Address to the Deists," Sermons, (Wilmington: John Adams,
1788), pp. v and 199ff.

At a later date Lorenzo Dow ridiculed proposed toleration acts in a similar way:

> Suppose a bill was brought into any Legislature
> entitled an 'Act to tolerate or grant liberty to
> the Almighty, to receive the worship of a Jew or
> a Turk,' or 'to prohibit the Almighty to receive it'
> all men would startle and call it blasphemy. 30

In a work published long after Dow's widely circulated
tract, Methodist Billy Hibbard's argument followed Dow's
so closely that the former must have been relying on the
latter or both were aware of a common third source:

> If the Governor and several Doctors of Divinity
> were to present a bill to the Legislature entitled
> an act to grant liberty to the Almighty to receive
> the worship of the Methodists and Quakers, every
> one would startle and call it blasphemy, but
> toleration implies this. 31

Such extended satirical arguments normally employed
reductio ad absurdum; but on occasion argumentum ad
hominum was employed as in the following case.

The use of Lemuel Haynes' celebrated sermon Universal
Salvation reveals a connection between two other seemingly opposite ideas: Calvinism and Universalism. The
satirical dimension of the text is realized only when one
keeps in mind that it was preached immediately following
a sermon by the prominent traveling Universalist Hosea
Ballou in West Parish of Rutland, Vermont, June 1805.
As the Universalist sat down, Haynes rose, eyed Ballou,
read out the scripture, "And the Serpent said unto the
Woman, ye shall not surely die" (Genesis iii.4), and
announced his sermon title, "Universal Salvation, A Very
Ancient Doctrine; with some account of the life and
character of its author." Parallels between the snake
and Ballou to whom he continually glanced, were stressed
throughout the sermon:

---

30. Lorenzo Dow, "Analects Upon Natural, Social and
Moral Philosophy," The Dealings, p. 51.
31. Billy Hibbard, Memoirs of the Life and Travels of
B. Hibbard, (New York: Piercy & Reed, 1843), p. 309.

Happy were the human pair amidst this delightful
Paradise, until a certain preacher, in his journey,
came that way, and disturbed their peace and tran-
quility, by endeavoring to reverse the prohibition
of the Almighty, as in our text -- Ye shall not
surely die. 32

When God enquired of this persevering preacher, Job
ii.2. From Whence comest thou? He answered and
said, From going to and fro in the earth, and from
walking up and down in it. He is far from being
circumscribed within the narrow limits of parish,
state, or continental lines; but his haunt and
travel is very large and extensive. 33

Lot preached to them; the substance of which was,
Up, get ye out of this place, for the Lord will
destroy this city, Gen. xix.14. But this old
declaimer told them -- No danger, Ye shall not
surely die. To which they generally gave heed, and
Lot seemed to them as one who mocked; they believed
the universal preacher, and were consumed. 34

To close the subject: As the author of the foregoing discourse has confined himself wholly to the
character of Satan, he trusts no one will feel
himself personally injured by this short sermon; but
should any imbibe a degree of friendship for this
aged divine, and think that I have not treated this
Universal Preacher with that respect and veneration
which he justly deserves, let them be so kind as to
point it out, and I will most cheerfully retract;
for it has ever been a maxim with me - Render unto
all their dues. 35

The text went through seven editions by 1810 and was
known outside Haynes' denomination. 36 Presbyterian
John Johnston was well aware of the "serpent sermon" and
its satire; and as a staunch Calvinist, he applauded its

32. Lemuel Haynes, Universal Salvation, A Very Ancient
Doctrine; with some account of the Life and Character of
its Author, (Newburyport: W. & J. Gilman, 1819), p. 3.

33. Ibid., p. 4.

34. Ibid., p. 5.

35. Ibid., p. 7.

36. Timothy Mather Cooley, Sketches of the Life and
Character of the Rev. Lemuel Haynes, A. M., (New York:
Negro Universities Press, 1969), p. 96.

sentiments. [37]   But it is doubtful that Haynes, Johnston
or any other Calvinist would have appreciated the context
in which the sermon was later used.   In 1827 The Dagon
of Calvinism was published with Hayne's "Universal
Salvation"included.   Peter Cartwright heartily enjoyed
the entire work and sent it to all Kentucky and Illinois
Methodist preachers under his charge.[38]   Consisting
chiefly of poetry ridiculing the doctrines of election
and predestination, the book included Haynes' sermon
because the editor viewed "Calvinism as a modification
of fatalism, and as leading directly to Unitarian and
to Socian and Arian opinions." [39]

Among those using and spreading pulpit humor, Methodists
were not alone in recognizing the connections of Calvinism and Universalism.   In serious passages of their
preaching, Charles Finney and Baptist Jacob Knapp
expressed similar insights into how the Calvinist over-
emphasis on divine sovereignty animated Universalism;
Knapp argued:

> Universalism was the logical result of those hyper-
> Calvinistic tenants which constituted the staple of
> pulpit ministrations.   Resolving all questions of
> religious experiences into the decree of divine
> sovereignty. . . 40

> It seems as if almost any person of ordinary capac-
> ities could not help seeing the absurdity of the
> distinction between the saved and the lost, if this
> distinction arises not from their character, but
> from the arbitrary pleasure of Deity.   And when
> this sentiment is taught, the Universalist concludes
> that if the salvation of any turns upon the arbi-
> trary pleasure of God, without any regard to char-
> acter or conduct, it will be the pleasure of God
> to save all, and that all will be saved.   41

37. James Carnahan, ed., The Autobiography and Ministerial
Life of the Rev. John Johnston, D.D., (New York: M.W.
Dodd, 1856), p. 206.

38. William Strickland, ed., Autobiography of Peter
Cartwright, p. 198.

39.The Dagon of Calvinism, or the Moloch of Decrees,
(n.p., 1837), p. iii.

40. Knapp, Autobiography, p. 38.

41. Ibid., p. 334.

Charles Finney wrote:

> Universalism is another logical and irresistable inference from these dogmas. Assuming as a fact, that men are constitutionally depraved, unable to obey the gospel, under the necessity of waiting for a physical regeneration, one must either adopt the conclusion that God is an infinite tyrant, or that all will be saved. 42

As we see more fully in chapters two and four, the development of Universalism from Calvinism caused both moderate Calvinists and anti-Calvinists to look more skeptically at the logic and language on which they had been relying and led to a wider recognition of logic's limits and an increased use of humor in argument.

Exempla: Black and White

Humorous exempla are evident in both black and white preaching; but the pattern of borrowing these stories was not a simple flow from whites to blacks as some have supposed. [43] While the last portion of this chapter suggests that white use of humor in the pulpit led some blacks to feel free to use humor in their own sermons, the records of actual preaching reveal as much white borrowing from blacks as black borrowing from whites. But there was little borrowing evident in either direction. Unreliability of person, places, and times in any exemplum adds to the difficulty of explaining its history

42. Charles G. Finney, "Traditions of the Elders," Sermons on Important Subjects, (New York: John S. Taylor, 1835), p. 82.

43. J. Mason Brewer, The Word on the Brazos: Negro Preacher Tales from the Brazos Bottoms of Texas,(Austin: University of Texas Press, 1953). A similar early white assumption that spirituals simply flowed from white to black in camp meetings (e.g. George Pullen Jackson, White and Negro Spirituals, New York: J. J. Augustin, 1943) has been challenged by black scholarship which has shown the ironic and satiric dimension added in the black use and the originality of many black spirituals. (c.f. Russel Ames, "Protest and Irony in Negro Folksong," Science and Society, xiv, Summer 1950, pp. 193-213 and John Lovell, Jr., "The Social Implications of the Negro Spiritual," The Social Implications of Early Negro Music in the United States, New York: Arno Press and the New York Times, 1969, pp. 128-137.)

or its relationship to other exempla. Some of the most
popular black exempla were drawn from European and Middle
Eastern stories that are not evident in white American
preaching. The black borrowing from white preaching was
a subject of one humorous exemplum which played upon the
garbled nature of the results. Another exemplum helps
us laugh at the impropriety and futility of trying to
trace these folk phenomena to an original source.
Absence of the sermon context in which these exempla
were used makes the purpose of each exemplum uncertain.

A few of the same exempla are found in both black and
white collections of pulpit humor. But precise dating of
such materials is not possible so as to determine which
collections hold precedence or if either collection was
dependent upon the other. The white collection was not
published until 1950; and the black collection published
in 1953 was drawn together in the 1930's by black folklore pioneer J. Mason Brewer who dated the exempla from
the last quarter of the nineteenth century. From the
exempla common to both collections, two pairs of anecdotes are reproduced to illustrate problems inherent in
comparing them to discern origins. The first pair
appear to attack the exaggerated eulogies at funerals:

"The Wrong Man in the Coffin"

One time dere was a han what died on de old McPherson
fawm by de name of Ken Parker. De membership of de
Salem Baptis' Chu'ch think Ken's a good man, 'caze
he hab a fine big family an' he 'ten' chu'ch regluh
as de Sundays come. De pastuh think he a good
Christun, too. So when he git up to preach Ken's
funeral, he tell 'bout what a good man Brothuh Ken
was, 'bout how true he was to his wife, an' what
a good profiduh he done been for his family an 'all
lack dat. He keep on an' he keep on in dis wise,
but Ken's wife Sadie know de pastuh done errored;
so she turn to de ol' es' boy, Jim, an' say, "Jim,
go up dere an' look in dat coffin an' see if'n
dat's yo' pappy in dere."   44

---

44. Brewer, The Word on the Brazos, pp. 9-10.

"Right Man: Wrong Eulogy"

A prominent old-timer in industry on the Pacific
coast recently died. At the funeral service in the
church were gathered many old acquaintances and
employees. The clergyman, in making his address,
spoke in a most impassioned manner of the merits of
the deceased, lauding his kindness, generosity, the
interest he had taken in the welfare of his employees, his untiring efforts in the interests of the
community; a truly magnificent presentation of a
long life filled with excellent deeds. In conclusion he expressed the usual formality that anyone
wishing a last view of the deceased should now pass
the coffin.

Three old men at the rear of the church, who had
known the dead man intimately for a number of years,
exchanged questioning glances. After an uneasy
moment or so, one said to the other with the deter-
mined air of a man desiring to settle an uncertainty:
"I think one of us had better go and have a look,
for, judging from what the preacher said, they've
got the wrong man." 45

The second pair appear to attack not only man's pride
but also the self depreciation with which religion cloaks
accomplishment:

"The Preacher and His Farmer Brother"

. . .de Revun say, "Sid, youse got a putty good
cawn crop by de he'p of de Lawd." Den day goes on
down to de cotton patsh and de Revun looks at hit
an' low, "Sid, youse got a putty good cotton crop
by de he'p of de Lawd." Den dey moseys on down to
de sugah cane patch an' when de Revun eye dis, he
say, "Sid, youse got a putty good cane patch by de
he'p of de Lawd." An' when he say dis, Sid eye 'im
kinda disgusted lack, an' say, "Yeah, but you oughta
seed hit when de Lawd had it by Hisse'f." 46

"Who Was the Junior Partner"

A farmer had taken over a very neglected and unpro-
ductive farm, and after five years of back-breaking
labor had transformed it into a very rich crop-
bearing and well paying farm. One day when he was
visited by his minister he showed him around his
farm and very proudly pointed out the improvements
he had effected during the short time of his owner-
ship. "Look at that field of corn," he said.
"When I took it over it was nothing but craggy soil
and now, by means of hard work, I have been able to

---

45. Weisfeld, The Pulpit Treasury, p. 182.
46. Brewer, The Word on the Brazos, pp. 9-10.

make a real cornfield out of it."
"Yes," said the minister gently, "you and your
partner, God, have done much." The farmer frowned
but said nothing. He took him to another field and
again contrasted it with what it had been years
before. Again the minister said, "Yes, you and
your partner, God, have really worked miracles."
With that, the farmer could no longer restrain himself and turning to the minister, he exploded.
"Mebbe so, Reverend, but you should have seen the
terrible place this was when my partner had it all
to himself." 47

Not knowing the sermon context in which each anecdote
was used, we may not safely assume that the purpose of
using the similar sounding anecdotes was the same; for
earlier in this chapter we encountered many similar
anecdotes used for different purposes.

Lorenzo Dow, cited as the source for southern black
pulpit humor, also drew on materials generated within the
black community as shown in his argument against predestination and the purposeless preaching of some Calvinist
Baptists, his competitors:

This reminds me of a story I heard concerning a
Negro who had just returned from meeting -- his
master said, Well Jack, how did you like the minister? "Why massa, me scarcely know, for de minister say God makey beings, calla man, he pickey
out one here, one dere, and give dem to Jesus Christ,
and dey cant be lost. He makey all de rest repro-
bate, and giving dem to de Devil, dey can't be
saved. And de Devil he go about like a roaring lion
seeking to get away some a Christ, and he can't.
De minister, he go about to get away some de Devil's
and he can't; me dono which de greates' fool, the
Preacher or de Devil." 48

In his October 5, 1879 opening sermon in Cleveland,

---

47. Weisfeld, The Pulpit Treasury, p. 93. The anecdotes
have been so thoroughly adapted to the language and
the setting of their tellers that the futility of speaking about origin of these anecdotes should be obvious.

48. Lorenzo Dow, "The Chain of Reason," The Dealings,
p. 12. The following cite Dow as the source of the
black use of pulpit humor: Brewer, The Word on the Brazos,
pp. 1-2. Arthur Palmer Hudson, ed., Humor of the Old
Deep South, (New York: The Macmillan Co., 1936), p. 225.

Dwight Lyman Moody credited a colored minister as the
source for one of his humorous illustrations:

> One of the most difficult things we have in preach-
> ing the gospel is to get people to hear for them-
> selves. They are willing to hear for other people.
> I once read of a colored minister who said that a
> good many of his congregation would be lost because
> they were too generous; and the way he explained it
> was that they were too very generous with the
> sermon; that they generally gave the sermon to their
> friends and neighbors, and did not take it home to
> themselves. And there are a great many white
> people, I think, who are just as generous as the
> colored people. 49

With some exempla, the specifics of a story were modified by the teller of the tale for his environment. For
instance, one exemplum features Henry Ward Beecher to
put down those who led others to look at creation without reference to the creator:

> Henry Ward Beecher, the famous preacher, and Robert
> G. Ingersoll, the agnostic, were warm personal
> friends -- although, of course, they disagreed on
> religious matters, and especially on the question
> of the creation of the Universe.
>
> A friend of the preacher's presented to him a
> beautiful celestial globe, showing the sun and moon,
> the planets and the stars. It was a wonderful
> piece of work, and Ingersoll admired it greatly.
> He said to Beecher, "Who made it?" "Nobody," said
> the minister; "it just happened." 50.

The foregoing probably was an elaboration of an exemplum
which William Taylor knew and used in his March 2, 1851
sermon in the Portsmouth Square Plaza, San Francisco:

---

49. Dwight Lyman Moody, "Opening Sermon", The Great
Redemption; or the Gospel Light, Under the Labors of
Moody and Sanky, (Chicago: The Century Book and Paper
Co., 1888), p. 51.

50. Israel Harold Weisfeld, The Pulpit Treasury of Wit
and Humor, (New York: Prentice Hall, 1950), p. 23.

It is said that Sir Isaac Newton had a friend who
professed to be an atheist. Sir Isaac, anticipating
a visit from his friend, placed a beautiful new
globe where he knew it would arrest the attention of
his visitor. When the atheist saw it, he exclaimed
with admiration, 'Sir Isaac, who made this beautiful
globe?' "O, it was not made at all, Sir!' 51

Because exempla are not historically accurate in any

detail, attempting to trace origins by such data is

futile.

One popular black exemplum not evident in white preaching

appears to stem from Middle Eastern or European sources

and shifts attention from preoccupation with self to

service for others -- a dominant purpose of pulpit humor

seen in chapters four and five:

Mose Johnson was the outshoutin'es member of the
St. James Baptist Church up at Pinewood. He was the
only man in the church who could outshout the sisters
and was known far and wide for his unique ability.
Mose often said that he knew he was going to walk
the golden streets when he got to heaven because he
had been such a loyal Christian down here on earth.
The members of the church and the people in the
community thought the same thing, but when Mose
died and went to heaven, the gates did not fly open
to welcome him as he thought they would

Mose was very surprised that no one paid attention
to him. So, after sitting down in front of the
Heavenly Gates for a long time, he walked up and
tapped on the wall. The guardian angel who was on
watch at the time said, "What do you want?" "Ah
wants in," replied Mose. "Ah's Mose Johnson, an'
Ah wants to git in de gate."
"What have you done to deserve entering the High
Gates of Heaven?" inquired the angel.
"St. Peter knows all 'bout me," replied Mose. "Ast
him 'bout what Ah's done."
So the angel called St. Peter and asked him if he
knew Mose Johnson. "Seems like to me I remember a
little something about him," replied St. Peter, "but
I don't recall what it is just now. Let me call St.
James and have him look up his record." He then
called St. James and told him to look it up. In a
few minutes St. James came back with the record book
and St. Peter asked him what the record said about
what Mose had done for the Lord. "He didn't do much

---

51. William Taylor, Seven Years' Street Preaching in San
Francisco, California, (New York: Phillips and Hunt,
1856), p. 105.

o' nothin'" replied St. James, "but I see here
where he did give a dime one time." "A dime!"
yelled St. Peter. "That ain't enough for him to
get into Heaven. Just give the dime back to him
and let him go to Hell!" 52

A similar exemplum is found in Moslem and Jewish
sources. 53

At least one exemplum in the black church made fun of the
garbled gospel which resulted when post civil war black
preachers borrowed their materials from whites. In the
story, an Uncle Jonas of Plantersville Church, Georgetown County, was chosen as pastor. He could not read or
write and relied on a listening to white pastors to form
his sermons which took interesting turns:

> The first white preacher to whom he listened took
> for the subject of his text, "Oh Ye Generation of
> Vipers." So when the next Sunday came, Uncle Jonas
> took his place in the pulpit and said, "Brothers
> and Sisters, de subject fer mah text dis mawnin' be:
> 'Oh Ye Jimme, don't you bite me.'" The next Sunday
> when he rose to give his text entitled, "There was
> a man of the Parisees named Nicodemus who came to
> Jesus by night and said, Rabbi —" he said, "Mah
> text fer de mawnin' be: 'There was a man name Nick
> who caught a musk an' come to brudder Jays's an'
> sister Sue's house one night an' say rabbit." 54

Also reflecting an awareness that black ministers borrowed some of their sermon material, another exemplum
cautions us not to inquire too seriously into the sources
of exempla but to sit back and enjoy them. In this
exemplum Elder Morrow has come to a bounteous chicken
dinner at the Robinson home. After helping himself to
a fourth serving, he addresses his host:

---

52. Henry D. Spalding, ed., Encyclopedia of Black Folklore and Humor, (Middle Village, New York: Jonathan David
Publishers, 1972), p. 107. J. Mason Brewer collected
this anecdote on one of his trips in the Carolinas.

53. cf. Habeeb Khalif, Moslem Laughter, New York, 1906
and Henry D. Spalding, Wit and Humor of Jewish Humor,
New York, 1969, Jonathan David Publishers. It had been
published earlier in Marshall Brown's Wit and Humor of
Ireland, (Chicago: S. G. Griggs & Co., 1884).

54. Spalding, Encyclopedia, p. 103.

"Humph, dis sho' am good chicken; Brothuh Deacon,
whar you git good chicken lack dis?"
"Now look a heah, Elduh, " say Brothuh Robinson,
"youse goin too far! Ah comes to chu'ch an' Ah
lissens to yo' sermons, an' Ah enjoys 'em, but Ah
don't ast you whar you gits 'em." 55

Humor from Other Periods and Places

Although a few of our ninety-one preachers indicated an
awareness of earlier European pulpit humor, no evidence
remains that they used in their own sermons any of that
humor except for medieval exempla. This limited use may
result in part from the preachers' purposeful use of
humor to deal with their contemporary problems to which
the humor of previous periods did not as directly apply.
When used, some of the older humor was altered by the
preacher to serve his purpose -- a tendency we note in
the preachers' handling of biblical humor as well.

From the eighteenth, seventeenth and sixteenth centuries,
humorous sermons of Robert South (1634-1716), Antony of

---

55. Brewer, The Word on the Brazos, p. 64.

56. Richard Salter Storrs, Jr., Orations and Addresses,
(Boston: The Pilgrim Press, 1901), p. 545. George W.
Bethune, "The Eloquence of the Pulpit, with Illustrations
from the Apostle Paul" (An oration before the Porter
Rhetorical Society of the Theological Seminary at Andover,
Mass., September, 1842), Orations and Discoveries, (New
York: George Putnam, 1850), p. 232. Haven, Life of Father
Taylor, pp. lxxvi and 332. William Taylor, The Model
Preacher, (Cincinnati: Swormstedt and Poe, 1860), pp.
285-303 (esp. pp. 288 and 300). Fish's work was published
by M. W. Dodd, New York, 1856. Many editions of South's,
Hall's and Latimer's sermons were in print from their
time through the 19th century. The South volume familiar
to Taylor may have been the 1819 edition of Selected
Sermons in John Wesley's A Christian Library (volume 26).
For other editions see British Museum, General Catalogue
of Printed Books, (London: Balding and Mansell, 1964),
column 467. The most readily available Latimer volumes
during Storr's time were those two edited by John Watkins:
The Sermons and Life of the Right Reverend Father in God
and Constant Martyr of Jesus Christ, Hugh Latimer, Some
Time Bishop of Worchester, (London: Aylott, 1858). For
those many other Latimer volumes available, consult
British Museum, General Catalogue, cxxxvii, columns 140-
142. Hall's Sermons,(Volume 5 in his published Works,
(Oxford: n.p., 1837) was the most complete of dozens of
collections that might have been read in the nineteenth
century.

Vieira (1608-1697), Bishop Joseph Hall (1574-1656), and
Bishop Hugh Latimer (1485-1555) were admittedly read
(although not noticeably used) by several of our 18th
and 19th century American preachers who used pulpit humor.
Congregationalist Richard Storrs, Jr. read sermons of
Anglicans South and Hall; Bethune cited the humor of
Hall's sermons; Edward Taylor's daughter read to him
sermons of South and Latimer; and in his work on preach-
ing but not in his sermons, William Taylor cited specimens
of Latimer's pulpit humor which were widely circulated in
Henry C. Fish's Masterpieces of Pulpit Eloquence. [56]
In sermons, Jonathan Mayhew and Presbyterian Samuel
Porter referred to Antony Vieira's humorous "Sermon to
Fishes"; but neither included passages from the work. [57]
From the early church fathers, humor of St. Basil and
pulpit humor of St. John Chrysostom were reported by
Richard Storrs, Jr.; but the passages occur not in Storr's
sermons but in his lecture on Chrysostom. [58]

57. Jonathan Mayhew, Popish Idolatry (Boston: Draper,
Edes, Gill and Fleet, 1765), p. 36. Samuel Porter, A
Discourse on the Decrees of God, the Perseverance of the
Saints Perfection,(Pittsburgh: n.p., 1793), p. 22. No
sermon collection of the Portuguese-Brazilian Jesuit was
available in English or even French until after the period.
But the "sermon to fishes" was printed in Edwin Paxton
Hood, "Wit, Humor, and Courseness in the Pulpit," : Lamps
Pitchers, and Trumpets: Lectures on the Vocation of the
Preacher,(New York: M. W. Dodd, 1869), p. 268, and may
have been found in humor books. The best modern study
on Vieira's sermons is Raymond Cantel's Les Sermons de
Vieira; etude du style, (Paris: Edicones Hispano-Ameri-
canos, 1958).

58. In his speech "The Puritan Spirit," Storrs recounted
Basil's purported response to the Cappadocian deputy
who threatened to cut out his liver: "Thanks! You will
do me a favor. Where it is it has bothered me ever since
I can remember." Storr's, Orations, p. 432.
Storrs cites Chrysostom's ridicule of the people's
reliance on their houses for security. At a time when
the Emperor was expected to destroy Antioch in response
to the riots, Chrysostom mockingly said, "Let your
houses stand by you! Let them deliver you from this
threatening peril!" Ibid., p. 527.

Also probably familiar with Chrysostom's humor was
Charles Nisbet if the report is true that he read during
his college days all of Chrysostom's homilies. [59]

Medieval Exempla

Traces of humorous medieval pulpit exempla are found in
the sermons of Dwight Lyman Moody, Henry Ward Beecher, and
traveling Methodist evangelists Lorenzo Dow and Billy
Hibbard, who served in New York. But we do not know how
they came to know the exempla or whether they knew the
stories to be from medieval pulpit literature. Santero
art of the Southwest indicates at least one medieval
humorous exempla was known by the Indians there. And the
exempla was probably related in the priests' preaching
among the Indians; but the church records in Spanish
California show none of the exempla known or used there.
One additional exempla was used by traveling Dominican
evangelist Thomas Nicholas Burke in his 1872 preaching
tour through eastern American cities.

In his preaching, Lorenzo Dow used several medieval
sounding exempla; but the truncated form in which he
recorded two and the altered form of a third cloud any
certain identification of his immediate source for the
exempla and leave it uncertain whether he knew that his

---

59. Samuel Miller, Memoirs of the Rev. Charles Nisbet,
D.D. Late President of Dickinson College, Carlisle, (New
York: Robert Carter, 1840), p. 307. In the early
twentieth century, the Rev. George Hodges, dean of the
Episcopal Theological School, revealed his acquaintance
with Chrysostom's sermon ridicule of Eutropius. Geroge
Hodges, The Early Church from Ignatius to Augustine,
(Boston: Houghton Mifflin Co., 1915), p. 231. cf.
Donald Atwater, St. John Chrysostom the Voice of Gold,
(Milwaukee: The Bruce Publishing Co., 1939), p. 54.

material was used in the medieval pulpit. [60]   His version
of what is known today as the Matron of Ephesus exempla
is reproduced below from his tract "Reflections on
Matrimony" and is followed by the standard version
from Jacques de Vitry's thirteenth century exempla
collections which served as the model for many medieval
preachers.

> Wept night and day at the tomb -- no more comfort --
> all my love and joy is for ever gone -- but after-
> ward formed favorable ideas of the Sergeant -- who,
> to understand female nature, had scraped acquaintance
> and found he would smoke tobacco -- wished to be off;
> and observed that he was a deserter from the army,
> -- and two pounds offered to place his head on a
> pole at the forks of roads! She replied,-- dig up
> my husband, etc. and they will not know but the head
> is yours -- Mary wept and yet cut off the head. 61
>
> There was once a woman who loved her husband greatly
> during his life, and after his death would not leave
> his grave day or night. It happened at that time
> that a certain knight, who had deeply offended the
> king, was hung on a gallows set up near the cemetery.
> The king commanded one of his knights to guard the
> man who had been hanged, so that his relatives could
> not carry his body away, saying: "If you do not
> guard him well, I shall do unto you as I did to him."
> After the knight had guarded the hanged man for some
> time, he grew very thirsty one night, and seeing a
> light in the cemetery went there and found the woman
> mourning over her husband. While the knight was
> drawing and drinking some water, the relatives of
> the hanged man came secretly and took his body away.
> When the knight went back to his post and did not
> find the hanged man, he returned in consternation to
> the woman and began to lament and weep. She, casting

---

60. The truncated stories were those about the man and
his wife who disputed whether it was a mouse or a rat
that ran across the hearth, (Dow, "Reflections on Matrimony," Dealings, p. 42), and the miser who recounted his
gold so often that he wore it away (Ibid., p. 37). A
more fully stated tale appears in "Of Petticoat Love"
and concerns the man who made love to his wife whom he
thought was his neighbor's wife with whom he had arranged
an affair   (Ibid., p.46).

61. Dow, "Reflections on Matrimony", The Dealings, p. 42.
The Matron of Ephesus exempla served as the basis for
Christopher Fry's play A Phoenix Too Frequent, (New York:
Oxford University Press, 1960).

her eyes on the knight said: "What will you do for
me if I can deliver you and all your goods from the
king's hand?" He answered: "Whatever I can do, I
will do willingly; but I do not see how you can help
me." The woman replied: "Swear you will marry me,
and I will free you from the danger of the king's
anger." After he had sworn to marry her, she said:
"Let us take my husband's body and hang it secretly
upon the gallows." They did so, and the king
believed that it was the body of that malefactor,
and so the knight escaped. 62

The medieval story was used to help the people laugh at
death and the over reaction to it exemplified by the
widow's original intentions to stay with the body for
ever; but Dow used the tale to ridicule fickle wives who
were unfaithful to their husbands and mistreated their
memory.

In a few recorded sermons of Hibbard and in the extensive
verbatim sermons of Moody and Beecher, we find only three
additional exempla that may stem from the medival pulpit;
but none of the preachers explicitly credited the medieval
pulpit for their material. In his attack on "Christians"
who attended the theatre, Beecher told one tale:

I am told that Christians do attend the theatres.
Then I will tell them the story of the Ancients.
A holy monk reproached the Devil for stealing a young
man who was found at the theatre -- He promply
replied, "I found him on my premises, and took
him." 63

To the critics of his tract against Quakers, Hibbard
announced:

And it will be with them as it was with a fool I
heard of: the fool got angry with Providence, and
spit up towards the heavens, and the spittle fell
in his own face. 64

And with this story in "The Gospel of the New Testament,"
Moody defended repetition of ideas in sermons:

62. Thomas Crane, ed., The Exempla or Illustrative
Stories from the Sermons Vulgar of Jacques de Vitry,
(London: David Nutt, 1890), p. 228.

63. Henry Ward Beecher, "Popular Amusements," Lectures
to Young Men on Various Important Subjects,(New York:
J. B. Ford and Co., 1873), p. 174.

64. Hibbard, Memoirs, p. 312.

I heard of a minister who preached the same sermon
three times, and some of the brethren went to him
and told him he had better preach another sermon,
and he said when his congregation believed that he
would preach another sermon, but he didn't propose
to do so until they did. 65

A few additional examples of medieval pulpit humor were
known in the nineteenth century; but there remains no
evidence that they were used in sermons on the period. 66

At least one retablo of the Southwest santero reflects a
medieval humorous exemplum which probably was in use by
nineteenth century Catholic priests in their teaching of
Indians. Jose Aragon's "St. Michael the Archangel" reflects the traditional humorous humiliation of the devil
beneath the feet of the triumphant St. Michael. 67
Aragon not only rendered visually the traditon from the
middle ages, 68   but also may have drawn upon Luke 10:19
in the painting of the amusing dragon figure with a
scorpion tail:

Behold I have given you authority to tread upon ser-
pents and scorpions, and over all the powers of
the enemies and nothing shall hurt you.

We should bring to our viewing of this retablo an acquaintance with the Christmas plays staged in the New

---

65. Dwight L. Moody, "The Gospel of the New Testament,"
Glad Tidings, (New York: E. B. Treat, 1877), p. 75.

66.This medieval exemplum was known and told about ministers: "There was once a priest who thought he sang well,
although he had a horrible voice like an ass's. One day,
while he was singing, a woman who heard him began to weep.
The priest, thinking his sweet voice incited her to tears
and devotion, sang the louder, and the woman wept the
more. Then he asked the woman why she wept, and she said:
"Sir, I am that wretched woman whose ass the wolf devoured
the other day, and when I hear you singing, I remember
that my ass was wont to sing so." Crane, The Exempla,
p. 157.

67. Jose Aragon, "St. Michael the Archangel," Tempura
over gesso on hand-adzed pine. 27-15/16 x 15-3/4 ".
Museum of New Mexico, Santa Fe.

68. Granger Ryan and Helmut Ripperger, trans., The Golden
Legend of Jacobus de Voragine, (New York: Longmans
Green and Co., 1941), II, p. 578 ff.

42

Mexican churches, for these may have come to the mind of Aragon's contemporaries in viewing this work. Roland Dickey describes the Christmas play "Los Pastores" which with variations in costume dates from Aragon's period:

> The peak of excitement is a swordfight between Good and Evil personified by the Archangel Michael and Satan. A youth dressed in white and tinsel is Michael, and Satan is portrayed in a tight black suit, with red horns and tail. At the conclusion of the fight, the Archangel assumes the victorious pose in which he is shown in New Mexican santos one foot upon the prone but waggish Devil. It is Satan who is the comedian, teasing the performers and disturbing their ritual until exorcised by the Cross. 69

But in the extensive archives on California missions at Old Mission, Santa Barbara, there is no evidence that this or any other humorous medieval exemplum was in circulation among California priests in the nineteenth century. [70] Thomas Nicholas Burke's use of a medieval exemplum also reflected no alteration of the exemplum's original purpose and is considered in chapter five.

Evidences and Explanations of Missing Materials

The humorous pulpit materials discussed in this chapter and later chapters should be seen as forming the minimal contours which indicate a shape of the pulpit humor whose full dimensions we will never know. This study is based principally on the surviving written sermons of the

69. Roland F. Dickey, New Mexico Village Arts (Albuquerque University of New Mexico Press, 1949), p. 184.

70. In response to questions whether the archives revealed any knowledge or use of humorous medieval exempla in manuscripts, books or sermons, Father Maynard Geiger responded in the negative. Included in sermon books of seventeenth, eighteenth, and early nineteenth century which the priests had available to them were sermons by Antony of Vieira. In his thorough reading of archive materials, Father Geiger has been observant of humor as his article on unintended humorous glosses demonstrates: Occasional Newsletter for the Friends of the Santa Barbara Mission Archive-Library, (Fall, 1972), Vol. II, No. 1, pp. 4-6. But Father Geiger has discovered no intentional use of humor in 18th and 19th century California Catholic sermons. Letter, Maynard Geiger to Doug Adams, December 10, 1973.

ninety-one ministers known by their contemporaries for use of humor in the pulpit.[71] The amount of humorous materials borrowed from the tradition of Christian preaching through the nineteenth century was probably greater than we have found. These prominent preachers may have set the style copied by lesser known preachers whose sermons have not survived. Even in the surviving written sermons of the ninety-one, much humor of the oral preaching was eliminated by ministers, their editors, and biographers. By reliance on hearers' recollections, we have been able to restore only part of this humor. The desire to make lasting original contributions which scholars would take seriously mitigated against inclusion of humor -- expecially humor that was borrowed from others. And similar motivations probably affected the reporting of pulpit humor from the sermons of those ministers known for humor outside the pulpit.[72] But the redirections of preaching in the nineteenth century (which will be explored in chapter two) and the linguistic base of some historic pulpit humor (which does not survive translation) also account for the minimal awareness and use of humor from the history of Christian preaching.

Having published some of George Whitefield's sermons, Benjamin Franklin was but one of several who noted that Whitefield's written sermons failed to include the many humorous anecdotes which the evangelist included in his his oral presentations.[73] While some of Whitefield's

71. Appendix one lists the ninety-one and their periods of preaching.

72. Appendix two presents the numbers and percentages of ministers noted for humor both in and outside the pulpit.

73. Clarence Edward Macartney, Six Kings of the American Pulpit, (Philadeplphia Westminster Press, 1942), pp. 31-32, and J. B. Wakely, Anecdotes of the Rev. George Whitefield, (London: Hodder and Stoughton, 1879), p. 30. Joseph Gurney's Eighteen Sermons, preached by the late Rev. George Whitefield, (Newburyport: Blunt, 1797) was the only volume to preserve much of Whitefield's humor.

humor was used to deal with interruptions to his preaching and was understandably left out in the interest of presenting an uninterrupted train of thought in published sermons, Whitefield explained the elimination of other anecdotes in the introduction to the 1743 second edition of his Nine Sermons, published in Boston:

> I will not say word for word of what was delivered from the Pulpit; for, as I had occasion in America, Scotland, and England, to preach upon the same subjects, I was obliged, according to the freedom and assistance given me from above, to enlarge or make excursions, agreeable to the People's Circumstance amongst whom I was preaching the Kingdom of God. 74

While Whitefield used the same basic ideas many times in preaching on an estimated 18000 occasions and left slightly different versions of over 100 distinct sermons,[75] the Rev. Charles Nisbet, a Scotch divine who came to America to serve as president of Dickinson College, allowed only one of his American sermons to be published because he considered them to be unoriginal. [76] Nisbet was known for using much humor in his sermons; and his humor may have been borrowed from the tradition of Christian preaching.

John Ross Dix, who attended on the pulpit ministrations of several prominent preachers of the nineteenth century, noted the humor which filled Lyman Beecher's preaching.[77] But any person who has read through Beecher's sermons must concur with Dix's appraisal of the published versions:

> The Doctor does not print his wit, he utters it and leaves it; and most of his published papers are

74. George Whitefield, Nine Sermons, (Boston: Kneeland and Green, 1743), pp. i-ii.

75. Wakely, Anecdotes of the Rev. George Whitefield, p. 22.

76. Sarah Woods Parkinson, Charles Nisbet, First President of Dickinson College, (n.p., 1908), p. 8.

77. Dix, Pulpit Portraits, p. 159.

quite free from that with which his pulpit
services abound. 78

Beecher's son-in-law, Harriet's husband Calvin Stowe,
confirms Dix's appraisal of Beecher's frequent use of
anecdotes which were eliminated in the published sermons
and observed that Beecher showed extreme caution in
preparing anything for publication. 79

Those who heard Lemuel Haynes' "Universal Salvation"
found that the published version left out a few of the
happiest illustrations in the interest of reducing
controversy and personal acrimony.80   Charles Finney,
Jabez Swan, Jacob Knapp, Sam Jones, and Dwight L. Moody
were all critical of many newspaper reports of their
sermons -- the humorous sections of which they felt had
been distorted to discredit them and to inflame controversy which they wished to avoid.81   We have no evidence to determine if the newspaper accounts of the
humor were accurate or if the ministers altered their
oral presentations in editing the texts for publication
to escape criticism from colleagues or others. But in
the introduction to his Sermons on Important Subjects,
Charles Finney stated clearly his primary consideration
in publishing the sermons:

> Garbled extracts of some of them had been given
> to the public by note-takers and reviewers, which
> had entirely misrepresented their doctrines. 82

While Finney's published sermons show traces of humor,
we will never know the humor eliminated to appease his
friends, such as Nathaniel Beman who warned him against

---

78. Ibid., p. 152.

79. Calvin E. Stowe, "Sketches and Recollections of Dr.
Lyman Beecher," The Congregational Quarterly, (July,
1864), Vol. VI, No. III, pp. 221-222.

80. Cooley, Sketches, p. 96.

81. Finney, Sermons on Important Subjects, p.v Knapp,
Autobiography, p. 107; Swan, The Evangelist, p. 241.

82. Finney, Sermons on Important Subjects, p. v.

46

"the indulgence of anything like wit in the pulpit." [83]
In contrast to Finney, Sam Jones resisted pressures to
eliminate humor "to maintain the dignity of the pulpit."
He rejoined:

> Dignity is the starch of the shroud. The more
> dignity a fellow has the nearer dead he is. I
> expect to be as dignified as any of you when I get
> into my coffin. [84]

Elimination of humor was sometimes more evident when it
was carried out by editors or biographers, for in these
cases we often have the ministers' notes or complete
sermons from which the editors worked. In some cases the
editors' failure to include the humor was unavoidable;
but in other cases the elimination raises questions
about the editors' or biographers' motivations. Some
editing was necessary in order to reduce the minister's
orations to manageable size. For instance, Finney com-
plained that the published version of his Lectures on
Revivals contained less than a third of what he had said
each evening. He estimated that each printed lecture
would take about thirty minutes to read while he had
lectured at least an hour and three quarters on each
occasion.[85]   And one hardly faults the editor of
Parker's West Roxbury sermons for leaving out the humorous anecdotes; for in the margins of the sermon notes he
left, Parker simply noted that at this or that point he
used an anecdote, but did not specify the anecdotes.

Similarly, it is understandable that editors may have
eliminated passages whose sense and nonsense depended on

---

83. Letter, Beman to Finney, Oct. 23, 1829, Finney Papers,
Oberlin College Library. (cf. McLoughlin, p. 139).

84. Sam P. Jones, "The Fruits of the Spirit," Sermons
and Sayings, p. 108.

85. Charles Grandison Finney, Lectures on Revivals of
Religion, (Cambridge: Belknap Press of Harvard University Press, 1960), p. lvii.

the manner of delivery. When he prepared his sermons
for publication, Bethune was tempted to alter his sermons
precisely because they were originally written for oral
delivery; and without the aid of living gesture and
emphasis, he feared that the meaning would be lost.[86]
John Price Durbin's biographer, John Roche, gave an
example of the problem of conveying Durbin's oral humor
on the printed page:

> His pronunciation of a sentence would sometimes
> produce an amazing effect. An Elocutionist gave an
> example of this power in a speech of Senator
> Preston's. It was in the presidential campaign of
> 1840. Crittendon had spoken. Webster had occupied
> about two hours, but the people were still attentive.
> Preston rose and uttered but the name "Martin Van
> Buren!" This he thrice did; the first time with the
> accent of incredulity. The people shouted. The
> second time with the accent of scorn. The people
> stormed. But when the third time he exclaimed,
> "Martin VanBuren!" with the accent of contempt, the
> vast assembly was wild. They clapped, they stomped,
> they threw their hats into the air, and were at a
> loss for any adequate demonstration. It was
> Climax on a Word. 87

That editors should eliminate enigmatic passages such as
"Martin VanBuren, Martin VanBuren, Martin VanBuren" from
a speech or sermon would be understandable. And one must
acknowledge that this study of humor no doubt misses some
of such oral humor known only to those who observed the
gleam in the eyes of the preacher or the intonation in
his voice. Of Lyman Beecher's humor, Dix observed,
"there is a peculiar mannerism in the preacher, --
humorous, sometimes cover sly and glancing and sometimes
bold and open, which are not without their influence on
his popularity." [88] Fortunately observations of this
kind from those who heard the oral delivery supplement
the texts, and caution us to approach other passages

---

86. George Bethune, Sermons, (Philadelphia: Mentz and
Rovoudt, 1846), p. 5.

87. Roche, The Life of John Price Durbin, pp. 243-244.
Methodist Durbin served as editor of the Christian
Advocate and president of Dickinson College.

88. Dix, Pulpit Portraits, p. 152.

with the possibilities of humorous interpretation in mind.
But when an editor is interested only in the principle
ideas and timeless quality of a man's preaching, the
humor may be edited out; for the humor is generally
associated with an attack on a concrete problem rooted
within the timely issues of the day. This editing
process may be seen most fully in the handling of Jonathan
Mayhew's sermon on "Unlimited Submission and Non-resistance to the Higher Powers,"[89]   which John Adams
described as "seasoned with wit and satire superior to
any in Swift and Franklin."[90]   We will fully discuss
the sermon in chapter three; but we note here that a
recent edited version of the sermon eliminated nearly all
the humor of the original;[91]   and Charles W. Akers,
the biographer of Mayhew, quoted at length Adams' ap-
praisals of Mayhew's sermon but did not include the
portion dealing with the humorous dimension of the
material.[92]   While Adams' appraisal of Mayhew's wit
and his additional comment that the sermon "was read by
everybody"[93]   revealed Adams' Boston centricity,
Aker's slighting of Mayhew's satirical side may reveal a
concern for his critics; for calling the subject of
one's study "humorous" was not likely to forward the

---

89. Jonathan Mayhew, A Discourse Concerning Unlimited
Submission and Non-Resistance to the Higher Powers,
(Boston: Fowle and Gookin, 1750). Mayhew served as
pastor of West Church, Boston, and is classed with
Unitarianism though during his lifetime he considered
himself a Congregationalist.

90. John Wingate Thornton, ed., The Pulpit of the American Revolution,(Boston:Gould & Lincoln, 1860), p.45.

91. Peter N. Carroll, ed., Religion and the Coming of
the American Revolution, (Waltham: Ginn-Blaisdell, 1970),
pp. 30-52.

92. Charles W. Akers, Called Unto Liberty: A Life of
Jonathan Mayhew 1720-1766, (Cambridge: Harvard University
Press, 1964), pp. 93-94.

93. Thornton, The Pulpit, p. 45.

scholarly estimate of either the subject or the author.[94]
Finally, the directions of preaching in the nineteenth
century (which we survey in chapter two) did not encourage a minister to probe historic sermons from previous
periods in hopes of finding appropriate illustrations.
Those directions (toward particular individuals at camp
meetings on the frontier and against particular contemporary Infidel ideas attacked in the preaching of those
who followed Dwight) would have more likely led ministers
to rely on their own resources or to look to the sermons
and the experiences of their contemporaries who faced the
same particular problems. Not having access to books
containing historic pulpit humor would be one obvious
reason for the absence of its use in the pulpit; but
having access to the sermons of some ministers would
have done nothing to stimulate awareness and use of humor
in the pulpit if one did not read the minister's sermons
in the original language. The language barrier may
explain the absence of any acquaintance with the humor
in some reformation preaching. For instance, the humor
of Zwingli's sermons, marked by many plays on the words,
was dependent on the language and does not survive
translation.[95]

---

94. A similar hesitation to elaborate or highlight a
minister's humorous side (especially in the pulpit) may
be seen throughout the letters contained in Sprague's
Annals of the American Pulpit, I-IX. Such hesitation
should caution one to consider the numbers cited in
Appendix II as bare minimums. Other letters note that
the humor has been eliminated in volumes on the life or
sermons of ministers (e.g. Ibid., II, p. 433.).

95. Reading the passages in translation, one is apt to
dismiss the author's argument where translators fail to
note this. Oskar Farner, Zwingli the Reformer: His Life
and Work, trans. by D. G. Sear,(London: Lutterworth Press,
1952), p. 103f. (cf. Fritz Schmidt-Clausing, Zwingli's
Humor, Frankfort: Lamect, 1963 , passim.) The same problem may be seen in the awareness and the use of Luther's
humor for those who do not read German. And even in the
original language, the humor may be lost in editing as
has been the case with the Table Talk: Preserved Smith,
Luther's Table Talk, a Critical Study,(New York: Columbia
University Press, 1907), p. 95.

Patterns of Shared Humor

Reflecting on all of the foregoing instances in which
humorous materials were borrowed and used in sermons, we
are struck by several patterns. Nearly all of the users
of borrowed materials were Methodist; and nearly all of
the materials were borrowed from other nineteenth century
preachers (not exclusively Methodist). The medieval
exempla were the only exceptions to a pattern of no use
of humorous pulpit literature which originated prior to
1800. Most of the shared materials were altered from
the original purpose if not the original form to deal
with particular opposition which the preachers faced.
And the form of humor was pointed to put down the
opposition.

Methodists Dow, Cartwright, Gruber, Cravens, Hibbard,
Jones, Edward Taylor, William Taylor, Upham, and black
preachers all used others' pulpit humor and made no
noticeable effort to prevent such borrowed materials from
appearing in their published works. They show little in
common with Presbyterian Lyman Beecher's concern to edit
out humorous anecdotes or Presbyterian Charles Nisbet's
concern to keep from publication sermons which he considered unoriginal. Showing less concern with being judged
original, serious scholars, the Methodists demonstrated
a greater freedom in using humorous anecdotes. The
common evangelical thrust of their work and the wide
ranging frequent contacts with colleagues to whom their
circuit and episcopal systems exposed them stimulated
Methodists to be the most frequent users of borrowed
material. At the end of this chapter we note the contacts
which these Methodists had with each other; and at the
beginning of chapter two we note how the evangelical
nature of their preaching led to conflict and the employ-
ment of humor. While some Baptists traveled as widely
as Methodists and held their evangelical meetings in
settings where nearly as much conflict arose as in Methodist meetings, they had far fewer opportunities for
association with their fellow clergy because of the

larger size of their circuits.[96]

Those in other denominations concentrated in the east
had frequent contact with their brethren within a limited
geographic range; but they carried out their preaching
in settings where they rarely had to deal with interruptions or immediate advocates of opposing ideas. (The
case of Haynes' Universal Salvation was a notable exception.) Humor, which we note in this study was often
used to deal with opposition, was less immediately required for crowd control in the eastern churches which
attracted those already committed to the particular
denomination. This use of pulpit humor was highlighted
by Professor George Fishers' comment in the Independent
that his close friend Leonard Bacon's sharpest humor,
which he so often displayed in debate and essay, was
rarely shown in his sermons because in the pulpit Bacon
lacked the stimulus of opposition.[97]

The use of the medieval exempla in the nineteenth century
may be understood when we remember that these exempla
made their original appearance in the pulpit in situations
somewhat congruous to those which nineteenth century
Methodists faced. Jacques de Vitry set the style of using
the exempla in his preaching on evangelical missions
among sometimes hostile crowds largely uneducated in the
orthodox Christian faith. The exempla had the explicit
purpose of attracting the people's attention and keeping
it focused on the preaching when the people might other-
wise be distracted. And the exempla, which were used
sparingly by Jacques de Vity and other educated clergy,
came into more frequent use after the black plague had
decimated the more educated clergy in the fourteenth

---

96. H. K. Stimson, From the Stage Coach to the Pulpit,
(St. Louis: R. A. Campbell, 1874), p. 289.

97. Leonard Bacon: Pastor of the First Church in New Haven,
(New Haven: Tuttle, Morehouse and Taylor, 1882), p. 213.
Bacon followed Nathaniel Taylor as pastor of First
Congregational Church, New Haven, Connecticut.

century and when often uneducated clergy were hastily trained to minister to the needs of the people.[98]

The ease with which a short humorous story may be remembered argued for the use of the exempla by and among those whose abilities in reading barred them from reference to written sermon sources and helps to explain the survival of many exempla. As we have noted in several instances, the purpose of many eighteenth and nineteenth century preachers in using the exempla or anecdotes to put down particular opposition or ideas within a religious meeting is highlighted by the alterations we have noted in the humor's original point. And this shifting of the point without necessarily altering the form of the anecdote reveals the importance of studying the sermon texts within which the humorous materials were set.

Handling of Biblical Humor

> Young man: "Father Taylor, what did you think of my sermon this morning?" Father Taylor laid his hand gently and tenderly on the young man's shoulder and said: "My dear young Brother, if your text had the smallpox, your sermon never would have caught it. Good Morning." [99]

Father Taylor's quip could be applied to many eighteenth and nineteenth century American preachers from George Whitefield through Henry Ward Beecher. The focus of the awakenings (especially the second awakening) was on conversion of the particular persons in worship. The focus of much of New England preaching

---

98. Jacques de Vitry and others normally used only one exempla to recapture the attention and enforce the message of the sermon. cf. Jos. Mosher, The Exemplum in the Early Religious and Didactic Literature of England, (New York: Columbia University Press, 1911), p. 99.

99. Haven, Life of Father Taylor, p. vii.

after Edwards was elaboration of Edwards.[100]
And the focus after Dwight was shifted to an attack on
Infidel ideas. With the attention on potential converts,
Edwards' ideas, or Infidel arguments, there were few eyes
free for biblical exegesis. While some limited expository preaching may be noted,[101] the Biblical texts
were generally used as pretexts to attend to the major
purposes outlined in the preceeding sentence. The use of
biblical humor may be seen within this general handling
of scripture. There is no awareness of most of the
biblical humor which careful modern exegesis has revealed.[102]
Frequently preachers would cite Old and New Testament
precedents where God, or Elijah, or Jesus laughed or
helped others laugh at someone or group. But there was
never exegesis and only slight exposition of the passages.
Occasionally the bilical humor would be applied with some
integrity to congruous nineteenth century situations;but
as often the passage would be used to make a point that
had nothing to do with the text's meaning. Occasionally
even wholly extraneous bits of humor would be introduced
into the reading of scripture in worship. These uses of

---

100. As a teacher of New Testament, Calvin Stowe decried
what he saw as a degeneration from the Puritan fathers'
attention to the Bible as the source for preaching. "The
prime cause of this degeneracy lay in the fascination
and success of Edward's metaphysical writings." Stowe,
"Sketches," The Congregational Quarterly, p. 224. In
Oldtown Folks Henry May characterized Calvin Stowe's
criticism succinctly: Edwards' followers were doing
exegesis of Edwards and not the Scriptures. Henry May,
ed.,Oldtown Folks,(Cambridge: Belknap Press, 1966),p.10.

101. e.g. works of New York's Dutch Reform George W.
Bethune, "True Glory: A Sermon Preached Before the Third
Reformed Dutch Church of Philadelphia, Feb. 3, 1839 on
the occasion of the death of Stephen Von Rensselaer,
Orations, pp. 37-53. George Bethune, Sermons,(Philadelphia
Mentz and Rovoudt, 1846), and some sermons of Robert
Henderson, A Series of Sermons on Practical and Familiar
Subjects, (Knoxville, Tenn: Harskell and Brown, 1823)
I and II.

102. Jakob Jonsson, Humor and Irony in the New Testament,
(Reykjavik: Bokautgafa Menningarsjods, 1965); John Dominic
Crossan, The Dark Interval, (Chicago: Argus, 1975).

54

the Bible should not be taken to mean that the preachers
were not people of the book. Some of these uses developed
precisely because these people lived in constant communion with their Bibles.

Instances of derision or ridicule were the most frequent
Bible passages cited in sermons as illustrations of the
appropriateness of exciting laughter in worship. At the
prideful plans of man, "He who sits in the heavens laughs,
the Lord holds them in derision." Psalm 2:4 was cited
in several sermons by Whitefield and others as a model for
the minister's own ridiculing of the people's pride:

> The Lord Jesus sits in heaven, ruling over all, and
> causing all things to work for his childrens' good;
> he laughs you to scorn, he hath you in the utmost
> derision, and therefore so will I. 103

Proverbs 1.24-26 was another popular scripture for revealing laughter as a holy and appropriate response to
man's calamity. Dwight, Dow, Jones, and Presbyterian
Reuben Tinker cited the passage:

> "Because I have called," says the awful and final
> Judge, "and ye refused; I have stretched out my
> hand and no man regarded: but ye have set at naught
> all my counsel, and would none of my reproof: I
> also will laugh at your calamity; I will mock when
> your fear cometh." 104

"Answering a fool according to his folly," (Proverbs 26.5)
was still another passage used to justify the weapons of
ridicule in the pulpit.[105]   And passing mention was
made of Solomon's quips, Zechariah's sarcasm, Mordecai's

103. George Whitefield, "Saul's Conversion," Fifteen
Sermons Preached on Various Important Subjects, (Glasgow:
James Duncan & Son, 1792), p. 73, and The Works of the
Reverend George Whitefield, M.A., (London: Edward and
Charles Dilly, 1772), p. 146, and Reuben Tinker, Sermons,
(New York: Derby and Jackson, 1856), p. 167.

104. Timothy Dwight, Sermons, (New Haven: Hezekiah House
& Durrie & Peck, 1828), II, p. 266; Tinker, Sermons, p.
327; Sam P. Jones, Tabernacle Sermons, p. 336; and Dow,
"The Chain of Reason," The Dealings, p. 18.

105. William Taylor, Seven Years, p. 46.

irony, and Isaiah's satirizing of idol worship.[106]

Elijah's ironic mocking of the priests of Baal (I Kings xviii.27) was commonly cited as evidence of the appropriateness of biting humor in the mouths of God's ministers; but the text was not read out, much less exegeted.[107] Jacob Knapp justified his use of a little sermon irony by reference to Elijah. After a narrow escape from being ridden out of town on a rail during an extended meeting in Auburn, New York during 1834, Knapp wrote:

> In addressing the congregation on the next evening,
> I indulged in a little irony (as did Elijah before
> the priests of Baal); I told them that it was a
> hard thing to fight against God; that they were
> fainthearted set of fellows; that if they had even
> succeeded in getting me on their pole, they would
> have probably fainted and let me fall and break my
> neck. 108

But it was Charles Finney who made the most extended application of the text; and he applied it to Calvinists who cautioned the people about the possibilities of conversion experiences:

> I have often thought such teachers needed the rebuke
> of Elijah when he met the priests of Baal. "Cry
> aloud, for he is a God; either he is talking, or he
> is pursuing, or he is in a journey, or peradventure
> he sleepeth, and must be awakened." The minister
> who ventures to intimate God is not ready, and then
> tells the sinner to wait God's time, might almost as
> well tell him, that now God is asleep, or gone on a
> journey, and cannot attend to him at present. 109

George Bethune and Robert Dabney, Union's Professor of Pastoral Divinity, recognized that Jesus led people to

---

106. Bethune, Orations, p. 232; Whitefield, The Works
V-VI, p. 373; Tinker, Sermons, p. 99; Robert L. Dabney,
Sacred Rhetoric; or A Course of Lectures on Preaching,
(Richmond: Presbyterian Committee of Pub., 1870), p. 288.

107. Bethune, Orations, p. 232; Dabney, Sacred Rhetoric,
p. 288.

108. Knapp, Autobiography, p. 69.

109. Finney, Lectures on Revivals, p. 342.

laugh at gnat straining, camel swallowing hypocrites and
embarrassed scribes who questioned him on the baptism of
John or the paying of tribute; but both urged caution in
using such devices of ridicule.[110]   As professor of
rhetoric at Andover, Ebenezer Porter attacked any regular
use of sarcasm or satire which could be safely employed
only by the inspired.[111]

In sermons, Dwight Moody attempted the most extensive
exposition of the humorous depths of Jesus' stories.
Based on Luke: 14.16-24, Moody's humorous handling of
men's excuses for not responding to God's invitation did
little violence to the text and even revealed humor that
may be called integral to the passage. Of the first
man's excuse, Moody observed:

> I can imagine this man was a very polite man and he
> said, "I wish you would take back this message to
> your Lord, that I would like to be at that feast.
> Tell him there is not a man in the kingdom that
> would rather be there than myself, but I am so situ-
> ated that I can't come. Just tell him I have bought
> me a piece of ground, and that I must needs go and
> see it." Queer time to go and see to land, wasn't
> it? Just at that supper time. They were invited
> to supper, you see. But he must needs go and see
> it. He had not made a partial bargain and wanted to
> go and close the bargain. He did not have that
> good excuse. He had bought the land, and he must
> needs go and see it. Could he not have accepted
> this invitation and then gone and seen his land?
> If he had been a good business man, some one has
> said, he would have gone and looked at the land
> before he bought it. 112

Likewise, in his updated application of the Good Samaritan story, we may be inclined to see his casting of

---

110. Bethune, Orations, p. 232; Dabney, Sacred Rhetoric,
p. 288. In preaching on II Corinthians, xiii.5, Charles
Wadsworth, Minister to Calvary Church, San Francisco, saw
an ironic side to Paul's question to Corinthians, "Know
Ye Not Your Ownselves?", "Self Knowledge," Sermons,(New
York: A. Roman, 1869), p. 112. But Paul was not cited
for humor by any others in our period.

111. Lyman Mathews, Memoir of the Life and Character of
Ebenezer Porter, (Boston: Perkins & Marvin, 1837),pp.286-7.

112. Moody, "Excused," The Great Redemption, p. 105.

roles to ridicule the upper classes as not far removed
from Jesus' intentions in other passages if not in this
one:

> Suppose a Methodist had been down there trying to
> get that poor fellow on his beast and wasn't quite
> strong enough to lift him up, and a Presbyterian had
> come along and the Methodist says, "Help me get him
> on the beast." "What are you going to do with him?
> What church is he going to join?" asks the Presby-
> terian. "I haven't thought of that," says the
> Methodist; "I am going to save him first." "I
> won't do it. I shan't help him till I know what
> church he is going to join."
>
> An Episcopal brother comes along and wants to know
> if he has been confirmed. "We haven't got time to
> talk about that," says the Good Samaritan. "Let us
> save him." "What inn are you going to take him
> to?" asks another. "A Congregationalist, Methodist,
> Baptist, or Episcopal inn?" Isn't that the spirit
> of the times? 113

But other expositions or applications of New Testament
texts verge far from what a Calvin Stowe or other Bible
scholar would approve. At one conference meeting, Jacob
Gruber preached the following sermon to ridicule fashionable preachers and their conduct. The full text is
given to show to what lengths some ministers would go in
their use of scripture for their own purposes:

> A great many years ago a bold blasphemer was smitten
> by conviction when he was on his way to Damascus to
> persecute the Christians. He was taken to Damascus
> in great distress. Ananias, after hearing of the
> concern of mind under which Saul was laboring,
> started out to find him. It seems that he was
> stopping at the house of a gentleman by the name of
> Judas, not Judas Iscariot, for that person had been
> dead several years. The residence of this gentleman
> was in the street which was called Strait. I sup-
> pose it was the main street, or Broadway of the
> city, and hence it was not difficult to find. Arriv-
> ing at the mansion he rang the bell, and soon a
> servant made her appearance. He addressed her thus:
> "Is the gentleman of the house, Mr. Judas within?"
> Yes, sir," responded the servant, "he is at home."
> Taking out a glazed, gilt-edged card, on which was
> printed, Rev. Mr. Ananias, he handed it to the

113. W. H. Daniels, Moody, His Words, (New York: Nelson
and Phillips, 1877), pp. 213-214. Moody was never ordained and avoided alignment with any one denomination.

servant and said: "Take this card to him quickly."
Taking a seat, with his hat, cane, and gloves in
his left hand, his right being employed in arranging
his classical curls so as to present as much of an
intellectual air as possible, he awaited an answer.
Presently Mr. Judas makes his appearance, whereupon
Mr. Ananias rises, and making a graceful bow, says:
"Have I the honor to address Mr. Judas, the gentleman of the house?" "That is my name, sir; please
be seated." "I have called, Mr. Judas, to inquire
if a gentleman by the name of Mr. Saul is in his
chamber and a guest in your house." "Yes, sir;
Mr. Saul is in his chamber, in very great distress
and trouble of mind. He was brought here yesterday,
having fallen from his horse a few miles from the
city on the Jerusalem road." "O, I am very sorry
to hear of so painful an accident. I hope he is not
dangerously wounded." "No, sir, I think not, though
the fall has affected his sight very much, and he
complains considerable and prays a good deal." "Well,
I am very sorry; but that is not very strange, as
I believe he belongs to that sect of the Jews called
Pharisees, who make much of praying. How long
since he received this fall, Mr. Judas?" "About
three days since, and all the time he has not taken
any refreshment or rest." "Indeed! you don't say
so! he must be seriously hurt. May I be permitted
to see Mr. Saul?" "I will ascertain his pleasure,
Mr. Ananias, and let you know if you can have an
interview." After being gone a short time Mr. Judas
returns, and says, "Mr. Saul will be much pleased
to see you." When he is ushered into his presence
Saul is reclining on his couch in a room partially
darkened. Approaching him, Ananias says: "How do
you do, Mr. Saul? I understand you had done our
city the honor of a visit. Hope you had a pleasant
journey. How did you leave all the friends at
Jerusalem? How did you leave the high Priest? We
have very fine weather, Mr. Saul. I thought I would
call and pay my respects to you, as I was anxious
to have some conversation with you on theological
subjects. I am extremely sorry to hear of the
accident that happened to you in visiting our city,
and hope you will soon recover from your indispo-
sition." 114

What we consider as a rather light treatment of a text
should be seen within other humorous nineteenth century
handling of Bible texts -- handling which grew out of
living closely or exclusively with the Bible so that it
formed the media for one's lightest as well as one's

---

114. Strickland, The Life of Jacob Gruber, pp. 312-314.

most serious moments. Henry Ward Beecher's irrepressible
mirth could burst forth in the midst of a scripture
reading. For instance in his sermon on "The Ends and
Means" he was quoting Matthew 10.34-38 with this result:

> I am come to set a man at variance against his
> father, and the daughter against her mother, and
> the daughter-in-law against her mother-in-law
> (which might not require much!). A man's foes
> shall be they of his own household. 115

Beecher did not defend such mirthful outbursts in reading
scripture; and he did not see any of the purposeless
jesting in the Bible. [116]   Although mirth or levity (**the**
purposeless use of humor) was advocated in serious sermons
in the early eighteenth century by Congregationalist
Benjamin Colman and in the middle of the nineteenth century by Horace Bushnell, we find   little of mirth in
the sermons by Colman, Bushnell, or any other preacher
of the period. [117]

Word play on biblical phrases was the most common form
of mirth in what some might call less educated circles.

---

115. H. W. Beecher, Plymouth Pulpit: Sermons Preached in
Plymouth Church, Brooklyn, March-September, 1875, (Boston:
Pilgrim Press, 1875), III, p. 202.

116. Henry Ward Beecher, "The God of Comfort," The Sermons
of Henry Ward Beecher, First Series, 1868-69, (New York:
J. B. Ford, 1869), p. 13. John Donne's humor burst forth
in similar ways while reading scripture in worship. And
though it had a point, it was not related to the text or
sermon at hand. In a sermon at the lawyers' Lincoln's
Inn, Donne remarked: "Depart not for the literal under-
standings of those words of our Saviour: "If any man
sue thee at law for thy coate, Let him have thy cloake
too; for if thy adversary have it not, thine advocate
will." The Sermons of John Donne, (Berkeley: University
of California Press, 1955), II, p. 154.

117. Benjamin Colman, The Government and Improvement of
Mirth According to the Laws of Christianity, (Boston: B.
Green, 1707); Bushnell, Work and Play, p. 31f. In his
book about homiletics, Wm. Taylor cited many Old and New
Testament instances where laughter was a spontaneous
appropriate response to God or Christ for the mercy they
show to men or women. William Taylor, The Model Preacher,
pp. 189-192.

60

Such puns may not impress us (e.g. "Who is the shortest man in the Bible?" "Nehemiah."); but playing with words was a pastime on the frontier.[118]   Such mirth entered into one black pulpit exemplum:

> One Sunday he passes a bunch of lil' ole boys on de plannuhtation playin' marbles for keeps. So he ast em dey names an' writ 'em down on a paper bag he hab in his han' an' brung 'em 'fore de deacon boa'd for trial. De Major say de parent 'sponsible for de chile till he come to be sebun yeahs ole; so all dese lil' boys was five an' six an' dey papies had to 'ten de meetin' wid dey chilluns. When dey all don 'sembel, Revun Galloway, de pastuh, say, "Brothuh Buford, what's de 'ditement 'gainst dese chillun?"
> "Dey was playin' marbles on a Sunday for keeps," 'low de Major, "an' de Bible say, 'Don' do dat!'"
> "Show us whar 'bouts in de Holy Writ do hit say not to play marbles," 'low one of de pappies of de lil' boys, name of Silas Andrews.
> "Awright," de Major reply, "Ah'm gonna turn to hit rat now." So he turns ovuh to a passage of Scripture an' han' hit to de pastuh an' tell 'im to read what hit say.
> De pastuh tuck up de Bible an' lookin' at de passage de Major hab mark, turnt back 'roun to'a'ds de Major an' say, "Look heah, Brothuh Buford, dis passage don't say, 'Marble not, 'dis heah passage say 'Marvel not.'"
> "Huh, Ah knowed hit all de time," chuckled de Major. "Huccome you didn' know?"
> 'Nothuh time we was all in a Sunday School teachuhs' meetin' an' evuhbody haftuh ast a question 'bout de Word. So when Major Buford's turn come, he say, "Who kin tell me de name of de dog what lick Lazurs' sores?" Dis heah puzzle evuhbody, eben down to de pastuh. So fin'ly dey say, "We gibs up. What was his name?"
> "Look a heah," say de Major openin' de Word an'

118. Charles Francis Potter, a founder of the Humanist Society of New York, took an interest in these puns which were in circulation in his father's period at the end of the nineteenth century, "Fun Among the Fundamentalists," American Mercury, (May, 1939), 47, pp. 37-42. For discussion of frontier word play, see Wm. Henry Milburn, The Lance, Cross, and Canoe, (New York: N. D. Thompson Publishing Company, 1892), p. 473. There are some five hundred puns in the Old Testament and some two hundred in the New Testament. E. Russell, Paranomasia and Kindred Phenomena in the New Testament, (Chicago: University of Chicago Press, 1920).

p'intin' to a verse. "Don' you see whar hit say heah "Mo' Rover de dog lick Lazrus' sores'?" 119 Although this sort of word play entered the pulpit on rare occasions as in the foregoing black exemplum, usually pulpit humor was used in dealing with the most serious matters with the most serious of purposes as we see in subsequent chapters.

Encouragement and Communication of Humor
Professional Training and Association

When Dr. Nathaniel Emmons was asked "Why is it that young clergymen feel so small after talking with you?" he responded, "Because they feel so big before they come here." 120 Some humor was used in the professional training and continuing association of ministers to temper the pride of those who would be looking down on their people from pulpits. And the humor that permeated education and association of ministers outside the pulpit encouraged the use and appreciation of humor in the pulpit. We will note how many of our ninety-one users of humor experienced each other's humor in education, association and preaching. While much of the humor experienced outside the pulpit was never repeated in the pulpit, the humor is important for our consideration because it affected not only the ministers' attitudes toward humor but also the way in which some listeners approached even the preacher's solemn sermons. One of Congregationalist David Parsons' parishioners observed:

> I believe that his passion for drollery never came out in the least degree in the pulpit; though it may reasonably be doubted whether his jokes out of the pulpit, with which the memories of his hearers were stored, did not sometimes occur to them in the meeting house, to neutralize, in some degree the effect of his solemn appeals. 121

119. Brewer, The Word on the Brazos, p. 24.
120. Letter, Elam Smalley to Wm. Sprague, (November 9, 1852), Sprague, Annals, I, p. 705.
121. Letter, Samuel Osgood to Wm. Sprague (February 29, 1856), Sprague, Annals, II, p. 122. There was a similar expression concerning Nathan Strong's humor: Letter, Daniel Waldo to Wm. Sprague, (November 7, 1851), Sprague, Annals, II, p. 40.

After delivering his sermon, a young preacher came into
Nathaniel Emmons' study:

> The Doctor turned to the preacher, and very blandly
> remarked, "I liked your sermon this morning very
> much. It was well arranged, well argued, and well
> delivered. I have but one fault to find with it --
> it was not true." 122

In more formal educational training at Drew seminary
nearly a century later, Samuel Upham was noted for the
same style of response to sermons: "He would always find
something good to say about the sermon, namely the
text." 123   We have already read Jacob Gruber's prayer
for a young preacher's soft heart and head; and we have
noted Edward Taylor's evaluation of one young man's
careful expository preaching. Taylor regularly invited
young Harvard Divinity students to preach at his Sunday
morning service; and his audible comments during their
sermons combined with his closing prayers to keep young
preachers from too great a pride. 124 At one Bethel
prayer meeting, a young divine was exhorting the people
with an appropriate anecdote which had made the rounds in
the religious magazines. Father Taylor sighed out, "Lord,
deliver us from stale bread." 125 Students reported
that a similar deflating humor was a regular ingredient
in the more formal education under Dwight at Yale, Nisbet
at Dickinson, Porter at Andover, and Bacon at Yale. 126

122. Letter, Elam Smalley to Wm. Sprague, (November 9,
1852), Sprague, Annals, I, p. 705.

123. Ezra Squier Tipple, ed., Drew Theological Seminary
1867-1917, A Review of the First Half Century,(New York:
The Methodist Book Concern, 1917), p. 134.

124. Haven, Life of Father Taylor, p. 331.
125. Ibid., p. 159.
126. Letter, Denison Olmstead to William Sprague, (October
27, 1849), Sprague, Annals, II, p. 160; Miller, Memoirs
of the Rev. Charles Nisbet, pp. 218 and 327; Letter,
Ralph Emerson (professor at Andover) to William Sprague
(January 12, 1848), Sprague, Annals, II, p, 357; Leonard
Bacon, pp. 229 and 233. Bacon taught theology at Yale
from 1866 through 1871. (For more on Dwight's classroom
humor, see Sereno E. and W. T. Dwight, "Memoir of the
Life of President Dwight," Timothy Dwight Theology
Explained, I, pp. 21 and 47.)

In the tradition of training under a parish minister
during the late eighteenth century, Lemuel Haynes studied
with Congregationalist Daniel Farrand, whose humor in
and out of the pulpit was credited with encouraging the
development of Hayne's own humorous potential.[127]
Although we do not know if Haynes heard the following
anecdotes, they are samples of Farrand's biting humor in
evaluating first a student's preaching and then Ethan
Allen's The Oracles of Reason which the general had
proudly brought him. The preacher had spoken on the evil
spirits and the swine:

> Mr. Farrand declined expressing his opinion, remark-
> ing at the same time, that he was not in the habit
> of dealing in compliments. This increased, rather
> than diminished, the preacher's anxiety to hear his
> remarks, and he injected his request with still
> greater energy. "Well," said Mr. Farrand, "if you
> insist on hearing my opinion, I must say that I
> think you made worse work with the Scripture, than
> the devils did with the swine." 128

To General Allen's inquiry on Farrand's reaction to the
general's book, the minister replied:

> The paper of the book was rather poor in quality --
> otherwise he thought it a pity that so much of it
> should have been spoiled. 129

In more formal education, we see in chapter two how
Dwight's method of humor in preaching in the early
eighteen hundreds may have influenced one of his students,
Lyman Beecher. And at the close of the century President
Tipple noted that his seminary's graduates salted their
sermons with Samuel Upham's witty sayings. Among those
sayings were the following:

> Put off the old man, brethren, but don't put on the
> old woman. What is man to do if his ass falls into
> the pit on the Sabbath? Should he not pull it out?
> Yes, of course. But if he persists in falling in
> every Sunday, I would do one of two things: either
> fill up the pit or kill the ass. 130

127. Cooley, Sketches, pp. 60-62.
128. Letter, David Boardman to William Sprague, (March
29, 1953), Sprague, Annals, I, p. 492.
129. Ibid.
130. Tipple, Drew, p. 134; and Joy, Teachers of Drew,
p. 19.

And Upham's wit even at his death was publicized well
into the twentieth century through the Stylites column
of Halford Luccock, who picked up this bit of tradition
while teaching at Drew a decade after Upham:

> The beloved Dr. Samuel Upham lay dying; friends and
> relatives were gathered about the bed. The question
> arose whether he was still living or not. Someone
> advised, "Feel his feet. No one ever died with
> warm feet." Dr. Upham opened an eye and said, "John
> Hus did." These were his last words, and glorious
> ones too. They tell a lot about the relation of
> humor to faith. 131

Exposure to additional ministerial humor at association
meetings or other gatherings further stimulated the
development of attitudes that humor was not alien to the
minister's professional role. While differences in
denominational polity affected the geographic breadth
from which the ministers would be drawn together, the
minister's own mobility added additional contacts. With
the broadest geographic representation at such meetings
and the greatest personal mobility, Methodists reported
by far the largest number of contacts with humorous
colleagues -- contacts which may account in part for the
greater number of common anecdotes which they shared in
sermons.

Leonard Bacon noted the constant flow of humorous anecdotes that Lyman Beecher contributed at meetings of the
Connecticut Association Meeting.[132]He noted that few of
his colleagues cared to travel to other states and other
denominational meetings to serve as observers. 133
The Congregational and Presbyterian reports of other
living ministers' humor were generally confined to those
with whom they lived and worked closely. Storrs noted
Bacon's humor from their association as editors of The
Independent. [134]   Harriet Beecher Stowe wrote that her

---

131. Simeon Stylites, (Halford Luccock), "Research;
Human Interest and Humorous Stories of the Church,"
Christian Century, (July 7, 1954), p. 817; and Tipple,
Drew, p. 136.

132. Leonard Bacon, p. 126.

133. Johnston, Autobiography, p. 206.

134. Leonard Bacon, p. 197.

brother Henry Ward Beecher's humorous bent was encouraged
by fellow ministers with whom he gathered to await the
mail at a local store in Indianapolis:

> On one occasion Mr. Beecher, riding to one of the
> stations of his mission, was thrown over his horse's
> head in crossing the Miami, pitched into the water
> and crept out thoroughly immersed. The incident of
> course furnished occasion for talk. (His good friend
> the Baptist Minister greeted him at the store),
> "Oh, ho, Beecher, glad to see you! I thought you'd
> have to come into our way at last; you are as good
> as any of us now." A general laugh followed his
> sally. "Poh, poh," was the ready response, "my
> immersion was a different thing from that of your
> converts. You see, I was immersed by a horse, not
> by an ass. 135

Close friends in Scotland before coming to America,
Nisbet and John Witherspoon carried on in a humorous
vein; for example in his letter to Witherspoon on December
3, 1793, Nisbet wrote:

> I suppose that you have already heard of the arrival
> of Dr. Priestley's son in this country from France
> and that his father is expected soon to follow him
> from England. Is it not somewhat surprising that
> this young man, who, scarcely a year ago, gave
> public thanks to the National Assembly of France,
> for the immense honor they had done him, by adopting
> him as a French citizen, should have so soon become
> sick of 'liberty and equality,' and come over to
> this country, where we have only liberty?. . . By
> the way, I have seen the plan of the Federal City,
> and agree that it resembles the New Jerusalem in
> one respect; for as St. John testifies, that 'he
> saw no temple there', so I find no plan or place
> for a church in all that large draught. 136

135. H. B. Stowe, Men of Our Times, (Hartford: Hartford
Publishing Company, 1868), p. 549.

136. Miller, Memoirs, p. 231. Witherspoon's humor, well
illustrated in his satirical "Ecclesiastical Characteristics" did not appear in his sermons because he was
constitutionally unable to control himself once started
in a humorous direction. Therefore, he restrained himself from any such emotion in the pulpit. John Witherspoon, The Works of John Witherspoon, (Edinburgh: Ogle
and Aikman, 1804), I, p. xxxi. "Ecclesiastical Characteristics" appears in volume six of this nine volume edition,
pp. 139-284. For his American sermons, see volume four.

And at one association meeting, the following exchange
between the two was reported:

> Dr. N. -- I don't feel very well, I have a ringing
> in my head.
> Dr. W. -- Don't you know what that is a sign of?
> Dr. N. -- No sir, what is it a sign of?
> Dr. W. -- It is a sign that it is hollow.
> Dr. N. -- Why sir, does yours never ring?
> Dr. W. -- No indeed, never, never.
> Dr. N. -- And don't you know what that is a sign of?
> Dr. W. -- No, what is it?
> Dr. N. -- It is a sign it is cracked. [137]

A few other anecdotes reveal the same sort of cutting
retort in conversational humor that we noted as charac-
teristic of the pulpit humor. C. A. Bartol reported to
Mrs. Bushnell the following example of Bushnell's play-
fulness with a Presbyterian minister:

> "What have you been doing with my friend Bartol?"
> "I have not been doing anything but laying out the
> Presbyterian creed to him," was the reply. "You
> mean that you have been putting a shroud on it, I
> suppose; for that's what they do when they lay
> things out." [138]

And Unitarian Andrews Norton, Dexter Professor of Sacred
Literature at Harvard set back one smart student who
was known for partying:

> (the student) met Norton, who was proverbial for
> total abstinence, one morning after there had been
> some rather jubilant meetings, and said to him,
> 'Well, Norton, I understand you were intoxicated
> last evening.' To which he replied, "Well, K---l,
> I understand you were not, and I should like to know
> which of the two facts is the most singular." [139]

---

137. Parkinson, Charles Nisbet, p. 11. The Discussions in
the General Assembly of the Church of Scotland (where
professional lawyers were engaged to debate) were credited
with developing ministers' skills in ridicule and satire.
Miller, Memoirs, pp. 354-355.

138. Mary Bushnell Cheney, Life and Letters of Horace
Bushnell, (New York: Harper & Brothers, 1880), p. 186.

139. Letter, Jacizaniah Crosby to Wm. Sprague, (July 22,
1864), Sprague Annals, VIII, pp. 432.433.

By late nineteenth century, Leonard Bacon felt that the
incessant joking throughout the installation services in
the churches at the expense of those being installed
should be curtailed. [140]

In contrast to the Congregational and Presbyterian
patterns, Methodists reported humor from numerous contacts with their colleagues across the country. For
example, from the 1860 Methodist Conference Meeting in
Buffalo, the Daily Christian Advocate reported the lengthy
humorous presentations by Father Edward Taylor and
Peter Cartwright, who were called upon to help the assembly laugh at some of the pretenses of regionalism.
Below are reproduced a few humorous highlights which the
Advocate reporters noted as producing laughter. Father
Taylor was the first to speak:

> "After you have said Niagara, all that you may say
> is but the echo. It remains Niagara, and will roll
> and tumble and foam and play and sport till the
> last trumpet shall sound. It will remain Niagara
> whether you are friends or foes. So with this
> country. It is the greatest God ever gave to man;
> for Adam never had the enjoyment of it; and, if he
> had he could not have managed it. 141

> Oh, you will never find the match of our gospel!
> New England -- I don't know much about the West. I
> am at school yet; for I am only a school-boy -- I
> have been in New England only fifty years. 142

> "God bless the East! God bless the West! God bless
> the North! God bless the South! And oh for a gulf
> as deep as from here to Sirius, where all bickering
> and dissension and hair-splitting shall be forever
> buried! . . . Let us have a funeral first, and
> then a rejoicing. Bury the dead and open the
> prisons. Throw wide the gates, and take the long-
> itude off your faces. 143

---

140. Leonard Bacon, p. 121.
141. Haven, Life of Father Taylor, pp. 214-215.
142. Ibid., pp. 215-216.
143. Ibid., pp. 216-217.

Cartwright responded immediately after Taylor's Address:

> When Father Taylor was speaking, I was forcibly
> reminded of a remark made by a foreign lady, who
> visited this country a few years ago. She said
> there were but two cataracts in the United States,
> Niagara and Father Taylor; and I verily believe it.
> I mean to detain you but a few moments, but I am
> amazed at the ideas of Father Taylor about New
> England. I would bear his expenses over the moun-
> tains and through the West to infuse into his head
> some knowledge of that great world out there. New
> England is but a pea-patch compared to the West;
> and, if he could get so eloquent over New England,
> over the West he would get so eloquent that he
> would astonish the nations. I know the sun rises
> in the East; but it does not stay there long, and
> they have the sun, moon, and seven stars in the
> West. They have a world there.
>
> I cannot illustrate the matter better than by a
> description a man gave me of his farm in New England.
> He said he had about two acres and three quarters of
> land. He had three pigs and four chickens; and he
> raised on this great farm so many peas, oats, and
> potatoes, that, after supporting his wife and his
> wife's mother, he cleared from it one hundred
> dollars! Why, sir, in the West we would hardly make
> a pig pen of such a farm as that. 144

Humorous handling of regional and other antagonisms at
the Methodist conferences was not uncommon. At the 1844
General Conference, southerner George F. Pierce climaxed
an attack on northern Methodists with the words "let
New England go." Bald New Englander Jesse T. Peck objected heatedly to such an unbrotherly speech. Mr. Pierce
responded in a way that released the tension in a burst
of laughter:

> Mr. Pierce rose and, with amicability and wit,
> acknowledged he might owe an apology for his unfor-
> tunate expression about New England, but added, "if
> my speech has shocked the nerves of Brother Peck,
> my explanation will not ruffle a hair upon the
> crown of his head." 145

---

144. Ibid., p. 219.
145. Roche, Durbin, p. 127.

And in 1820 at the Baltimore general conference meeting
torn apart by heated arguments over whether presiding
elders were to be elected or not, Brother Axley of
Tennessee knelt to lead the closing prayer:

> Now, O Lord, thou knowest what a time we have had
> discussing, arguing, about this elder question;
> and thou knowest what our feelings are, we do not
> care what becomes of the team -- it is only who
> drives the oxen. 146

The Methodist system of shifting ministers from one post
to another (often at a great distance) also aided their
acquaintance with the humor of their brethren. Cravens
reported the humorous sermon preached by his presiding
elder Jacob Gruber in Virginia before Cravens was trans-
ferred to the Illinois circuit to serve under Peter
Cartwright. 147 Later Gruber served at St. George Church,
Philadelphia at the same time that humorous George
Cookman served the same church. 148 Samuel Upham served
in Boston during the last years of Edward Taylor's
ministry and appreciated his humor. Taylor had in the
early years of his ministry appreciated the humorous
preaching of Lorenzo Dow as did Methodist Abner Chase.149
Methodists Gruber and William Taylor knew of Dow's
preaching but discredited even his early efforts after
he began attacking the Methodist church.150 William

---

146. Wm. Henry Milburn, The Pioneers, Preachers, and
People, (New York: Derby and Jackson, 1860), p. 374.

147. Wakely, Bold Frontier Preacher, p. 53.

148. In 1828 they served the church together. Henry D.
Ridgeway, The Life of the Rev. Alfred Cookman; With Some
Account of His Father, The Rev. George Grimston Cookman,
(New York: Nelson and Phillips, 1874), p. 34; and
Strickland, The Life of Jacob Gruber, p. 293.

149. Haven, The Life of Father Taylor, pp. 87,88,and 95;
and Abner Chase, Recollections of the Past, (New York:
Conference Office, 1846), p. 43.

150. Strickland, The Life of Jacob Gruber, p. 27; and
Taylor, The Model Preacher, p. 74f.

Taylor's own career demonstrated Methodist mobility.
Beginning his ministry in Baltimore and moving to San
Francisco where he was famous for his street preaching,
Taylor returned East and preached to Father Edward
Taylor's Boston sailors and to Cartwright's young Illinois
circuit riders before serving in South America and becoming Bishop for Africa. [151] The mobility of those in the
Baptist denomination resulted in some similarly far flung
contacts. Hiram Stimson, who began his preaching in
New York State and was influenced by Jacob Knapp's
humorous style of preaching at Rochester, New York, removed to pastorates in Michigan and Wisconsin before
settling in Kansas. On return to New York to raise
funds for a Kansas college, he experienced Jabez Swan's
preaching. [152]

Publications

Religious publications were occasionally the channel for
humor to flow into the pulpit, but a less significant
channel than was personal contact. We have noted how
Haynes' "Universal Salvation" was spread from New England
through the Midwest by being included in The Dagon of
Calvinism. For the conclusion of his sermon Haynes had
borrowed a humorous parody of the Beatitudes which had
appeared in Theological Magazine:

> The tottering drunkard shall to glory real, And
> common trumpets endless pleasure feel.
> Blest are the haughty who despise the poor,
> For they're entitled to the heavenly store.
>
> . . .Blest all who hunger and who thirst to find
> A chance to plunder and to cheat mankind;
> Such die in peace -- for God to them has given
> To be unjust on earth, and go to heaven. [153]

151. William Taylor, Story of My Life, (New York: Eaton
and Mains, 1896), pp. 227 and 247.

152. Stimson, From the Stage Coach to the Pulpit, pp.308
and 381. Swan's humorous preaching had been approvingly
received by Knapp early in his career although Knapp
preceded Swan through Hamilton College and into the
ministry. Knapp, Autobiography, p. 41.

153. Haynes, Universal Salvation, p. 8.

Another jingle common in both Dow's and Finney's preaching may have been found in the religious press as an
attack on Calvinism:

You can, and you can't
You shall, and you shan't
You will, and you won't
You'll be damned if you don't. 154

Dow used this against Calvinist Baptists in the South
while Finney directed it against the Ultra Orthodox
Calvinists in New England. Sam Jones' source for
Beechers humor probably was an issue of Plymouth Pulpit
or one of the published volumes noted in our discussion
of Jones' expansion of Beecher's material.

The evidence reveals that little from the period's popular humorists or humorous novelists found its way into
sermons. Leonard Bacon's conversation was full of humor
from the novels of Scott and Dickens; [155] but nothing
from these sources appeared in his sermons. Sam Jones
used one of Josh Billings' quips in a sermon:

> Josh Billings says, the old miser that has accumu-
> lated his millions, and who then sits down with his
> millions at last without any capacity of enjoying
> it, reminds him of a fly that has fallen into a
> half barrel of molasses. 156

154. Finney, Sermons on Important Subjects, p. 81; Finney,
Lectures on Revivals, p. 205; Dow, "The Chain of Reason,"
The Dealings, p. 11. The jingle was aimed at the Ultra
Calvinist denial that man had the free will to convert
although he was viewed as responsible even if predestined
to hell. The tension was most obvious within Presbyterianism where the Old School extended divine sovereignty
to a virtual absolutism denying free will after the fall
and the New School insisted that God operated through a
moral government dependent on man's exercise of free will.

155. Leonard Bacon, p. 213.

156. Sam P. Jones, "Laying Up Money," Tabernacle Sermons,
p. 252.

And Jones used a bit of Burn's wit:

> Ouch! Mankind are but unco' weak
> And little to be trusted;
> When self the wavering balance shakes,
> It's rarely right adjusted. 157

The negligible use of humor from popular novels is better
understood when we remember that Methodists were most
inclined to use others' humor; and for Methodists, novels
were not the sorts of books with which one should spend
time. When John P. Durbin commented at a Baltimore
tract society meeting that he would rather a boy read
novels than nothing at all, Bishop Waugh sharply repri-
manded him. Durbin quickly responded and brought down
the house:

> What I want, Mr. President, is to give the mind a
> start; it is then in the wrong direction, to be
> sure, but I hope to head it off and turn it back
> and press it into the right course. 158

To turn people around and head them in a different
direction was the purpose of much ministerial humor as
we see in turning to chapter two.

---

157. Sam P. Jones, "What Is It to Be in Christ,"
Tabernacle Sermons, p. 121. From serious philosophical
volumes, some humor entered sermons. Jonathan Mayhew
quoted one humorous excerpt from John Locke: Jonathan
Mayhew, Sermons, (New York: Arno Press & The New York
Times, 1969), p. 37. A third or more of the stories in
the more popular eighteenth and nineteenth century jest
books concerned the clergy; but we have no evidence that
any of these jest book stories were used by clergy in
sermons: e.g. The Galaxy of Wit, (Boston: J. Reed,
1830), I and II; and H. Bennet, trans., The Treasury of
Wit, (London: Charles Dilly, 1786), I and II. Popular
jest books probably were a source for the regular
columns of "Humor" in the religious press: e.g. The
Catholic Northwestern Chronicle, (January 28, 1882),
XVI, No. 11, p. 6.

158. Roche, Durbin, p. 204.

CHAPTER II

MOTIVATIONS FOR HUMOR IN THE PULPIT

Once when Henry Ward Beecher was in the midst of an
impassioned flight of oratory, a drunken man in the
balcony waved his arms and crowed like a rooster.
Instantly Beecher stopped, took out his watch, and
remarked: "What -- morning already? I wouldn't
have believed it, but the instincts of the lower
animal are infallible." 1

Beecher's purported humorous handling of a drunken disrupter of his sermon opens our consideration of the motivations for humor in the pulpit. This anecdote is chosen
because in the East as often as on the frontier, humor
was used to gain a hearing: to attract and hold attention against all disruptions and to lead the people to
hear and to accept the Gospel with all of its controversial ideas and personal criticisms. This use of humor
to gain a hearing we explore as "evangelical motivation."
This motivation led to a style of preaching called hortatory which centered on persons present and which
justified its rambling style on the grounds that it was
after a rambling people. [2] Humor was necessary because
man was human. A recognition of reason's limits and the
resulting unresolvable conflicts on the logical level was

1. Weisfeld, The Pulpit Treasury, p. 19. As one would
expect, no record of this disruption is found in any
collection of Beecher's sermons; but this purported
response is not uncharacteristic of Beecher's behaviour
with his congregation. During the period of announce-
ments which often occupied up to half an hour of the
worship service before his sermon, Beecher engaged in
banter with members of his congregation. Fowler, The
American Pulpit, pp. 176 and 171.

2. The justification was given in a sermon by Congrega-
tionalist Samuel Moody and reported by Letter, Jotham
Sewell to Wm. Sprague, July 13, 1850, Annals, I, p. 246.
Such a justification was also credited to George White-
field in the popular American joke book, The Galaxy of
Wit, p. 96.

73

the basis for what we explore as "theological motivation" for humor. At the opening of the nineteenth century, Yale President Timothy Dwight heightened this use of humor by counselling Christians to turn their attention away from defending and elaborating Christian doctrine and toward attacking Infidel positions which were attracting adherents. Both "evangelical" and "theological" strategies attempted to secure the sovereignty of God at the center of the people's minds and lives and fight the encroachment of a host of idolatries. Reason was insufficient not only to put down conclusively Infidel ideas, but also to put down the idolatries which competed for the allegiance of eighteenth and nineteenth century man. The last section of this chapter reveals the patterns of preferences that were explicitly identified as the period's idols. Chapters three, four and five demonstrate how a high percentage of the period's pulpit humor was directed at putting down these idolatries of power, wisdom, and wealth.

The Evangelical Motivation

William Strickland characterized much nineteenth century Methodist preaching as hortatory: a preaching focused on the people and concerned with inciting or encouraging them to change. [3] This focus of the preaching on the people explains the presence of much humor and the absence of much exegesis. In defending this style of preaching with all its humor, Sam Jones noted:

> I hold up the looking glass, and you people laugh at your carcasses reflected there. [4]
> Don't criticize me, but criticize yourself. You can pick a thousand flaws in my sermon, but I don't care whether my sermon goes to heaven or not. [5]

---

3. Strickland, The Life of Jacob Gruber, p. 47.
4. Jones, Sermons: Wise and Witty, p. 32.
5. Ibid., p. 34.

Different patterns of worship in settled and unsettled
areas accounted for some different patterns of humor
used by ministers to attract and keep attention and
introduce controversial comments; but the differences
in the uses of humor were in degree and not in kind.

Attracting Attention

In camp meetings and street preaching in less settled
environments, a minister used humor at the beginning of
a sermon to draw the crowd together; and he used humor
throughout the sermon as needed to control the crowd and
keep its attention when he was challenged directly by
those who did not stand within the faith or his particular faith. Within the walls of the protracted meetings
and formal worship of more settled areas, a minister
often used humor during the first of a series of sermons
to attract attention to the series. And other humor was
employed during the sermon to deal with distractions.
More of the preachers' humor in unsettled environments
was directed at those who intentionally interrupted the
proceedings by comments or actions; and more of the
preachers' humor in the settled environments was directed
at those who unintentionally distracted attention by
trying to walk out of the worship or by falling asleep.
But even the settled minister in prestigious eastern
churches faced occasional intentional disrupters. While
the humor was often intended to silence the disturbance
without force so that the serious message might be heard
by others, some serious controversial and critical comments were clothed in a humorous context or manner of
delivery so that the people heard the word.

Of his preaching at the camp meetings in the early 1800's
Peter Cartwright recounted:

> I commenced by relating several short anecdotes.
> They began to draw up nearer, and nearer still; the

anecdotes were all calculated to excite their risibilities. 6

William Taylor related a similar strategy as he mounted a whiskey or pork barrel to begin his sermons in the streets of San Francisco at mid century. [7] Those competing for initial attention Cartwright called by name; and he related their personal shames to silence them and further increase attention to his words. [8]

Jabez Swan and Jacob Knapp used similar strategies in protracted meetings among Baptists; but in their cases, the humor was sometimes directed against those who were absent on the first evening but who as a result were present on subsequent evenings. [9] In the first half of the century, protracted meetings were to Baptists what camp meetings were to Methodists and Cumberland Presbyterians. [10] Whereas the camp meeting on the frontier would extend several days with massive round-the-clock outdoor services and small tent prayer meetings, the protracted meetings in the eastern cities offered indoor preaching at least once a day for a period of weeks if not months. By the last half of the century, the revival patterns of Methodists as well as Baptists were modeled on the protracted meetings which were better adapted to settled city life.

In this protracted meeting pattern, Sam Jones and Dwight Lyman Moody conducted their revivals and used humor extensively in sermons for the first evenings. The first few sermons were also the most rambling and least based

6. Strickland, Cartwright, p. 218.

7. Taylor, Seven Years, passim.

8. Sydney Greebie and Marjorie Greebie, Hoofbeats in the Canebrake, (Penobscot: Traversity Press, 1962), p. 176.

9. Knapp, Autobiography, passim, and F. Denison, The Evangelist; Or Life and Labors of Rev. Jabez S. Swan, (Waterford: William Peckham, 1873), p. 414.

10. Ibid., p. 207.

on any biblical text. For instance, in Sam Jones' revival at Loveland, Ohio ,(outside of Cincinnati) during
August, 1885, his first sermon was called the most humorous, though it was not extensively reported. [11] His
first sermon in a Nashville series was extensively reported with the dozens of interruptions by laughter. No
single thought was developed through the first sermon;
and it was characterized by evocative criticisms clothed
in humor:

> I know a merchant by the name of Lee. I once saw a
> customer come into his store to buy a plough, and
> he asked whether the blade was hard enough. "It
> seems to be too soft," was Mr. Lee's reply. Wasn't
> he a strange merchant? I asked him why he hadn't
> told the man that perhaps it wasn't hard enough, or
> something of that sort, but he wouldn't tell a lie.
> I should think a merchant of that kind would feel
> lonesome in most places -- lonesome about in spots.
> (Laughter) A man can lie and never open his mouth.
> That's the way a horse trader lies -- not knowing
> that to keep his mouth shut is the biggest sort of
> a lie. (Laughter) 12

> His wife one morning suggested that it was her
> birthday, and he said to himself: "I've got a good
> wife; she has been kind, self-sacrificing and true
> in all respects. I must buy her a present." So he
> went down town that day, and walked into a store and
> bought himself a new hat, consoling himself that
> nothing would more please a good wife than to make
> her husband a present of a new hat. (Great laughter
> -- especially among the married ladies) He's the
> meanest man I ever saw, (laughter) and there are a
> great many men just that way.

> We are too often unjust to our children, exacting
> of them things we don't do ourselves, and berating
> them with our tongues when they don't understand
> what we want. And then we are too mean to say ten
> words to make one of them happy. Oh, how unjust we
> are to wives, husbands, and children!

> If you'll put a little downright justice in your
> conduct with your children you'll have happier homes.

---

11. Jones, Sermons: Wise and Witty, p. 51.
12. Ibid., p. 6. "Lonesome about in spots" was the report
of the minister's words however ungrammatical.

Did you ever start anywhere with your wife and keep
hurrying her up when you ought to know she has not
only to dress herself, but five children besides,
while you have nothing to do but get ready? "Hurry
up, hurry up: I don't want to be late! If you
don't hurry I'll go on by myself." And after a
while she tells you to "go on, husband: I'm afraid
I can't get ready in time for you: I don't want to
hinder you." I've done just that way. (Laughter.)
I have walked off, out the gate and fifty yards down
the road, and then I'd stop and think. I'd say:
"Sam Jones, you are the meanest man living, and you
shan't go to church nor anywhere else till you learn
how to behave yourself." And then I walk back and
go in and find worry in my wife's face and tears in
her eyes, and I go up and put my arms around her and
kiss her -- there's nobody there but us two (Laughter)
and say: "Wife, I'm as mean as a dog, I know I am,
and I want you to forgive me," and she forgives me,
and we get ready and go -- and find ourselves the
first ones there. (Laughter.) 13

Dwight Lyman Moody's first sermon of a series was of a
similar character. [14] These initial sermons must be
considered in the context of the whole series, the later
sermons of which were invariably less humorous and more
concerned with developing a single theme. [15]

Handling Disruptions

In settled and unsettled areas, ministers faced disruptions during worship services and used humor to silence
disrupters and restore order. While the setting of outdoor worship in unsettled areas admitted disruptions
(such as dog fights) unknown in the midst of more formal
places of worship, the walled in worship of settled
communities occasioned disruptions uncommon in outdoor
meetings; for while a person might inconspicuously come
or go in the wall-less camp meeting or street preaching,
a person could not so easily leave an indoor formal
worship service without attracting attention.

13. Ibid., p. 7.
14. Moody, "Opening Sermon," The Great Redemption.
15. This pattern is most clearly seen in the verbatim
reporting of Moody's Boston revival and Jones' St. Louis
revival: D. L. Moody, To All People, (New York: E. B.
Treat, 1877); and Sam Jones, Tabernacle Sermons.

Intentional Disruptions

While a few examples of his humorous retorts survive,
George Whitefield's style of outdoor preaching and use of
humor to handle disruptors of his meetings was cited by
a few other Methodists to justify their own style. [16]

Whitefield crossed the Atlantic thirteen times in the
course of a thirty-four year ministry, preached in the
colonies from Georgia to Massachusetts, and further
identified himself with America by being buried beneath
the pulpit of old South Presbyterian Church, Newburyport, Massachusetts, in 1770 according to his request.
His example of humor in the pulpit rather than John
Wesley's injunction to soberness is reflected in the fact
that Methodists in America demonstrated as much humor in
the pulpit as most other groups of American clergy. [17]
Wesley advised that one's "whole deportment before the
congregation be serious, weighty, and solemn;" [18] and
Methodists wrote Wesley's principles into their "Form of
Discipline": "Be serious, let your motto be, holiness
to the Lord. Avoid all lightness, jesting and foolish
talking." [19] But anecdotes about Whitefield's and even
Wesley's ability to use humor to deal with an adversary
provided the context in which the "Form of Discipline"

16. Taylor, Seven Years; and Wakely, Anecdotes of the Rev.
George Whitefield, p. 123. Whitefield's Nine Sermons,
his Sermons on Various Subjects, and his Five Sermons on
the Following Subjects, (Philadelphia: Bradford, 1740),
were the best selling books in the colonies from 1739-
1741.

17. See Appendix Two.

18. John Wesley, The Works of the Rev. John Wesley, A.M.,
(New York: B. Waugh and J. Mason, 1835), VII, pp. 224-225.

19. H. Shelton Smith, Robert J. Handy, and Lefferts A.
Loescher, American Christianity, (New York: Scribner,
1960), I, p. 457

80

was set. Included among the Whitefield anecdotes was the
following which showed a cutting side to his character:

> On Whitefield's arrival in Boston, where he had not
> yet preached, he met, while walking through the
> streets a famous Doctor of Divinity, who not only
> had a deep seated prejudice against him, but was
> also his enemy. Recognizing each other at once,
> the doctor remarked, "I am sorry to see you here."
> Whitefield replied, "And so is the devil." 20

No less cutting nor less humorous was John Wesley's
response which Methodist preacher and United States
Senate Chaplain George Cookman related in his sermon
before the fifth anniversary meeting of the Methodist
Preacher's Aid Society of Baltimore assembled in Light
Street Church, Baltimore, on November 3, 1835:

> It is related of Mr. Wesley, that, riding one day to
> preach, he met a pompous country magistrate, mounted
> on his stately charger, who looking with ineffable
> scorn upon the little apostle of Methodism, exclaimed
> in a rough tone of voice, "I shall not give the road
> to a fool." Wesley very calmly reined his horse to
> the left, and quietly replied, "But I will." 21

Cookman commended for his hearers' emulation Wesley's
way of dealing with the lofty. Such sharp retorts
reported as coming from the most prominent members of
their denomination freed Methodist ministers to engage in
similar ways when the occasions arose.

Incidents in which humor was helpful to put down dis-

---

20. Wakely, Anecdotes of the Rev. George Whitefield,
p. 142. The encounter cannot be confirmed by reference
to sermons; but Wakely appears to be a reliable source
for Whitefield's humor. Although Wakely did not cite
the sources for the anecdotes by sermon titles that could
be readily checked, a thorough reading of Whitefield's
sermons in their various editions shows that many of the
anecdotes Wakely cited are historically valid.

21. George G. Cookman, Speeches Delivered on Various
Occasions,(New York: George Lane, 1840), p. 74. Whether
these anecdotes about Wesley or Whitefield were true was
less important than the fact that they were circulated
among Methodist preachers and associated with these
leaders.

rupters came frequently in camp meetings. A challenge
to the minister's ordering of the meeting took various
forms in the course of worship. We have noted how humor
was used to draw the camp meeting to order and how Cartwright and Gruber used humor to put down young men in
ruffled shirts who insisted on peering about from the
tops of benches. Young ladies were put down in analogous ways:

> When the time had come for preaching, every effort
> of the elder failed to get the congregation orderly
> arranged. Quite a number were standing on the seats,
> and among them several ladies. Gruber again lifted
> up his voice, the squeaking German accent of which
> immediately arrested attention, and said: "If
> those young ladies there only knew what great holes
> they have in their stockings they wouldn't be
> standing on the bench where they can be seem by
> everybody." They all dropped suddenly as if they
> had been shot. Order was restored, and all was
> quiet. After the discourse was ended one of the
> preachers asked how he knew the young ladies had
> holes in their stockings. "Why," said he in his
> quizzical manner, "did you ever know stockings with-
> out holes in them?" 22

To bring men and women to their knees, Peter Cartwright
may have employed humor in the following way to shame
even hecklers to conform:

> "And now," said Peter, "I must remind you that you
> are going to get down on your knees." His eyes
> traveled from the tight silk sheaths with no petti-
> coats under them hobbling the knees of the girls in
> front to the tightly enclosed thighs and hinder
> parts of the young gentlemen hecklers. "And from
> what I can see from here there's going to be a
> mighty busting of seams from the waist down. If
> there's anybody here that don't dare trust their
> pants and their pet--" Here he gave a roguishly
> embarrased glance to the girls and dropped his long
> black lashes on his cheeks bashfully, "and their
> no petticoats to the mercy of the Lord, I give them
> the opportunity to leave." The girls tittered
> hysterically. Some of the young men's faces were
> scarlet. No one left. "Very well," said Peter,
> "We will now risk the power of God." 23

---

22. Strickland, The Life of Jacob Gruber, p. 88.

Direct challenges to the minister's control occurred
when bystanders interrupted the sermon; but the humor
put down many such challenges. At a mid-century California camp meeting in the Bodega Hills, Methodist
"Father" Cox was interrupted in the first moments of
his sermon:

> Many souls have been converted, and now I want them
> all to join the Church. When I was a boy, I learned
> that it was best to string my fish as I caught them,
> lest they should flutter back into the water. I
> want to string my fish -- that is, take all the
> young converts into the Church, and put them to work
> for Christ, lest they go back into the world" --
> "you can't catch me!" loudly interrupted a rowdyish
> looking fellow who sat on a slab near the rostrum.
> "I am not fishing for gar!" retorted Father Cox,
> casting a contemptuous glance at the fellow, and
> then went on with his work.
> The gar-fish is the abomination of all true fisher-
> men -- hard to catch, coarse-flavored, bony, and
> nearly worthless when caught. The vulgar fellow
> became the butt of the campground, and soon mounted
> his mustang, and galloped off, amid the derision
> even of his own sort. 24

Methodist William Milburn reported the humorous handling
of one camp meeting Infidel who interrupted a minister
in the midst of his sermon. The use of reductio ad
absurdum to answer the Infidel's initial comment was
similar to the strategy employed in the most sophisticated
eastern pulpits:

---

23. Greenbie, Hoofbeats in the Canebrake, p. 279. Sydney
Greenbie died before publishing the final volume in this
trilogy on Cartwright's life. The third volume was to
include the citation of all his primary sources. This
anecdote did not come from the two primary sources on
Cartwright's ministry: Strickland, Autobiography of
Peter Cartwright, and W. S. Hooper, ed., Fifty Years A
Presiding Elder, (Cincinnati: Cranston and Stowe, 1871).
But Greenbie claimed that all of the direct address
portions of his works were historical even though some
of his narrative portions were fictional to fill historic
gaps with probable occurrences. Inquiries about this
anecdote by letters to Marjorie Barstow Greenbie through
Traversity Press have gone unanswered. "Their no petti-
coats" was the report of his words.
24. O.P. Fitzgerald, California Sketches, (Nashville:
Southern Methodist Pub. House, 1880), p. 86.

"I know Latin and Greek, and the soul only means the
wind or air -- you might say a smelling bottle."
The preacher, nothing daunted, answered, "Then let us
see how my text would read: For what is man profited if he gain the whole world and lose his own
smelling bottle; or, what shall a man give in exchange for his smelling bottle?" 25

The strategy was not to dignify the interrupter and his

comment with serious treatment. As we all will explore

further in chapter four, an unbeliever's problem was

seen as one which reason could not solve. The taking of

one's self too seriously was seen as part of the infidel's

problem; and so the humorous response was a part of the

treatment for this sin of pride.

While there are fewer reports of direct challenges to

the minister's control of the meeting in settled eastern

churches, when such disruptions occurred the minister's

use of ridiculing humor restored his control. Henry

Ward Beecher's response to the drunk in Plymouth church

has been cited. To a more sober challenge, Baptist

Jabez Swan responded with sharp humor:

Preparatory to his final appeal however, he paused
and did the uncommon thing of calling upon all in
the house to testify their assent to his argument
and conclusion by rising up. All in the house rose
up save Mr. B., who was sitting in the end of a body
slip next to the south aisle. He, instead of rising,
slammed back the slip door, slid out into the aisle
and sat down on his feet. Elder Swan, observing
him, invited the congregation to be seated. Then
calmly while his eye glowed with animation, he spoke
briefly of the children of God as sheep, and the
Savior as the Shepherd. Then lifting up his sten-
torian voice, he exclaimed, "Whoever in God's world
saw a sheep sit back on his haunches?" and at the
same time imitated the posture of Mr. B. Rising
again, with double strength of voice, he added,
"Beware of dogs." 26

The strategy of ridicule brought disturbers not only to

silence but also on occasion to submission. Swan's

25. William Henry Milburn, The Lance, Cross and Canoe,
pp. 366-367.
26. F. Denison, The Evangelist; Or life and Labors of
Rev. Jabez S. Swan, p. 213.

84

editor noted that the man whom Swan held up to ridicule
became his friend and followed him into the Baptist
ministry. [27]

To the man who raised speculative questions which would
focus attention on others or abstract issues, the minister responded in ways that turned attention to the critical issue of the man's personal salvation. In his
Boston Bethel on the occasion when singer Jenny Lind was
in the congregation, "Father" Edward Taylor was interrupted by a tall man who stepped onto the lower pulpit
stairs and inquired whether a person could go to heaven
if they died while attending one of Jenny Lind's con-
certs. Taylor glared at the man and responded:

> A Christian will go to heaven wherever he dies; and
> a fool will be a fool wherever he is, -- even if he
> is on the steps of the pulpit. [28]

A similar concern to keep the mind focused on personal
salvation was reflected in Congregationalist William
Rogers' response to a question at the close of his
exhortation on temperance in a school house to which his
reputation had attracted many hard drinkers. One of the
drunks cried out, "Mr., can you tell me the way to hell?"
"Yes," said Rogers, "keep right on, Sir." [29]

Unintentional Disruptions

From his mid-century San Francisco street preaching
experiences, William Taylor illustrated the unintended
disruptions which occurred in that setting and which he
turned to some advantage by a humorous comment to regain
attention. On one Sunday afternoon in 1853 at the "Long
Wharf," Taylor was launched into his sermon. A man
attempting to ride through the crowded street provided
the preacher with an illustration:

---

27. Ibid.
28. Haven, Life of Father Taylor, p. 130.
29. Letter, Rev. W. A. Stearns to William Sprague, August
24, 1854, Sprague, Annals, II, p. 734.

"Gentlemen, I stand on what I suppose to be a cask
of brandy. Keep it tightly bunged and spiled, and
it is entirely harmless, and answers some very good
purposes; it even makes a very good pulpit. But
draw that spile, and fifty men will lie down here,
and drink up its spirit, and then wallow in the
gutter, and before ten o'clock tonight will carry
sorrow and desolation to the hearts of fifty families. So that man there, trying to urge his horse
through the audience," "all eyes turned from the cask
to the man, "if he had kept his mouth shut, we might
have supposed him a very decent fellow; but finding
the street blocked up with this living mass of
humanity, he drew the spile, and out gurgled the
most profane oaths and curses. But, while there is
now all the difference between outwardly moral and
out-breaking sinners, as between a tightly bunged
and an open cask of brandy, I would invite your
attention to a time when there will be no material
difference between them. 30

On another occasion a man on a jack-ass tried to get

through a street crowded by Taylor's audience and re-

ceived a similar treatment. The ass finally refused to

go further; and Taylor noted:

See there, that animal, like Balaam's of the same
kind, has more respect for the worship of God than
his master, who only lacks the ears of being the
greater ass of the two. 31

When a dog fight down the street from one of his meetings

attracted the attention of some boys and threatened to

draw more of his crowd away, Taylor used humor not only

to check the movement of the crowd but also to draw

some comparisons between that occasion and the criticisms

of Methodist meetings (often attacked for the enthusiasm

and animal excitement they engendered):

"Run boys, run! We are all seeking enjoyment, and
trying to be happy! There's a rare opportunity!
You are under a high excitement of animal feeling!
A glorious entertainment that! What an intellectual
feast it must be to enlightened, highminded American

---

30. Taylor, Seven Years, pp. 40-41.
31. Ibid., p. 130.

gentlemen, to see a couple of dogs fight!" 32
The setting of Eastern churches produced other varieties
of unintentional disruptions which passed unnoticed in
the noisy street or camp meeting settings. Within the
walls of "Father"Taylor's Bethel, a woman whispering did
distract attention which Taylor regained by fixing his
eyes upon her and saying:

> If that lady on the third row, sitting on the end
> of the seat, with a yellow bonnet, don't stop
> whispering, I'll point her out. 33

And late comers, who in a camp meeting or street preaching would be welcomed if noticed at all, occasioned
critical comment in formal church settings. Samuel
Moody resorted to humor to deal with a young man who
showed off his new clothes and shoes by always arriving
after the worship service began:

> He came in as he usually did, one morning during
> the prayer, and had to walk a considerable distance
> in the house before he reached his seat. The moment
> he stopped in his seat, Mr. Moody with an elevated
> tone of voice, exclaimed, "O Lord, we pray thee,
> cure Ned Ingraham of that ungodly strut." 34

Those who left the service early as well as those who
came in late were targets of pulpit humor. Seeing several persons leaving one of his sermons, Edward Taylor
noted:

> "I have observed down around the wharves, when the
> tide rises, the chips float off. There they go
> now," he says, "rag, tag, and bobtail." 35

On several occasions, Taylor greeted the departure of
men at the middle of his sermon by saying, "Small vessels

---

32. Ibid., p. 53.

33. Haven, Life of Father Taylor, p. xxvi.

34. Letter, Rev. Jotham Sewall to Wm. Sprague, July 13,
1850, Annals, I, p. 248.

35. Haven, Life of Father Taylor, p. xxvi.

are easily filled." [36] Similar expressions were later
common in the sermons of Sam Jones (". . . when your
little cup is full, you can just back out."). [37] Jabez
Swan used a different metaphor to make the same point
when several walked out from his sermon ". . . every
sheep would come back to the fold, while only the goats
preferred wandering." [38] Samuel Moody developed a
preventative measure to deal with the problem of parishioners departing before worship was concluded. He
announced that he would preach his sermon to two groups
-- first to the sinners and then to the saints. Having
reached the time when many usually left the service, he
announced that he had finished preaching the portion of
his sermon to sinners and they could leave as he ad-
dressed the balance of his sermon to the saints. That
Sunday all sat attentively through the whole service. [39]

Samuel Moody also illustrated effectively one aspect of
what Henry Ward Beecher called the sacred mission of
humor: to keep the congregation awake on Sunday. [40]
In a day when sermons ran to an hour and a half or longer
such use of humor was especially important to arrest the
attention if not wake up the person. [41] On one occasion
noting a number of his congregation asleep, Moody stopped
his sermon and shouted:

> "Fire, Fire, Fire." One man, waking up out of a
> sound sleep asked in the utmost consternation,
> "Where?" "In hell, for sleeping sinners," answered
> the preacher. [42]

---

36. Ibid., p.162.

37. Sam Jones, "Turn Ye," Hot Shots.

38. Denison, The Evangelist, p. 205.

39. Letter, Jotham Sewall, Annals, I, pp. 247-248.

40. Henry Ward Beecher, Forty Eight Sermons, (Preached
Previous to 1867), (London: R.D.Dickinson,1871),I,pp.28-29.

41. Denison, The Evangelist, p. 414.

42. Letter, Jotham Sewall, Annals, I, p. 248.

In Parma, New York, during the eighteen thirties, Baptist
Hiram Stimson was faced with a similar problem of a
congregation accustomed to sleeping through sermons
which his predecessors had extended to two hours. He
resorted to having the choirister break in singing "Awake
my soul" in a booming voice after ten minutes of the
sermon had elapsed. Some of those who had already gone
to sleep awoke thinking that the service was over; but
amid chuckles from the congregation, he announced a
second text which he called more to the likening of some
brethren: "Sleep on now, and take your rest." Twenty
years later when he returned to the church for a brief
visit, many confided to him that that worship service
was the cause for their resolve never again to sleep
during sermons. [43] As humorous stories were long
remembered, so also the lessons learned from being the
targets of humor were not soon forgotten.

Introducing Controversial Comments

Another mission of humor which Henry Ward Beecher ex-
ploited in his preaching aided the introducing of controversial comments. In his sermon "The Courtesy of
Conscience" he detailed this dynamic humor:

> One of the best missionary influences vouchsafed
> to the human soul is wit and humor. I throw out
> wit and humor, and bring my hearers into a state of
> royal good nature; and through these elements I
> bring in the truth which men do not like; and they
> say, "Well, I don't believe it; but after all, let
> it go -- he is smart." Directly or indirectly, I
> begin to make a lodgment in the moral sense of these
> men. Although their conscience cannot be directly
> approached, I can get at it through the side of wit
> and humor; and while I keep on that side of them,
> so that I am good natured myself, I can pour in the
> truth on their minds, and can at last make a sure
> lodgment in their moral sense -- a thing which I
> could not have done by argument alone. In this case,
> wit and humor are auxiliaries; and decisions are
> borne in upon the moral sense through the element

---

43. Stimson, From the Stage Coach to the Pulpit, pp. 141-
142.

of wit and humor -- one of the most civilising of
all the influences in the soul of man. 44

Sam Jones identified this same dynamic more succinctly:

Some men open their mouths to laugh, and you can
drop a great brickbat of truth right in. 45

But while Jones dropped brickbats of truth on personal
and family ethics, Beecher introduced major political
issues and social controversies with humor.

On October 30, 1859, when John Brown was in jail and the
Republican Party was blamed, Beecher sought to vindicate
the party and place the Harper's Ferry Raid in perspective through his sermon "The Nation's Duty to Slavery."
And the perspective he shared was designed to help the
people laugh in a time of "crisis" and see that slavery
and not John Brown or the party was to be blamed and
eliminated:

There is an element of the ludicrous in this trans-
action which I think will effectually stop all
panic. Seventeen men terrified two thousand brave
Virginians into two days' submission, - that cannot
be got over! The common sense of common people will
not fail to see through all attempts to hide a
natural shame by a bungling make believe that the
danger was really greater than it was! The danger
was nothing, and the fear was very great, and the
courage was none at all. 46

Do what you please, -- muster a crowd of supposed
confederates, call the roll of conspirators, include
the noblest of men of these States, and exhibit this
imaginary army before the people, and, in the end,
it will appear that seventeen white men overawed a

44. Beecher, "The Courtesy of Conscience," Plymouth
Pulpit,(Boston: The Pilgrim Press, 1875), IV, pp. 38-39.
In his "Lyman Beecher Lectures" at Yale in 1872, Henry
Ward Beecher mentioned a similar reason for using illus-
trations and humor in sermons: cf. Henry Ward Beecher,
Yale Lectures on Preaching, (New York: J.B. Ford, 1872),
pp. 116, 167, and 179.
45. Jones, Sermons: Wise and Witty, p. 34.
46. H. W. Beecher, "The Nation's Duty to Slavery,"
Freedom and War, Discourses on Topics Suggested by the
Times,(Boston: Ticknor & Fields, 1836), pp. 3-4.

town of two thousand brave Virginians, and held them
captives until the sun had gone laughing twice
around the globe!

And the attempt to hide the fear of these surrounded
men by awakening a larger fear will never do. It is
too literal a fulfillment, not exactly a prophecy,
but of fable; not of Isaiah, but of Aesop.

A fox having been caught in a trap, escaped with the
loss of his tail. He immediately went to his brother foxes to persuade them that they would all look
better if they too would cut off their tails. They
declined. And our two thousand friends, who lost
their courage in the presence of seventeen men, are
now making an appeal to this nation to lose its
courage too, that the cowardice of the few may be
hidden in the cowardice of the whole community! It
is impossible. We choose to wear our courage for
some time longer! 47

One word more, and that is as to the insecurity of
those States that carry powder as their chief cargo.
Do you suppose that if tidings had come to New York
that the United States armory in Springfield had
been seized by seventeen men, New Haven, Hartford,
and Stamford, Worcester, New York, Boston, and
Albany would have been thrown into a fever and panic
in consequence of the event? We scarcely should
have read the papers to see what became of it. We
should have thought that it was a matter which the
Springfield people could manage. The thought of
danger would not have entered into our heads. There
would not have been any danger. But in a State
where there is such inflammable stuff as Slavery,
there is danger, and the people of the South know
it. I do not blame them so much for being afraid:
there is cause for fear where they have such a
population as they have down at the bottom of society.
But what must be the nature of State and domestic
institutions which keep brave men at the point of
fear all their life long? 48

In a sermon on "Christian Manhood in America", Beecher
used humor to clothe highly critical comments on California and Eastern attitudes and actions toward Chinese:

I am so astonished at these Chinese myself! They

---

47. Ibid., p. 4.
48. Ibid., p. 7.

have seen so many beautiful exhibitions of Christian
character, that they must be stupid not to admire
it. It must be that they are bereft of natural
reason, not to be fascinated with California piety,
and not to fall in love with the religion of the
emigrants from the East! Why what have we not done
to convert them? We have thrashed them and kicked
them; we have hung them on trees; almost every
gospel influence has been brought to bear upon them;
but the fellows will not be converted! Well, it
may be that some nations are outside of mercy. 49

In a discussion of "Apostolic Christianity," Beecher
again resorted to humor introducing his attitudes on
evolution: "I would as lief have sprung from a monkey
as from some men that I know of." 50 Beecher minimized
the importance of attack on apostolic succession and
evolution with its preoccupation on the past and instead
urged the focusing of attention and energies on the
future. And in answer to those who were upset by preaching on controversial subjects, Beecher used humor in
stating the prophetic duty of the church:

The church was built to disturb the peace of man;
but often it does not perform its duty, for fear of
disturbing the peace of the church. What kind of
artillery practice would that be which declined to
fire for fear of kicking over the gun carriages, or
waking up the sentinels, sleeping at their posts? 51

Tension produced by crisis periods or by the introduction
of controversial issues was relieved by other ministers
through laughter. 52 The laughter as a physical reaction

49. Henry Ward Beecher, "Christian Manhood in America,"
Kirk, ed., Beecher As A Humorist, p. 50.
50. Henry Ward Beecher, "Apostolic Christianity, "The
Sermons of Henry Ward Beecher in Plymouth Church, Brooklyn,
New York: J.B.Ford & Co., 1873), Eighth Ser. 1872 ,p.175.
51. Proctor, Life Thoughts, p. 173.
52. During the war of 1812 when a Norfolk congregation
feared a British invasion, Presbyterian Charles Coffin
made light of their fear and chided them for having
failed to build a church building: "Oh, happy people of
Norfolk! If an enemy should come into your harbour,
and bombarded your city, they could not batter down your
churches, for you have none to bear the brunt!" Sprague,
Annals, IV, p. 247.

could bring to the people's attention more dimensions
of themselves and the issues than they had on their
minds. In this sense, Dix called humor and human one;
for humor presented wisdom in a full bodied form and
brought to the attention more than an idea or abstract-
ion. [53]

The Theological Motivation

Attacking Infidel Arguments

Because he realized that reason could not resolve the
major theological disputes in favor of either the
Christians or the Infidels and that belief undergirded
the Infidel position as well as the Christian one, Timothy
Dwight urged Christians to follow him in going beyond
the usual defense of Christian Doctrines to an attack on
Infidel positions. In this attack, the humor of reductio
ad absurdum was frequently employed. Dwight recognized
that Infidel use of ridicule resulted because argument
was inadequate to decide conclusively the issues in their
favor. Knowing that such use revealed weakness in one's
position, Dwight restrained his own use of ridicule on
occasion; but in certain disputes where no other device
would do, he discarded restraint in order to carry on
the attack. By surveying the situations in which Dwight
and others turned to the use of humor in argument, we
identify some of the most deeply felt disputes in theological discourse which reason could not resolve.

In his second sermon on "The Nature and Danger of Infidel
Philosophy" delivered first in 1797, Timothy Dwight
mapped out not only the enemy's position but also a plan
for battle against the Infidels (a term loosely applied
to Unitarians, Philosophical Atheists, Jeffersonian
Republicans, or any others opposed to the established
order which Dwight championed). Dwight analyzed previous
encounters:

---

53. Dix, Pulpit Portraits, p. 115f.

The usual course of the controversy has been this.
Infidels have uniformly attacked, and Christians
merely defended; Infidels have found difficulties,
and Christians have employed themselves merely, or
chiefly, in removing them. Hence Infidels have
naturally felt, and written, as if the difficulties
lay solely on the Christian side of the debate. Had
Christians, with more worldly wisdom, carried their
arms into the fortress of their antagonists, they
would long since, and very easily, have proved them
to be everywhere weak and untenable. The sheds only,
and pens, of occasional marauders. 54

Earlier in the same sermon Dwight had shown that difficulties and disputes raised against scripture and doctrine arose not from what was known but from what was
unknown. 55   Therefore, in the debates, reason could not
resolve the issues:

> Neither they, nor we, know; both classes merely
> believe; for the case admits not of knowledge, nor
> can it be determined with certainy. The only
> question to be decided between the contending
> parties is which believe on the best evidence.56

The elaboration of Christian doctrine would hardly be
the chosen work of those who followed Dwight's analysis
of the theological situation. The task was to develop
the best means to attack Infidel positions. In this case
when reason was admittedly inadequate, ridicule became

---

54. Timothy Dwight, "The Nature and Danger of Infidel
Philosophy," Sermons,(New Haven: Hezekiah Howe & Durrie
& Peck, 1828), I, pp. 359-360.

55. Ibid., P. 345.

56. Ibid., p. 349. Dwight was free to admit on matters
of theological dispute that he did not know the answer
to some questions. There was no good reason to raise
certain questions for which there was no guidance from
revelation. Dwight, "The Ordinary Means of Grace,"
Theology Explained and Defended in a Series of Sermons,
(New York: Harper & Bros., 1849), IV, p. 71. The limited
nature of reason for Dwight should be seen within his
understanding that "theology is the science of the will
of God concerning the duty, and destination of man."

a means of carrying on the attack.

Dwight recognized why ridicule was used as a means in
debate. One resorts to ridicule against arguments "which
he is unable to confront with arguments of superior
force." [57] "When reasons fail, ridicule is still left."[58]
And Dwight pointed out how the Infidel use of this weapon
revealed a weakness in their position:

> The insolence and ridicule, exhibited universally by
> Infidel writers, is, at least to my view, a strong
> indication of the consciousness of the weakness of
> their cause, and of the insufficiency of their
> arguments. [59]

While Dwight scorned the Infidel use of ridicule against
Christianity, he was emphatic to "deny the propriety of
using it to decide any serious concern of mankind," [60]
and explicitly rejected the temptation to employ ridicule
in the pulpit on one occasion. [61] He nevertheless
succumbed to the temptation on numerous other pulpit
occasions when no other means was at hand to put down
the Infidel attack on scripture and doctrine. To illustrate Dr. Dwight's use of reductio ad absurdum and other
ridicule in attack on Infidel ideas, several selections
are cited from his Theology Explained and Defended in a
Series of Sermons. These passages are chosen because
the sermons in this series were the ones which Dwight's
Yale students heard:

> His practice was to preach one on the morning of
> each Sabbath in term time. By this arrangement he
> finished the course once in four years. Thus each

57. Dwight, Sermons, I, p. 352.
58. Ibid., p. 353.
59. Ibid., p. 371.
60. Ibid., P. 352.
61. Dwight, "Atheistical Objections and Schemes of
Doctrine Considered," Theology Explained, I, p. 98.

student, who completed his regular collegiate period, had an opportunity to hear the whole series. 62

Dwight reserved particular ridicule for Unitarian Joseph Priestly, who had abandoned Calvinism and gained international fame as a chemist as well as minister and advocate of revolutions before coming to America to join his three sons in 1794. Priestly denied that the soul was separable from the body and affirmed that the life of reward and punishment for present conduct was to be on earth. In his sermon "The Divinity of Christ: Objections to the mode in which the Unitarians Conduct the Controversy," Dwight dealt with Priestly's position:

> Dr. Priestly, commenting on John xiv.2: In My
> Father's house are many mansions; says, "Perhaps
> with a learned friend of mine we may understand the
> mansions in his father's house, of which Jesus here
> speaks, to signify, not places of rest and happiness
> in heaven, but stations of trust and usefulness upon
> earth; such as he was then about to quit," etc.
> Here the house of God is made to mean earth and
> mansions, stations; and Christ of course was going
> away, to prepare a place for his Apostles, here,
> where he and they then were; and was to come again,
> to receive them into the place, whither he himself
> was going, that they might be with him there, by
> continuing here. 63

In like manner, Dr. Dwight took terms which Unitarians were fond of substituting for "Christ" or "Word" and applied them systematically in passages until such substituted reasoning appeared ridiculous:

> In the beginning was a super-angelic creature . . .
> and this super-angelic creature was with God, and

---

62. Wm. and Sereno Dwight, "Memoirs of the Life of President Dwight," Dwight, Theology Explained, I, p. 26. Dwight shaped these sermons through two repetitions of the cycle as a pastor at Greenfield and two more repetitions of the cycle at Yale. That many had the opportunity to hear the sermons does not mean that many took advantage of the opportunity and heard the sermons.

63. Dwight, "The Divinity of Christ: Objections to the Mode in Which the Unitarians Conduct the Controversy," Theology Explained, II, pp. 46-47.

this super-angelic creature was God. The same was
in the beginning with God. All things were made by
this super-angelic creature, and without him was
not anything made that was made." I presume, I need
proceed no further. 64

Similarly he substituted the word "God" for "Word" with
this result: "In the beginning was God, and God was with
God, and God was God." When substituting "divine power"
for "word", he duplicated the gospel of John complete
through the fifteenth verse of chapter one. [65] To the
Unitarian assertion that references to the Holy Ghost
meant nothing more than "the divine power," Dwight
responded:

> According to what rules of construction are we, on
> this plan, to interpret the following passages; in
> which I shall substitute the word power for Ghost,
> or Spirit: always intending by it, however, the
> divine power.
>
> All manner of sin and blasphemy shall be forgiven
> unto men; but the blasphemy against the Holy Power
> shall not be forgiven unto men. Matt. xii.31.
> Baptizing them in the name of the Father, and the
> Son, and of the Holy Power, Matt. xxviii.19. Why
> has Satan filled thy heart, to lie unto the Holy
> Power? Acts v.3. God anointed Jesus with the Holy
> Power and with power, Act. x.33. Romans xv.13.
> That ye may abound in hope through the power of the
> wonders, by the Power of the Power of God. In
> demonstration of the Power, and the Power . . .
> More instances cannot, I think, be necessary to
> elucidate this part of the subject. 66

Applying this same sort of substitution to concepts as
he had to individual words, Dwight argued with irony:

> In the passage, quoted from St. Paul, it is said
> that Christ created all things, that are in heaven
> and that are in earth. This the Unitarians say,
> means no more, than that Christ published the
> Gospel, and constituted the Church. In the first

---

64. Dwight, Ibid., p. 39.
65. Ibid., p. 42.
66. Ibid., pp. 46-47.

verse in Genesis, it is said, <u>In the beginning God</u>
<u>created the heavens and the earth</u>. Thus, I say,
and upon their plan of construction, I am certainly
warranted to say it; means no more than, that in
the beginning God published the Gospel and constituted the Church. 67

Having an acquaintance with Dwight's strategy and style,
we have the background against which to view one of his
student's preaching. Lyman Beecher, who was a sophomore
when Dwight assumed the duties of the presidency at Yale,
followed Dwight closely; and in addition to the exposure
he had to Dwight's preaching during his remaining under-
graduate days, Beecher stayed on after graduation to
study divinity with Dwight. Years later when Beecher
was faced with arguing against prudent drinking, he
employed a style similar to his mentor's. Whereas abstinence from excessive drinking of hard liquor might be
reasonable and conclusively argued, abstinence from
"prudent drinking" of wine and even New England rum was
more difficult to argue -- especially when Beecher and
his colleagues had been drinking and serving such beverages to their parishioners for years. But as the temperance movement widened its scope to eliminate all
alcoholic content and Beecher championed the cause in a
series of sermons, he resorted to the tool which his
mentor had used when arguments would not do. And Beecher
rendered "prudence" as ridiculous a term as Dwight had
rendered "super-angelic angel":

> I know that much is said about the prudent use of
> ardent spirits; but we might as well speak of the
> prudent use of the plague -- of fire handled pru-
> dently around powder -- of poison taken prudently
> every day -- or of vipers and serpents introduced
> prudently into our dwellings, to glide about as a
> matter of courtesy to visitors, and of amusement

---

67. Dwight, "Divinity of Christ -- Objections to the
Doctrine of Unitarians," <u>Theology Explained</u>, II,
p. 22.

to our children. 68

And as Dwight had done, Beecher used humor chiefly in those portions of his sermons in which he dealt with Infidel objections to the doctrine or scripture. 69

In the next three chapters on the use of humor to deal with eighteenth and nineteenth century idolatries, we find others employing this method of reducing words, concepts, or modes of logic to the absurd. There we note that Presbyterians Samuel Porter and Reuben Tinker used it against arguments for universal salvation and against the sufficiency of the atonement, Jonathan Mayhew used it against simplistic ideas of salvation by grace, and Theodore Parker used it against absolutizing obedience to the law. The method is particularly obvious in chapter four's discussion of varieties in the idolatry of wisdom; for one could not put down the idolatry of reason and logic by seriously using reason and logic.

Identifying Idolatries

The majority of instances in which eighteenth and nineteenth century American ministers employed humor in the pulpit dealt with man's preferences which they explicitly identified as idolatries. Incongruities are the basis for humor; and from the religious standpoint, all idolatries in the culture are incongruous and therefor subjects of humor. These subjects which assumed idol-

---

68. Lyman Beecher, "The Signs of Intemperance," Lectures on Political Atheism and Kindred Subjects Together with Six Lectures on Intemperance,(Boston: John R. Jewett & Co., 1852), Vol. I in Beecher's Works, p. 372. In his lectures on intemperance, Beecher rewrote his own personal and family history as well as the New England history of involvement with ardent spirits. From the lectures one would never suspect that Beecher had been in charge of keeping his Yale classmates well supplied with the spirits of their choice or that he took pride in mixing the hot rum punches for his parishioners. Beecher, Ibid., p. 360. cf. John Hull Brown, Early American Beverages,(New York: Crown Publishers, 1966), pp. 13-20.
69. Charles Beecher, ed., Autobiography, II, p. 115.

atrous proportions to which men bowed had a life within
the ongoing idolatries of the day: excesses of political
and ecclesiastical power, pretensions of wisdom, and
burgeoning manifestations of wealth. In the remainder
of this chapter we survey the patterns of preferences
identified as idolatries and so lay a background against
which to appreciate the point of the humor in chapters
three through five.

In eighteenth and nineteenth century American terms,
idolatry meant giving a supreme attention, preference,
love, regard, and trust to something other than God. At
the close of his attack on Popish idolatry, Jonathan
Mayhew broadened his definition of idolatry:

> Whatever usurps that place, that preeminence in the
> affection of men, which is due to God alone; that
> is their idol, that is their God. How many idol-
> aters are there then even among protestants? 70

In his sermon on the first commandment, Timothy Dwight
defined gods as "all the objects of supreme regard,
attention, or esteem" and later called idols those things
to which men bow. [71] The preferring of some being other
than God was called the spirit of idolatry by Presbyterian Robert Henderson:

> Now if it be correct to view this as idolatry, are
> there not many of us idolaters? Do not many of us
> prefer some other being to God, in our affections?
> Some perhaps a wife, some a husband, some peradven-
> ture, our money, some perhaps a little popular ap-
> plause, or a little elevation on the pinnacle of
> glory. Now, sirs, according to my humble views, it
> matters but little what the object is which we
> prefer to God. I conceive we may justly be said to
> be guilty of the spirit of this crime whenever we
> give any created being a higher place in our affec-
> tions than we give the great God, whatever may be

---

70. Jonathan Mayhew, Popish Idolatry, pp. 51-52.

71. Timothy Dwight, "The Law of God -- The Decalogue --
The first Commandment," Theology Explained, III, p. 165;
and "On the Love of Distinction, "Sermons, I, p. 502.

the subject. [72]

Putting trust in creatures to the dishonor of God was setting up idols in George Bethune's preaching on "Love of Human Praise, Fatal to Faith;" [73] and Reuben Tinker classified as idols whatever the mind was enslaved to acquiring. [74] And by the end of our period, Henry Ward Beecher defined idolatry as bestowing on some other what was due to God. [75] And Dwight Lyman Moody continued to identify as idols anything man thought more of than God:

> People who live in America think there is no such thing as idolatry. They think they have to go off into China, Japan, or some heathen country to find idols. Don't flatter yourselves. We have idols in America. You have not to go far from Cleveland to find them. You will find a thousand idolatries, I was going to say, where you find one true Christian that worships the God of the Bible. Anything that a man thinks more of than he does God is his idol. [76]

With these definitions of idolatry, many preferences were labeled idolatries. We group these preferences under the general headings of Power, Wisdom, and Wealth -- the overall terms used by Lyman Beecher, Reuben Tinker, George Bethune, and others to characterize the major idolatries in which Americans gloried. (Jeremiah 9: 23-24 was cited by several who summarized the American idolatries in a way analogous to Israel's glorying in wisdom, might, and riches.) [77] In 1839 Bethune noted:

---

72. Robert Henderson, "The Anxious Sinners Earnest Enquiry for Salvation," A Series of Sermons on Practical and Familiar Subjects, II, pp. 131-132.

73. George Bethune, "Love of Human Praise, Fatal to Faith," Sermons, p. 203.

74. Reuben Tinker, "The Great Good," Sermons, p. 172.

75. Henry Ward Beecher, "The Love of Money," The Sermons of Henry Ward Beecher, First Series, p. 171.

76. Dwight Lyman Moody, "Tekel," The Great Redemption, p. 155.

77. Reuben Tinker, "The Gospel, The Hope of Salvation," Sermons, pp. 404 and 415; Bethune, "True Glory," Orations, pp. 37 and 45.

If the pride of wisdom be the most natural, and the
pride of power the most intoxicating, the pride of
wealth has come to be the most general. 78

Timothy Dwight had identified ambition as "a fatal idolatry of the world." [79] During the eighteenth and nineteenth centuries, various persons or institutions were
identified as idols ambitiously aspiring to power or
elevated to power by others. Early in the period, Mayhew
examined Popish idolatry and the pretensions of royal
English power as both threatened to establish themselves
further in America. [80] Later, Horace Bushnel cited
Jefferson and new political sects as the object of popular idolatry during a period when democracy was in the
ascendancy. [81] Tinker and Bacon both cited the institution of slavery as a hideous idol which the people and
legislators sought to reverence. [82] And Stimson cited
the idolization of George McClellan when the General's
political fortunes were once again on the rise. [83] One
should note that the power criticized as an idol was a
power in the ascension; and these idolized aspiring

78. Ibid., p. 45.

79. Dwight, "Long Life Not Desirable," Sermons, p. 276.

80. Mayhew, Popish Idolatry, and Unlimited Submission,
passim.

81. Horace Bushnell, Crisis of the Church, (Hartford:
Daniel Burgess and Company, 1835), p. 11.

82. Tinker, "The Gospel, Hope for Salvation," Sermons,
p. 419; Bacon, "The Pastor Retiring from His Original
Work," Four Commemorative Discourses, (New Haven: T. J.
Stafford, 1866), p. 58. Bacon's sermon was given at
the close of the Civil War but was a reflection on earlier experiences in the ministry.

83. Stimson, From the Stage Coach to the Pulpit, p. 262.
McClellan reentered politics in the early 1870's and
was elected governor of New Jersey by 1877. Stimson's
book was published in 1874.

powers were the subject of humor explored
in chapter three.

Archbishop John Ireland identified another idolatry in
America as the aristocracy of mind or learning:

> This is an intellectual age. It worships intellect.
> It tries all things by the touchstone of intellect.
> By intellect, public opinion, the ruling power of
> the age, is formed. 84

Having identified this and other American idolatries,
Ireland did not set out to exorcise them but rather
urged Catholics to do them homage in an effort to become
accepted as Americans and so come to positions of
influence:

> The Church herself will be judged by the standards
> of intellect. Catholics must excel in religious
> knowledge; they must be ready to give reasons for
> the faith that is in them, meeting objections from
> whatever source, abreast of the times in their
> methods or argument. They must be in the foreground
> of intellectual movements of all kinds. 85

One reason for the absence of much humor in Catholic
sermons of the period may be traced to this tendency to
identify with rather than exorcize American idolatries.86

---

84. John Ireland delivered this sermon on November 10,
1889 in Baltimore on the centennial of that see. "The
Mission of Catholics in America," The Church and Modern
Society, (St. Paul: Pioneer Press, 1905), p. 92.
85. Ibid. After speaking of the way in which the age was
wedded to its idols, Ireland urged Catholics to prove
they were heart and soul in sympathy with movements of
the age. He spoke thus in 1893 in Baltimore: John Ireland,
"The Church and the Age," The Church and Modern Society,
pp. 121-122.
86. Neither American Catholic Church historian Monsignor
John Tracy Ellis nor John B. McGloin could furnish the
names of any Catholic preachers who used humor in the
American pulpit during the 18th & 19th centuries. One
must agree with Monsignor Ellis that "doubtless there
were such -- the Roman Catholics could hardly have had
a perfect record of humorlessness..." Letter, John Tracy
Ellis to Doug Adams, August 15, 1973. (cf. Letter, John
B. McGloin to Doug Adams, December 9, 1973.) The use of
humorous medieval exemplum has been seen among Southwest
Catholic Priests of the nineteenth century.

But while Ireland identified intellect as what Americans
worshipped and urged Catholics to emulate the idolatry,
those in other religious traditions who had no need to
prove their Americanism attacked the idolatry in its
various forms. Of ninety-one preachers studied, Dwight
was the first to label learning as an "idolatry". This
may be better understood if we realize that after the
Revolutionary War, some other distinctions were at least
temporarily swept away; but as Harriet Beecher Stowe's
Major Broad notes in speaking of education after the war:
"'Our only nobility now,' he said to my grandfather.
'We've cut off everything else; no distinction now sir,
but educated and uneducated.'" [87] Thus, while education
was not necessarily expanding as an idolatry after the
Revolutionary War, it was in the ascendancy when seen
against the relative position of other distinctions.

Besides labeling as idols the whole pantheon of eloquence,
learning, science, taste and criticism, [88] Dwight
singled out general and abstract terms as the idols of
the period:

> The idolatry of the heathen was occupied in the
> worship of a great variety of false Deities; such as
> men, brutes, stocks of wood, and images of stone.
> The idolatry of multitudes, who call themselves
> Christians, is rendered to Words, and Names: Par-
> ticularly to those which are called general and
> abstract terms. 89

While he publicly affirmed the Great Awakening with which
his grandfather Jonathan Edwards was associated, Dwight
differed widely from Edwards' certain reliance on the
mathematical precision of words and was far from the
ultra Calvinism of Edwards' followers Hopkins and Emmons.

---

87. Harriet Beecher Stowe, Oldtown Folks,(Cambridge:
Harvard University Press, 1966), p. 113.

88. Dwight, "On the Love of Distinction," Sermons, II,
P. 502.

89. Dwight, "On Conformity to this World," Sermons,
p. 433.

Much further from Calvinism, Orestes Brownson voiced
during his liberal period the Unitarian antagonism to
what he called the worship of specific words in Calvinist
Church creeds:

> There are few who do not worship their creed with
> more devotion than they do their God, and labor a
> thousand times harder to support it than they do
> to support the truth. 90

And many different doctrines and creeds as well as Infidel ideas which were reverenced became the target for
pulpit humor as we explore in chapter four.

Higher education which was acquired for no seemingly
useful purpose or at least no soul saving purpose by
those who then flaunted their elite learning was labeled
an idolatry particularly among Methodists and some black
clergy who were concerned with saving the many. [91] As
we have noted in chapter one, there was a particular
attack on ministerial education until such time as Methodist leaders were as educationally distinguished as
those of any other denomination. But widespread linger-
ing antagonism to an exclusive Calvinism led popular
ministers to deride "theology," "creed," and "doctrine"
as code words for Calvinism long after the leading strict
Calvinist had passed from the scene. And increasingly in
the nineteenth century, cultural expectations that education would solve the nation's problems reinforced the
idolatry of learning which was particularly attractive
to the people of the book.

The Bible itself was noted as an idol by Henry Ward
Beecher in the last half of the nineteenth century. And
although it figured less significantly in the preaching
of the ministers during the period as we have already
seen, the Bible no doubt did stand in a position for
some people that was idolatrous. But Henry Ward Beecher

90. Brownson, Orestes A. Brownson's Life, p. 199.
91. Hibbard, Memoirs, p. 356

was the only one of the preachers to call it an idol and
to exorcise it with humor in his preaching:

> The Bible is in many churches where men idolize and
> praise it, like an idol in the temple. One would
> think that it is a living thing. A man would not
> accidently sit down on a Bible without jumping up
> as if he had sat on a wasp. 92

We also deal with the idolatry of alcohol under the
heading of the idolatry of reason although such an idolatry may be seen as opposite to reason. Alcohol, which
was called a king or god in many lives, 93 was opposed
first and foremost because it clouded the reason which
was considered so important in an increasingly democratic
era when the unclouded reason of the majority needed to
be reached and trained in order to establish or reestab-
lish America as the kingdom of God on earth. Thus as we
see in chapter four, the temperance movement and increasing ridicule of drinking coincided with the extension of
the franchise and the attempted extension of religious
influence after disestablishment. And this movement
further heightens the idolatry of education.

Wealth and all the material trappings it provided was
cited by most ministers as the period's idolatry. Mayhew,
Dwight, and Tinker cited, as Paul's observation, that a
covetous man is an idolater (Ephesians V.5 and Colosians
III.5). 94 Presbyterian Tinker saw that "wealth was an
idolatry to which all hearts are prone." 95
And Tinker contended that the increased wealth among many
from the period of the Revolutionary War to the mid-
1830's promoted infidelity:

> For riches promote atheism. They are put in God's
> stead. They are idolized . . . The race after

92. Beecher, "Agnostic Faith," Kirk, ed., Beecher,p.115.
93. Taylor, Seven Years, p. 150. H. W. Beecher, "The Love
of Money," The Sermons, First Series, p. 170.
94. Mayhew, Popish Idolatry, p. 51; Dwight, Theology
Explained, III, p. 552; and Tinker, Sermons, p. 166.
95. Tinker, Sermons, p. 408.

riches, which this country was running till out of
breath, in 1836, and about that time, was a race
towards infidelity; the world was not only in it,
but the church was running . . . [96]

The pervasiveness of this preference among the people
was cited earlier by Presbyterian Conrad Speece during
his August 20, 1812 fast day sermons:

> The thirst of wealth, the vile idolatry of gold,
> must be mentioned as one of the extensive sins of
> our country. Our opportunities of acquisition of
> money in years past have been far greater than in
> former times . . . We seem to have taken up the
> notion that all happiness was included in being
> rich; and the rage of accumulation has spread its
> baneful infection into almost every heart. [97]

As we discover in chapter five, some ministers excused
the wealthy if they used their wealth in charitable ways
and others saw wealth as a sign of one's election or
favor in God's eyes; but for many of the ministers in
this study, wealth as an accumulation of money was itself
seen as evidence of idolatry. And the accumulation of
wealth with the design to provide for one's child was
exposed as an idolatry of both wealth and the child
which would lead to the ruin of both.

Speece had elaborated the idolatry to include "the
solicitude with which parents labor to provide large
fortunes for their children, to the detriment, very often
of their peace and usefulness through life."[98]   And by
the end of the period, Dwight Lyman Moody elaborated the
idolatries in a similar way and saw the idol of self
animating the idolatry of both wealth and children.[99]

That self was at the root of all the idolatries received

96. Tinker, Sermons, pp. 398-399.
97. Conrad Speece, A Sermon Delivered at Petersville
Church on Thursday, August 20, 1812,(Richmond: Blagrove
and Turehart, 1912), p. 10.
98. Ibid.
99. D. L. Moody, "Tekel," The Great Redemption, p. 155.

the most detailed elaboration in Timothy Dwight's sermon
on the first commandment. For example, in relation to
one's child, Dwight noted:

> This spirit manifests itself, however, in an almost
> endless variety of forms. The parent often idolizes
> his child; the beauty, her face, her form; the man
> of genius, his talents; the ambitious man, his fame,
> power, or station; the miser, his gold; the accom-
> plished man, his manners; the ostentatious man, his
> villa; and the sensualist, his pleasures. By all
> these, however, a single spirit is cherished, and
> discovered. The parent dotes upon his child, be-
> cause it is <u>his</u> child. Had it been born of other
> parents, it might, indeed, be occasionally agree-
> able to him, but would never have become an object
> of this peculiar fondness. 100

For Dwight and later for Henry Ward Beecher, the trappings
of fashion were simply another manifestation of the
idolatry of wealth and the idolatry of self. [101] And
Richard Storrs, Jr. and Dwight Moody explicitly spoke of
self-idolatry. [102] The idolatry of self was most obvi-
ously revealed by material display; therefore, chapter
five's discussion of wealth provides the setting in
which to explore this self-idolatry further.

Because self-idolatry animated many if not all the other
idolatries, humor which we call ridicule was commonly
needed to put the self in its place. Because the ministers wielded this weapon, they needed to be the first
targets of humor in their training and association.
George Whitefield labeled "Self-righteousness as the
last idol that is rooted out of the heart." [103] In

---

100. Dwight, "The First Commandment," <u>Theology Explained</u>,
III, p. 169.

101. Dwight, <u>Sermons</u>, II, p. 298; Beecher: "Six Warnings"
<u>Lectures to Young Men</u>, p. 55.

102. Richard S. Storrs, Jr., <u>Christianity: Its Destined
Supremacy on the Earth</u>,(New York: Almon Merwin, 1851),
p. 12; and D. L. Moody, <u>Glad Tidings</u>, p. 13.

103. George Whitefield, "The Lord Our Righteousness,"
<u>Fifteen Sermons</u>, p. 31.

ministerial training that idol was the first on which
the ministers worked. Their background in chapter one
should be kept in mind as we approach their use of
humor against others in chapters three through five.

CHAPTER III

THE USE OF HUMOR

IN EXORCISING IDOLATRIES OF POWER

0, Lord, grant that we may not despise our rulers;
and grant, O Lord, that they may not act so we
can't help it. 1

Words attributed to Lyman Beecher open consideration of
pulpit humor used to put down political authorities.
Assuming idolatrous proportions in the people's eyes or
in their own eyes, the political authorities of the
eighteenth and nineteenth centuries shifted from kings to
presidents, lesser politicians, and movement leaders.
The ministers' humor was often directed at the rising
authorities and extended to the Union itself, its law and
democratic political system when these institutions were
invoked on the side of an expanding system of slavery.

Implicit in most of these attacks was an understanding
of the sinful nature of man who invariably attempted to
go beyond his limits. But an opposite understanding of
rulers as too small undergirded the humor of radical
Unitarian Theodore Parker, who was foremost among those
using pulpit humor against political authorities. Parker
cited Psalm 2:2-4, a scripture which we have noted as
common among those using pulpit humor, to which he added
a phrase to stress the puny dimensions of many leaders:

"The kings of the earth set themselves, and the
rulers take counsel together, against the Lord, and
against his anointed, saying, Let us break their

---

1. This prayer is popularly attributed to Beecher, cf.
Florence Ryerson and Colin Clements, Harriet,(New York:
Charles Scribner's & Sons, 1943), p. 96; and Weisfeld,
The Pulpit Treasury, p. 86; but a search of scholarly
sources fails to yield a reliable reference to the
prayer.

bands asunder, and cast away their cords from us.
He that sitteth in the heavens shall laugh: the
Lord shall have them in derision."
He taketh up the isles as a very little thing and
the inhabitants of the earth are as grasshoppers
before them. 2

The likening of men to grasshoppers, worms, or other
illustrious creatures was more common during the period
among those of Calvinist persuasion, who applied the
terms to all men and distrusted democracy as much if not
more than they distrusted monarchy. In an increasingly
democratic nation, the passionate preoccupation with
politics extended to more and more people and so attracted humor from the pulpit. Whether political authority
was vested in one monarch or in millions of voters in a
democracy and whether the current crusade was for or
against slavery or some other cause, a sinful swelling
of men's pride was likely to emerge and be another target for ministerial humor. Even a modified Calvinist
viewpoint would nearly expect any man including a king
or president to show his fallen nature occasionally; but
Parker, whose theology attributed evil to social conditions or personal will which could be changed, was
harsher in his humorous attack. And in preaching on
"The Relation of Jesus to His Age and the Ages," Parker
identified the true follower of Jesus (the great new man)
as one who "refuses all masters; bows not to tradition,
and with seeming irreverence, laughs in the face of
popular idols." [3] While no other minister explicitly

2. Theodore Parker, "State of the Nation," Speeches,
Addresses, and Occasional Sermons,(New York: D. Appleton
and Company, 1864), II, p. 215.

3. Theodore Parker, "The Relation of Jesus to His Age and
all Ages," (December 26, 1844), Ibid., I, p. 3. Parker
does not explore the dimensions of evil in man very far.
He credits much evil to man's "perverse will" in combination with "deficiencies in religious power" without
defining those terms. Theism, Atheism and Popular
Theology, Charles Wendte, ed., (Boston: American
Unitarian Association, 1907), p. 350.

called for laughing at all masters, (and many would have
seen such a call as an open invitation for man's evil
inclinations,) the ministers studied did lead their congregations to laugh at those particular political powers
who were moving to master the popular mind.

Putting Down Political Deities

English Kings

> O Lord, bless thy servant, King George, and grant
> unto him wisdom; for thou knowest, O Lord, he
> needs it. 4

This prayer was credited to a Boston Whig minister, who
was forced by British troops to hold a worship service
and pray for the king during the American Revolution.
The use of humor against the king, which reached a climax
in secular literature during the American Revolution, [5]
had a life within churches long before the Revolution and
occasionally after it when English power reached beyond
accepted limits. We examine these cases to understand
what prompted the resort to humor.

When the British ordered that all ministers preach a
sermon praising Charles I and attacking those who beheaded Charles 100 years earlier, Jonathan Mayhew not
only employed humor to put Charles I in his place but
also used satire to put down the contention that Paul's
injuction to obey authorities (Romans 13:1-8) entailed
unlimited submission. According to Mayhew's thinking,
submission was due not to any entitled "rulers" but only
to those who lived up to his definition of "ruler" as
one who properly performed duties with justice for the

---

4. Harriet Beecher Stowe, (review of Sprague's Annals of
the American Pulpit, I and II), Atlantic Monthly, A
Magazine of Literature, Art, and Politics, (February,
1858), I, No. IV, p. 490.
5. Bruce I. Granger, Political Satire in the American
Revolution, 1763-1783, (Ithica: Cornell University Press,
1960).

good of society. In Mayhew's sermon, Charles' performance as king did not qualify him as a true ruler; and
much less did the king qualify as the saint which the
occasion would have made of him:

> "King Charles is upon this solemnity frequently
> compared to our Lord Jesus Christ, both in respect
> of the holiness of his life and the greatness and
> injustice of his sufferings; and it is a wonder
> they do not add something concerning the merits of
> his death also; but "blessed saint" and "royal mar-
> tyr" are as humble titles as any that are thought
> worthy of him . . . I fear it will be hard to prove
> this man a saint. And verily one would be apt to
> suspect that that church must be but poorly stocked
> with saints and martyrs which is forced to adopt
> such enormous sinners in her calendar in order to
> swell the number. 6

The British attempt to elevate Charles was by implication an attempt to elevate any king above the opposition
of the descendants of those Puritans by whom, in Mayhew's
words, Charles was "beheaded before his own banqueting
house." 7 Mayhew, who suggested the idea of Committees
of Correspondence to James Otis, died a decade before
the American Revolution; but his sermon, which has
regularly been classed as the first in a series of major
American sermons leading to the Revolution, 8 reduced
to the absurd an argument for unlimited submission to
rulers:

> It has often been asserted that the Scriptures in
> general, and the passage under consideration in
> particular, makes all resistance to princes a crime
> in any case whatever. If they turn tyrants and
> become the common oppressor of those whose welfare
> they ought to regard with a paternal affection, we
> must not pretend to right ourselves, unless it be
> by prayers, and tears, and humble entreaties. And

6. Jonathan Mayhew, "Unlimited Submission and Non-resistance to the Higher Powers," Sermons, pp. 44-45.

7. Ibid., p. 16.

8. Thornton, Pulpit; Carrol, Religion; Dean Kelley, ed.,
The Light in the Steeple: Religion and the American Revolution, (New York: Ecumenical Task Force, 1973).

if these methods fail of procuring redress, we must
not have recourse to any other, but all suffer ourselves to be robbed and butchered at the pleasure of
the "Lord's anointed," lest we should incur the sin
of rebellion and the punishment of damnation. 9

The resentment at the crown ordering the free churches
to preach or pray in particular ways was reflected not
only in Mayhew's satiric response of 1750 and in the Whig
minister's prayer for the Lord to give King George wisdom during the Revolution, but also in the words which a
future American, Charles Nisbet, used in his Scotch
sermon when a public fast day was ordered by the crown
to support the British effort against the American
Revolution:

> We are this day called by our superiors to fast and
> afflict ourselves: and they have not called us to
> this duty until they have given us abundant reason
> to do so. 10

After the American Revolution, the pulpit humor directed
at the kings occurred when British force threatened
either Americans or those to whom the American congregation were attached by recent immigration. Preaching
in Light Street Methodist Church, Jacob Gruber offered
up the following prayer when the booming canon interrupted his sermon and heralded the approach of British
troops into the American Capital in 1812:

> Lord, have mercy on the Sovereigns of Europe --
> convert their souls -- give them short lives and

---

9. Mayhew, "Unlimited Submission," Sermons, p. 16. In
this sermon of January, 1750, Mayhew refrained from
praising those who had overthrown Charles; and for purposes of further criticizing Charles by comparison,
Mayhew even praised the ruling monarch George II. But
just before his death, Mayhew preached a sermon on the
occasion of the stamp act in which he noted "God gave
the Israelites a king in his anger, because they had not
sense and virtue enough to like a free commonwealth."
Thornton, Pulpit, p. 46.

10. Parkinson, Charles Nisbet, p. 9.

happy deaths -- take them to Heaven, and let us
have no more of them. 11

And long after American ministers had shifted their
attack to American authorities whom they viewed as more
dangerous to the church and America than any foreign
king, traveling Dominican preacher Thomas Nicholas Burke
sarcastically spoke of the British rulers whose successors continued to threaten the Catholic church by supporting the spread of the Anglican church in his native
Ireland:

> A church and religion claiming to be of God with
> such a divinely appointed head as the saintly Henry
> the Eighth, such a nursing mother as the chaste
> Elizabeth, such gentle missionaries as the humane
> and tender hearted Oliver Cromwell, may have pre-
> sented difficulties to a people whose wits were
> sharpened by adversity, and who were not wholly
> ignorant of the Christian character, as is illus-
> trated in the history and traditions of their
> native land. 12

American Presidents

Pulpit humor directed against the early presidents of
the Republic (from Washington through Jackson) resulted
from their strong actions and ideas and the reverencing
of these presidents and their ideas by many people. But
that pulpit humor directed against later presidents
played on their weakness. During the period of these
later Presidents, other politicians were more prominent

---

11. Strickland, The Life Of Jacob Gruber, p. 98. Gruber
assigned the sovereigns to heaven; but Whitefield noted
with Dr. Watts that few kings made it to heaven. (cf.
George Whitefield, "The Good Shepherd," Eighteen Sermons,
p. 283.) American popular prints often portrayed political leaders in hell (with the most powerful personifying
the devil.) A root for such portrayal was identification
of all rulers as potentially the beast of Revelation: cf.
John Cotton, Exposition, 13th Chapter (London, 1656),p.72&77
12. Thomas Nicholas Burke, "St. Patrick," (sermon on
March 10, 1872, New York Cathedral), The Sermons,
Lectures and Addresses, p. 435.

than some of the presidents and became the target of
pulpit humor.

While George Washington came as close as any President
or American to be considered a saint in sermons, [13]
his ideas and the popular veneration of them was challenged in at least one instance from the pulpit although
the challenge came long after his death and in the context
of the Mexican American War. In his sermon "Following
Peace," Reuben Tinker reduced to the absurd Washington's
maxim "In time of peace, prepare for war":

> If it is our duty and that of all men to follow
> peace, we ought in time of peace to prepare for
> peace, and not for war. The maxim, "In time of
> peace, prepare for war," sounds like, "in time of
> temperance, prepare for drinking," or, "in time of
> praying prepare for swearing," or, "in time of
> doing right, prepare to do wrong." [14]

Tinker, who had served as a missionary in Hawaii, opposed preparation and glorification of war not only for
ethical reasons, but also because the spread of Christianity from a biblical perspective was most aided by a
climate of peace. [15]

The threat of another war (the War of 1812) and the
effects of the Embargo which Jefferson had imposed and
with which Madison had been associated, prompted another
moment of pulpit humor against a president. New England
Federalists were particularly frustrated because they
had little hope to regain national power; and the poli-
cies of the Jefferson-Madison administrations which led

---

13. Cf. John Glendy, An Oration on the Death of George
Washington, (Staunton: Wise, 1800); and Thomas Nicholas
Burke, Sermons, p. 21.
14. Tinker, "Following Peace," Sermons, p. 279. (cf.
Theodore Parker, "A Sermon on the Mexican War," Speeches,
I, p. 152.)
15. In the section dealing with "putting down other
powerful deities" we consider other instances where the
preachers helped the people laugh at the glorification
of war and the military heroes who were worshipped.

to the Embargo and then the war with England endangered
New England commerical interest so heavily dependent on
the uninterrupted movement of New England shipping. In
his strongly Federalist Church, Massachussetts Congregationalist Samuel Eaton offered up this prayer during a
fast day worship service called for by the state:

> O Lord, Thou hast commanded us to pray for our
> enemies, we would therefore pray for the President
> and Vice-President of these United States . . . 16

The popular acclaim of the leader as well as the leader's
own actions led to the use of pulpit humor to put down
reverence of leaders. Peter Cartwright enjoyed recount-
ing the way he humorously handled such acclaim of President Andrew Jackson when Jackson, still a general, had
walked into one of his worship services:

> My fastidious preacher whispered a little loud,
> said: "General Jackson has come in, General Jackson
> has come in." I felt a flash of indignation run
> all over me like an electric shock, and facing about
> to my congregation, and purposely speaking out
> audibly, I said, "Who is General Jackson? If he
> don't get his soul converted, God will damn him as
> quick as he would a Guinea negro."
> The preacher tucked his head down, and squatted low,
> and would, no doubt, have been thankful for leave
> of absence. The congregation, General Jackson and
> all, smiled or laughed right out, all at the

---

16. Letter Alpheus Packard to Wm. Sprague, (January 18,
1855), Annals, I, p. 616. Antagonism to Jefferson, his
party, and his ideas extended to democracy itself. The
broadening of the franchise undermined Federalist power.
Federalism and Calvinism were nearly synonymous in New
England; and the Calvinist ridiculing of democratic ideas
we consider under the later section entitled "Democracy."
Although in Federalist thinking only a few were considered
fit to rule, one should not identify this political
theory with the Calvinist idea that only a few are
chosen by God as the elect. Calvinist experience in
Europe and America was enough to convince them that some
of those in power were probably not among the elect,
and it is doubtful that many New England Calvinists
confused the elected with the elect.

preacher's expense. 17

After Jackson, presidents did not inspire such great
acclaim that humor was necessary to put down them or
their followers. Lincoln might have been an exception;
but the Civil War and the assassination may account for
the absence of pulpit humor directed at him. [18] Baptist
Hiram Stimson's comment summed up the attitude toward
many presidents of the period:

> I have voted for President of the United States
> from General Andrew Jackson to Grant, nine in all.
> I didn't vote for all that were elected! I am
> thankful for that. 19

Reflecting on nearly the same period a few years earlier,
Henry Ward Beecher was thankful to have Lincoln as President, a man the nation could trust; for trust had been
a rare commodity in Washington for decades. [20] And in
his sermon in the early 1850's on "The First Last, and
the Last First," Reuben Tinker observed:

> . . . that amount of piety which is often found
> among the low and obscure, and nothing thought of
> it, would render a president a prodigy, and the one
> hundredth part of some obscure widow's self denial
> would pass in them for unparalleled religion. 21

Whig Millard Fillmore, whose firm dedication to his
party's staunch anti-slavery platform may be measured
by his supporting and signing into law the fugitive

---

17. Strickland, Cartwright, p. 192. (cf. Milburn, The
Lance, Cross and Canoe, p. 396.)

18. Although it did not take the forms of humor, minis-
terial criticism of Lincoln did not end at his death.
"What was a decent person doing in a theatre?" Stimson,
From the Stage Coach to the Pulpit, p. 305.

19. Ibid., p. 383.

20. Beecher, Freedom and War, p. 218.

21. Tinker, "The First Last and the Last First," Sermons,
p. 120.

slave law and other features of the 1850 Compromise, was
likened along with his supporters to squash, Fillmore
Squash, by Jabez Swan. [22] When Lincoln was elected
President and about to assume office, Edward Taylor offered up a prayer of praise for him; but mentioned out-
going President Buchanan in this way: "But, O Lord, as
for this stuff that is going out, we won't say much
about that." [23] Henry Ward Beecher called Buchanan's
administration "imbecile in all but corruption." [24]
The best comment Beecher had for Andrew Johnson as he
prepared to make way for Grant's administration was a
prayer to God, ". . . accept our thanks that he that now
is President hath done so little mischief." [25] And
President Grant and his successors gave little reason to
fear that others would treat them as idols.

Other Politicians

If most of the presidents after Jackson were so weak as
to require no pulpit humor to put down idolatry and only
a little pulpit humor of any kind, other politicians
filled the power vacuum and became the targets of pulpit
humor. The reason for putting down the idolized politician was most explicitly stated by Theodore Parker in
his attack on Daniel Webster: "Men are continually led
astray by misplaced reverence." [26] As senator from
Massachussetts, Webster had spoken as New England's
voice against the growth of slavery. But on March 7,

22. Denison, The Evangelist, pp. 437-438.
23. Haven, Life of Father Taylor, pp. xlii and 279.
24. Henry Ward Beecher, Freedom and War, p. 132.
25. Beecher, The Sermons, First Series, p. 438.
26. Theodore Parker, "Daniel Webster," Historic Americans
Samuel A. Elliott, ed., (Boston: American Unitarian
Association, 1908), (Volume VII of the centenary edition),
p. 275.

1850, Webster spoke on the Senate Floor for the Fugitive
Slave Law and the other specifics of what was to be
called the Omnibus bill or Compromise of 1850 which
allowed the extension of slavery into areas ceded by
Mexico. In subsequent speeches Webster, who hoped to
gain southern support for the Whig nomination for the
presidency in 1852, spoke throughout the North urging
the people to support the Fugitive Slave Act. From
Parker's perspective, Webster's prestige and persuasive-
ness led the majority astray from anti-slavery sentiments
and into the betrayal of many blacks in the North.

Remembering that Webster's senate speech in support of
the Fugitive Slave Law was on March 7, that on his return
to Boston in a speech at Revere House he called the obey-
ing of the slave law "a disagreeable duty," and that a
provision of that law allowed ten dollars to the person
who informed on the whereabouts of fugitive slaves in the
North, we are prepared to appreciate Parker's sharp
ridiculing of the senator. [27] After the passage of the
omnibus bill in September, Theodore Parker preached his
Thanksgiving sermon on "The State of the Nation." Satirizing the position that all must obey the law, he
argued that James and John, Mary and Martha were weak
and wrong not to respond to the chief priests' and pharisees' commandment that anyone knowing the whereabouts of
Jesus should inform the authorities. Using phrases
from Webster's recent speeches, Parker reduced the senator's arguments to the absurd by applying them to the
events of passion week:

> Martha and Mary, could minister unto him of their
> substance, could wash his feet with tears, and wipe
> them with the hairs of their head. They did it
> gladly, of their own free will, and took pleasure
> therein, I make no doubt. There was no merit in
> that -- "Any man can perform an agreeable duty."
> But there was found one disciple who could "perform

---

27. Ibid., p. 323.

a disagreeable duty." He went, perhaps "with alac-
rity," and betrayed his Saviour to the marshal of
the district of Jerusalem, who was called centurion.
Had he no affection for Jesus? No doubt; but he
could conquer his prejudices, while Mary and John
could not.

Judas Iscariot has rather a bad name in the Christian world: he is called "The son of perdition,"in
the New Testament, and his conduct is reckoned a
"transgression;" nay, it is said the devil "entered
into him," to cause this hideous sin. But all this
it seems was a mistake; certainly, if we are to
believe our "Republican" lawyers and statesmen,
Iscariot only fulfilled his "constitutional obliga-
tions." It was only "on that point," of betraying
his Saviour, that the constitutional law required
him to have anything to do with Jesus. He took his
'thirty pieces of silver' -- about fifteen dollars;
a yankee is to do it for ten, having fewer prejudices to conquer -- it was his legal fee, for value
received. True, the Christians thought it was 'the
wages of iniquity,' and even the Pharisees -- who
commonly called the commandment of God of none
effect by their traditions -- dared not defile the
temple with this 'price of blood;' but it was honest
money. It was as honest a fee as any American
commissioner or deputy will ever get for a similar
service. How mistaken we are! Judas Iscariot is
not a traitor; he was a great patriot; he conquered
his 'prejudices,' performed "a disagreeable duty"
as an officer of "high morals and high principle;"
he kept the "law" and the "Constitution" and did all
he could to save the"Union;" nay, he was a saint,
"not a whit behind the very chiefest apostles."
"The law of God never commands us to disobey the
law of man." Sancte Iscariote ora pro nobis. 28

Later in a sermon entitled "The Chief Sins of the People"
Parker extended this argument:

Till the fugitive slave law was passed, we didn't
know what a great saint Iscariot was. I think there
ought to be a chapel for him, and a day set apart in
the calendar. Let him have his chapel in the navy-
yard at Washington. He has got a priest there already. And for a day in the calendar - set apart

---

28. Theodore Parker, "State of the Nation," Speeches,
II, pp. 212-213.

for all time the seventh of March. 29

Finally in his October 31, 1852 sermon Parker climaxed his attack on Webster two days after the former Senator and Secretary of State was buried at Marshfield:

> But after that day of St. Judas, Mr. Webster pursued the same course which Mr. Hill had followed forty years before, and the two enemies were reconciled. The Herod of the Democrats and the Pilate of Federalism were made friends by the Fugitive Slave Law and rode in the same "Omnibus," -"a blue-light Federalist," and "a genuine Democrat dyed in wool.30

The sharpness of Parker's attack was in his mind necessary to cut through the reverence being paid to Webster and his "accomplishments" by everyone else in Boston where Parker's words were the only discouraging ones heard. As the reverence paid to Webster had made the fugitive slave law respectable, so Parker was moved to ridicule of Webster to discredit that law.

And Parker's attack on Webster extended to the charges that Webster was bribed and a tool of the churches of commerce. As Webster had ridiculed Senator Seward's appeal to a higher law in the New Yorker's attack against the Fugitive Slave Law, so Parker ridiculed Webster's New York address as Secretary of State in which Webster had said, "The great object of government is the protec-[31] tion of property at home, and respect and renown abroad." Just ten days after Webster's speech, Parker's sermon contained this rejoinder to reduce the Secretary's "great object" to lesser dimensions in the public eye:

29. Parker, "The Chief Sins of the People," Speeches, II, p. 264. "The chapel in the navy-yard" was an attack on a Boston Unitarian doctor of divinity who supported Webster's position most vocally and was appointed chaplain to the Navy after Webster became Secretary of State, under Fillmore.

30. Parker, "Daniel Webster," Historic Americans, p. 340. Democrat Hill represented New Hampshire where Webster had begun his own career as a Federalist.

31. Ibid., p. 320.

> The distinguished Secretary of State, in a speech
> at New York, used these words: "The great object of
> government is the protection of property at home and
> respect and renown abroad." You see what the policy
> must be where the government is for the protection
> of the hat, and only takes care of the head so far
> as it serves to wear a hat. 32

No other individual politician of the period attracted
as much attention from pulpit humor as did Webster. The
reason may well be seen in Edward Taylor's evaluation of
Webster: "He was the best bad man I ever knew." [33]

From Webster's period, the ministers studied found it
difficult to speak of other leading politicians in any
serious way. And the attitude toward politicians after
the Civil War was similar. Surveying the instances of
pulpit humor against politicians in general, we see that
primarily the people's preoccupation with politics and
secondarily the relatively poor performance of the politicians evoked the humor from the pulpit.

With the emergence of the Whig party in 1840 as a national force after decades of personality politics within
a dominant Democratic party, a two party struggle for
the presidency fostered the idea of loyalty to party.
In his sermon on "American Politics," Horace Bushnell
the party system as further exciting the people for whom
politics was becoming the "chief passion, and highest
end, and strongest appetite." [34] The same election
prompted Methodist Senate Chaplain George Cookman to
direct his humor toward the political process:

> Statesmen are imitating the apostles of Christian-
> ity, and have become itinerating preachers of late,

32. Parker, "State of the Nation." Speeches, II, p. 209.

33. Haven, The Life of Father Taylor, p. 315.

34. Horace Bushnell, "American Politics," The American
National Preacher, (December, 1840), XIV,No.12, p. 190.

and . . . within a few months there have been many
convictions, many conversions, and no want of songs
and anthems (to the triumph of Truth). 35

The enthusiasm for politics displayed by many Americans
was often cited to ridicule the attack on Methodist
enthusiasts and others in religious revivals; [36] but
the preference of many Americans for political enthusiasm evoked the pulpit ridicule of politicians -- ridicule
which may be seen as an indirect way of putting down this
passion for politics. Bushnell ridiculed those who
entered politics to defend the interest of religion and
who as a result had no time for religion:

> But no, they are not here, and for this they have
> the best of all reasons, they fancy, viz. that they
> have to fight for the very existence of religion in
> the great campaign of politics! How can they pray,
> how meet with the church, how instruct their famil-
> ies faith, and cry hosannas in so many long pro-
> cessions of the people? 37

Bushnell likened the entire political enterprise to the
trial of Jesus in which the politicians (Herod and
Pilate) attended caucuses in the night and revealed their
weak wills so ingloriously. [38] The pulpit demeaning of
politicians as weak, corrupt, and inglorious reflected
not only some truth but also an effort to darken the
image of politics which was inordinately attractive to
so many Americans. By the end of the century over an
issue of the consolidation of Brooklyn with New York in
1896 -- a consolidation he opposed but which the State
Assembly was encouraging -- Richard Storrs, Jr., reflected on politicians in this flattering way:

---

35. Henry B. Ridgaway, The Life of the Rev. Alfred
Cookman, p. 74.

36. These instances are considered in chapter four.

37. Bushnell, "American Politics," The American National
Preacher, pp. 197-198.

38. Ibid., pp. 193-196.

Is this population to be deprived of self-government,
and moved about by politicians in Albany, hither and
yon, as a blind man is led along by a dog? I think,
myself, that some apology is necessary for that
comparison, but under the existing circumstances,
the apology, I am sure, is due to the dog. 39

Eleven years earlier, Sam Jones evoked laughter at
politicians with these words in a protracted meeting
in Ohio:

Well, if there is one class of people in this
country I cannot pray for it's politicians. These
politicians I cannot pray for. Some power whispers
back when I try to, "Don't talk to me about them."40

Still thirteen years earlier on March 22, 1872, in St.
Paul's Church, Brooklyn, Irish Dominican Thomas Burke
noted that it did not take long for a foreigner to
learn that the term "politician" ws not to be sought
after:

It is no credit to a man to be a politician. Some
time ago a fellow was arrested in France for having
committed a robbery. He was taken before a magis-
trate and jury, and the prosecuting officer said:
"The crime of the man indicted before you is this:
That on such a night he went to such a house for
purposes of robbery. "Yes," said he, "it is so; but
remember, there is an extenuating circumstance."
"What is it?" "I am no Jesuit." "Did you not robe
the house?" "Yes, I did; but thank God, I am no
Jesuit." This man had been reading the French
infidel newspapers; and he selected a priest as
something worse than himself. Bad as he was, in
order to make it appear that there was something
still worse, it was necessary to say, "he was not a
Jesuit." So if a man were arraigned for any con-
ceivable crime, he might urge as an extenuating
circumstance, "it is true; I did it; but I am no
politician!" 41

39. Storrs, Orations, p. 582. The comment came in one
of the few verbatim accounts of Storrs' orations. The
verbatim accounts reveal a great deal of humor which is
only occasionally evident in edited sermons and speeches.

40. Jones, Sermons: Wise and Witty, p. 24.

41. Thomas Nicholas Burke, "The Christian Man, The Man
of the Day," Sermons, p. 17.

And twelve years earlier, Henry Ward Beecher ridiculed
politicians on the occasion of the 1860 Thanksgiving Day
when the mayor of New York and many other Democratic
politicians found nothing for which to be thankful:

> Papers and parties are in full outcry, and nostrums
> are advertised, and scared politicians are at their
> wits' ends,(without having gone far, either). . . .42

This consistent attack of pulpit humor on politicians
may be taken as one testimony to the continued American
passion for politics.

Democracy

It should be noticed that the attack on politicians and
the American political passion was most fully articulated
by the sons of New England Calvinism who regularly found
their own views in the minority during the nineteenth
century. The attack on the idolization of democracy and
the majority may be explained in part by the minority
status of the attackers. But the suspicion of "the
majority" was deeply rooted also in the view of man or
any combination of men as far from perfect.

At the beginning of the period under study, Jonathan
Mayhew ridiculed the idea that the notions of the majority could be safely followed to determine the truth:

> If truth and right have no existence but in the
> opinions of men, then indeed they might depend upon
> number and multitude. But then it may be reasonably
> asked how many votes are necessary to change a great
> lie into a truth? How many to change a flagrant
> crime into a meritorious virtue? And a sinner into
> a saint? The church of Rome has been trying a great
> while to bring about these wonderful changes and
> revolutions; and has affected it to the satisfaction
> of many. 43

42. Beecher, Freedom and War, p. 36.
43. Mayhew, Sermons, p. 19. While Mayhew may be classed
as a forerunner of Unitarianism because of his opposition
to the doctrine of the trinity, he was far from Armin-
ianism in his doctrine of man.

Mayhew used the Calvinist argument of the imperfection
of man against those nominal Calvinists who felt secure
in numbers. And he ridiculed further the notion that
the majority position in any way revealed the truth:

> Infallibility cannot be the result of a great num-
> ber of fallibles: nor perfection be found in a
> large body of such as are each of them considered
> singly, imperfect. But never-the-less we daily see
> that the principle argument with which some endeavor
> to propagate their opinions, is that they are gen-
> erally received, i.e. in that particular place or
> country. . . .If we must needs be governed by num-
> bers in the choice of our religion, it is certainly
> reasonable to be governed by the greatest number.
> And if so, we must be neither Calvinist nor Arminian;
> nor Protestant; not Jew, nor Mahometants; but we
> must even turn Heathens at once, Paganism being the
> most universal Orthodoxy in the world. 44

The French Revolution provided an occasion for those of
Calvinist persuasion to further ridicule democratic
notions and the underlying assumption that truth was best
revealed by a majority. Dwight succinctly summed up the
attitude toward Infidel ideas, the reason of the majority
and the French Revolution. "3,000,000 dead, an illustrious instance of Infidel benevolence." [45] And Charles
Nisbet ridiculed equality in his reference to the stealing of Ashbel Green's horse before the May meeting of
the 1796 General Assembly of the Presbyterian Church:

> "No doubt," said he, "it was done by one of the
> sovereign people; he was taken, without your leave,
> by a pure act of sovereignty. But, sir, it was only
> a forced loan; it was an act of practical Liberty
> and Equality; the rascal thought that you had been
> riding long enough, and that, by all the laws of
> equality, it was his turn to ride now, and so he
> made use of his liberty to appropriate to himself a
> part of your property, without your consent. 46

---

44. Ibid., p. 20.
45. "Address" in New Haven, 1801. (cf. H. Shelton Smith,
Robert T. Handy, and Lefferts A. Loescher, American
Christianity, I, p. 535.)
46. Miller, Memoir, p. 312. Letter from Ashbel Green,
April 30, 1839.

But the most thorough humorous attack on the reverencing of democracy came from Horace Bushnell. Again it was idolization of democracy that attracted Bushell's attack which was based on the biblical insight that man is not only fickle as Mayhew had called him [47] but that the majority of men could be very wrong and carry out the greatest evil:

> The scene of Christ's trial and crucifixion shows us what to think of the sacredness of democracy. It has been given out, within the past year, with a profound philosophical bow to the people, and especially to Christian people, that "democracy is holy" . . .But when it is given out that democracy is holy, the insult offered to religion is too offensive to be suffered. What do we see? But yesterday the populace were all for Christ and followed him with their hosannas. Today they are with the Scribes and Pharisees crying "Crucify him, crucify him." And the cries of them and of the chief priests prevailed. Yes, they prevailed; they were a high majority. Democracy holy! . . .When did Jesus condescend to tell us that ours is the true form of govenment? When lend himself to any such mischievous flattery as this? When did he undertake to be a lecturer for democracy? And when his apostle dared to say of all forms of government, "the powers that be, are ordained of God" did he there controvert his Master's special predilection for democracy as the only holy form? [48]

Bushnell's ridicule of democracy did not necessarily mean that he preferred some other form of government. The ridicule was aimed at any attempt to elevate democracy to a level with the sacred and to trust it to produce infallable decisions. [49]

47. Mayhew, Sermons, p. 18.
48. Bushnell, "American Politics," The American National Preacher, pp. 199-200.
49. In a much earlier issue of The National Preacher appeared three of Lyman Beecher's sermons. The first raised the question "whence that idolatry of patriotism and talent, and forms of government and that continued jealousy of the Gospel.... "Propriety and Importance of Efforts to Evangelize the Nation," The National Preacher, (March, 1829),III, No. 10, p. 155. And the last was the famous attack on Sunday postal service with the closing lines: THUS ENDETH THE NATION THAT DESPISED THE LORD, AND GLORIED IN WISDOM, WEALTH AND POWER. Ibid., p. 160.

Putting Down Other Powerful Deities

The other two groups powerful enough to be labeled idols
and targets of pulpit humor were military leaders and
church leaders. The amount of humor directed against
these two groups was far less than that which dealt with
politicians. [50] And of these two additional targets of
humor, the military received less attention. The little
humor directed at a few other leaders (e.g. judges) was
within the context of slavery and is considered in discussions of that subject later in this chapter. But the
attack on military and church leaders did not usually
result from their actions or inactions in relation to
any issue. The attack on these leaders resulted from
the swelling pride inherent in their occupations.

The Military

Most of the ridicule of the military came at the times
when the govenment was inflating the significance of
serving one's country in order to raise an army on the
eve of war. The attack was less on particular leaders
than upon the glorification of military life and accomplishment. The inglorious performance of military in the
War of 1812 prompted no pulpit humor. But the Mexican
War, which the American military won with dispatch and
which some New Englanders opposed because they feared
the ceded territory would be used to expand slavery,
stimulated pulpit humor.

---

50. A direct relation seems to obtain between the amounts
of humor directed toward certain subjects and the significance of those subjects within a culture. Humor
has been especially directed toward those of rising
influence. For instance, humor directed against women
and monks in the medival period coincided with their
rising power. Similarly, the use of humor against
politicians in the nineteenth century coincided with
their increasing power.

To President Polk's call for troops "to defend" the
United States against "Mexican aggression" in mid 1846,
Theodore Parker responded with "A Sermon on War":

> If the President gets his fifty thousand volunteers,
> a thing likely to happen -- for though Irish lumpers
> and hod-men want a dollar or a dollar and a half a
> day, your free American of Boston will enlist for
> twenty seven cents, only having his livery, his
> feathers, and his "glory" thrown in -- then at $8
> a month, their wages amount to $400,000 a month. 51

Parker decried such expense which he noted was a hundred
times the cost of operating Harvard College. And the
amount was increased by those who were present to train
the young men in ways quite other than he approved:

> The officer, the surgeon, and the chaplains, who
> teach the soldiers to wad their muskets with the
> leaves of the Bible, will perhaps cost as much. 52

And in return for all of the cost, the country would
receive "three things, valor, glory, and -- talk; which,
as they are not in the price current, I must estimate as
I can, and set them all down in one figure = 0; not
worth the whiskey they cost." 53 Of previous military
ventures, Parker noted the glorious war with Florida
Indians which he estimated cost the country between
$30,000,000 and $40,000,000 "in fighting five hundred
invisible Indians!" 54 Ridiculing the glories and the
benefits of war, Parker went so far as to call most of
the Revolutionary War veterans "vile" because of their
war time experiences. 55 And Parker parodied the

51. Theodore Parker, "A Sermon on War," Speeches, p. 75.
52. Ibid., p. 76.
53. Ibid. Similarly, the cost of lavish patriotic cele-
brations commemorating wars on July 4 was ridiculed by
Jacob Gruber, who commented, "Does it give more real
pleasure to the mind to hear a great gun than it would
to hear a pop-gun? 'Vanity of Vanities.'" Strickland,
The Life of Jacob Gruber, I, p. 118.
54. Parker, "A Sermon on War," Speeches, I, p. 78.
55. Ibid., p. 90.

beatitudes to reduce to the absurd the glorification
of battle:

> Blessed are the men-slayers! Seek first the glory
> which cometh of battle. Be fierce as tigers. Mar
> God's image in which your brothers are made. 56

Parker used ridicule further to reduce to infamy the
famous "victories" which General Zachary Taylor "won"
in destroying villages when he invaded Mexico even before
Congress declared war:

> To butcher men and women and children, when they are
> coming home from church, with prayer books in their
> hands, seems an aggravation even of murder; a cow-
> ardly murder, which a Hessian would have been
> ashamed of. "But 't was a famous victory." 57

Preached in the same period and included in Horace
Bushell's first volume of sermons in 1858, "Dignity
of Human Nature Shown From Its Ruins" ridiculed the
heroics of war by comparing them to the deeds of ants:

> One race there is that figure in these heroics of
> war, in a small way, viz., the tiny race of ants
> whom God had made a spectacle to mock the glory and
> magnificance of human wars. 58

Bushnell called "little and contemptible" Napoleon and
others who needed to present themselves in the "digni-
fied" trappings of military dress. [59] And with some
irony Bushnell mocked the argument that men need the
glories and heroes of war. On the ruins he makes in war,
man raises "himself into the attitude of a god, before
the obsequious ages of mankind; for who of us can live
content, as we are tempted, without some hero to admire

---

56. _Ibid._, p. 91.
57. _Ibid._, p. 149.
58. Horace Bushnell, "Dignity of Human Nature Shown From
Its Ruins," _Sermons for the New Life_, (New York: Charles
Scribner, 1858), p. 56.
59. _Ibid._, p. 58

and worship." [60]

While the Civil War was not in itself an object of pulpit humor, some of those who served in the war were targets. At the outbreak of war, Henry Ward Beecher argued that salvation of the nation could not be expected from military power and that those in the army were far from saints who would deliver the nation from evil:

> . . . the papers do represent them as being made up of quite another class of men and that they will leave New York wonderfully purified when they go forth to do a patriot's duty in a distant state! [61]

Henry Stimson, who served as a captain and recruited many of his congregation with the hopes that the war would end slavery, reflected humorously about those who lorded it over others. To counter what he called the idolization of General George McClelland, who had commanded the Union forces and later run for president on the Democratic ticket in 1864, Stimson noted:

> In our opinion, he attained a greater and more sudden reputation, on a smaller capital, than any other man ever has on the American continent. . . He never ought to have fought with his _face_ to the enemy. Those in front of him had nothing to fear. He was dangerous only to those in his rear, as the Union cause can abundantly testify. [62]

---

60. _Ibid._, p. 57. In contrast to this exorcising of the idolatry of war and its heroes, Catholic John Ireland declared, "WAR IS SACRED." (cf. "The Patriotic Duties of the Catholic," _The Northwestern Chronicle_, September 11, 1896 , XXX, No. 44, p. 5. In this attitude toward war, we may see again the tendency noted in chapter two to identify American idolatries and then encourage Catholic emulation of the idolatry. Although a Catholic theology of submission to civil authorities as God's authorities also underlies this position on war, (_Ibid._, p. 5.), the pragmatic desire to avoid being called un-American should not be overlooked.
61. Henry Ward Beecher, "The Camp, Its Dangers and Duties," (May, 1861), _Freedom and War_, p. 144. (cf.p. 132).
62. Stimson, _From Stage Coach to Pulpit_, pp. 262-263.

132

And Stimson enjoyed repeating the story of how he handled
a Lieut. Colonel who criticized him for stepping out of
line to avoid a mud hole:

> The officer added, "As to Captain Stimson, if at
> any time he comes to a mud hole and thinks he can't
> go through it, if he will just speak to me, I will
> take him on my back and carry him over." I doffed
> my hat and said, smiling, "Thank you, Lieut. Col.,
> I have one objection to that. We are promised
> horses to ride, when we enlisted, and I should be
> ashamed to be seen mounted on a jackass." All the
> officers threw up their caps and cheered most
> lustily for the "old Captain." Did I say all the
> officers? I think the Lieut. Col. did not. 63

Church Leaders

There was little pulpit humor expressed against the Pope.
Jonathan Mayhew's attack in "Popish Idolatry" and other
sermons was not common with others:

> Sovereign princes must think themselves honoured in
> having the liberty to kiss the toe of an old Monk,
> who calls himself Christ's <u>Vicar</u>. And thus it is
> that the <u>Pope</u> imitates him who was <u>meek</u> and <u>lowly in
> heart</u>; and who condescended to <u>wash his disciples</u>
> feet. 64

And the humor expressed against the Anglican hierarchy
was confined to tracts and articles outside the pulpit.[65]
But the pulpit humor was directed at the group of church
leaders who had actual power in America during the
period: Protestant American Ministers.

---

63. <u>Ibid.</u>, p. 252.
64. Mayhew, <u>Sermons</u>, p. 59. (cf. <u>Popish Idolatry</u>.)
65. In the 19th Century, Leonard Bacon's articles were
cited as most sarcastic against Anglican and Episcopal
hierarchies. (cf. <u>Leonard Bacon</u>, p. 188; and Henry
Fowler, <u>The American Pulpit</u>: Sketches, Biographical and
Descriptive of Living American Preachers, New York: J.M.
Fairchild Co., 1856 , p. 483.) In the 18th Century the
Episcopal system and even the modest proposal for a
modified Presbyterian plan evoked the most humorous response from John Wise whose 1710 work was republished in
1770. <u>The Church's Quarrel Espoused</u>, Gainsville:
Scholars' Facsimiles and Reprints, 1966).

George Whitefield had noted ". . .we do not love the
Pope, because we love to be popes ourselves, and set up
our own experience as a standerd to others." [66] In
chapter four on the idolatry of education, we note how
ministers were often the target of pulpit humor because
of their pride in the development of theology which did
little in some cases but set up their own experiences
as a standard for others. But in a few instances, humor
(some of it self deprecating) was aimed at lessening the
distance which some ministers maintained from the congregation. And other anecdotes played upon the piety which
was advocated by, but not accomplished by church leaders.

We noted in chapter one that a great deal of humor was
used throughout the period studied among ministers
themselves in their training and association to put down
ministerial pride. But most of the uses of such humor in
sermons to help the lay people laugh at the minister,
date from after the Civil War. And such pulpit humor did
not aim to put the minister down any further than a level
with the people. In his inaugural sermon in 1825,
Leonard Bacon told his New Haven Congregation:

> You know too -- and I would not have you forget for
> a moment -- that your minister must be like other
> ministers, frail and sinful. And the longer you
> know me, the more distinct will be your conceptions,
> and the more thorough conviction of this. 67

And by the time of his retirement from the church in
1866, Bacon noted that because of some weaknesses in the
congregation the weaknesses of the minister had not
remained unknown: "everybody in the parish knows all
about him; and what the whole parish knows, everybody
else knows." [68]

---

66. George Whitefield, Eighteen Sermons, p. 128.
67. Leonard Bacon, "Inaugural Sermons," Leonard Bacon,
p. 60.
68. Leonard Bacon, "The Pastor Retiring from his Original
Work," Four Commemorative Discourses, (New Haven: T. J.
Stafford, 1866).

134

In the 1870's Henry Ward Beecher and Dwight Lyman Moody
used humor to stress their own humanity and poke fun at
ministers whose dignity kept them aloof or distant from
the people. Beecher made fun of himself in speaking of
his experience at trying to paint his own house in
Indianapolis:

> When I began to paint there I was so afraid that I
> should fall off from the platform, that I nearly
> rubbed out with my vest what I put on with the
> brush. 69

In a sermon which he repeated with different names to
suit the leading ministers in the cities he visited,
Moody aimed at the dignity of some clergy (a dignity
many people expected the ministers to maintain). In
this sermon on Joshua, Moody remarked in Boston:

> The ark was to come out, and the priests were to
> blow rams' horns. That was very absurd, wasn't it?
> Rams' horns. I think there are a people here, if
> they wanted anybody to blow anything, they would
> want them to blow silver trumpets. The idea of Dr.
> Webb, Dr. Pentecost, Mr. Brooks, Catholic divines
> and apostolic Protestants going around the streets
> and blowing rams' horns. Oh, no, they are too fine
> for that. They must blow beautiful silver trumpets.
> 70

With the same passage at the opening of his Brooklyn
meetings of 1875, Moody delighted the crowd by using the
names of local divines who were seated on the platform
with him: "How would Dr. Talmage and Dr. Budington and
Bishop Peter look marching in a single file, blowing
rams' horns?" 71

Advocating righteous living but falling short of such
living themselves was the occasion for additional humor
directed at church leaders. In one sermon, Henry Ward

69. Henry Ward Beecher, "Law and Liberty," (September 13,
1874), Plymouth Pulpit, (March -- September, 1875),
(Boston: Pilgrim Press, 1875), p. 17.
70. Dwight Lyman Moody, To All People, pp. 271-272.
71. Wm. McLoughlin, Jr.,Modern Revivalism, p. 242.

Beecher humorously remarked, "It is not well for a man to pray cream and live skim milk." [72] And in another sermon he helped the people laugh at the idea that the churches and the ministers were indispensable for God's work: "God works by churches and he works in spite of them. He works by ministers -- and it is hard work, often." [73] In his street preaching in San Francisco two decades earlier, William Taylor had held up to laughter the Christian who made a pretense to regular right living but who did not know how even to begin a prayer:

> Don't make a mockery of it as did a simple hearted old German, who, having a number of strange guests at his table, said to the one next to him, 'Friend, say grace.' The friend requested the one next to him to say it, and so it passed round till it came back to the old German, and he said: 'Vell, ve can do mit out dis time.' [74]

And a black pulpit exemplum from the last third of the century helped the people to laugh at the pastor who stood revealed as less than perfect. The pastor, elder Johnson, was asked by the people to ask the Lord for an easy way out of their troubles on the plantation:

> So Elduh Johnson say, "Aw-right," he gonna ast Gawd to show 'im a sign to hope de membuhship out. So sho' 'nuff, he ca'ie out his promus he done meck a pole on de wes' side of de Brazos rat whar de chu'ch hab its baptizin' de ver' nex' Sunday at three o'clock an' dat all de membuhs what tiahed of livin' and workin so haa'd kin climb dis pole to heabun if'n dey brings a box of chald an' mecks a mark for evuh lie dey done tole in dey life. But dey haf to be dere on time, 'caze de pole jes gonna stay for fifteen minnits. Elduh Johnson 'nounce dis to de membuhship at de prayer servus on a Wednesday night. So all dem what rathuh go on to heabun now gits 'em a box at de bapizin' hole long 'fo three o'clock dat Sunday, an' was stn'in dere waiting

---

72. Proctor, _Life Thoughts_, p. 64.

73. Henry Ward Beecher, "Soul's Growth," (March 7, 1875), _Plymouth Pulpit_, (March - September, 1875), p. 614.

74. Taylor, _Seven Years of Street Preaching_, p. 297.

'wid dey boxes of chalk. Zackly at three o'clock
de membuhs heah a loud noise lack a urfquake or su'n
nothin, an' jes' lack de pastuh say a great big pole
what rech so far to'a'ds de sky 'till you cain't
see de top comed up outen de groun' an' all de
membuhs what got dey chalk gits on de pole what habs
a rope ladder on hit an' staa'ts to climbin' an'
markin'. When de las one done clum up on de ladder,
de pole vanish jes' lack dat int' thin air an' you
don' see hit no mo'.
Dat ver' same night de Lawd come to de preachuh
again in a dream an' tell 'im dat dis same time
anothuh yeah he gonna meck a pole appear to de
membuhship again at de baptizin' place. De preachuh
'nounce dis dream to de membuhship at de Monday
night class meetin' an' when de time roll 'round de
nex' yeah for de pole to show up, dey was a bigguh
bunch of han's on de river banks dan dy was de yeah
befo'. When de pole pop up outen de groun' ez
befo', de fuss membuh of de chu'ch to staa't up de
pole was Elduh Roberts, what was de full pastuh of
Mt. Moriah Chu'ch. His whole fam'ly done die out,
so he say dey ain't no need of 'im stayin' heah no
longer. So, soon as de pole comed outen de groun',
he hobbles ovuh to hit, gits on de ladder an' staa't
to climb, but 'fo narry othuh han' kin git staa'ted
to climbin' dey looks up an' sees Elduh Roberts
almos' to de groun' again comin' down de pole, so
dey all wonduhs what de matta' wid de pole dis yeah.
But 'taint de pole, hit's Elduh Roberts.
When Revun Johnson, de pastuh spy Elduh Roberts
comin' down de pole, he yell, "What's de mattuh,
Elduh, ain't evuhthing awright up dere?"
"Sho', sho'," say Elduh Roberts, jumpin' down offen
de pole; "Ah'm jes' comin' back attuh some mo'
chalk." 75

Putting Down the Peculiar Institution

The issue of slavery prompted several different strategies of pulpit humor. This humor in the first half of
the nineteenth century was focused within the church
itself at those who held slaves or defended slavery as
right. The Fugitive Slave Law of 1850 and the Kansas-
Nebraska Act of 1854 shifted the focus of pulpit humor

---

75. Brewer, The Word on the Brazos, pp. 83-84. Hypocrisy
which is the basis for these humorous attacks need not
be seen in a totally serious light. cf. Elton Trueblood, The Humor of Christ, (New York: Harper and Row,
1964).

outside the church toward those who used the Union (its
law and courts) to defend and extend the influence of
slavery and the slaveholders' legal rights. And in this
later period, some humor was directed at the growing
groups of abolitionists and other radicals who equated
immediate action with Christianity and attacked fellow
churchmen who would not join this particular cause.

The Church

In the mid 1820's when Methodist circuit rider William
Cravens was transferring to Indiana from his native
Virginia, he engaged in the following conversation with
a stranger and so stated the place of slavery in his
Christian world view:

> Stranger, (addressing Mr. Cravens, inquired,)
> "Where are you removing to?"
> Cravens, "To Indiana."
> Stranger, "That is a fine country. I have just come
> from there, and have only one objection to it."
> Cravens, "What is that, for I am interested to know
> as I propose to make Indiana my future home."
> Stranger, "It is this: they will not let a man
> take his property there.
> Cravens, "But I am going to take my property there."
> Stranger, "I mean they will not let a man take his
> slaves there."
> Cravens, (raising his hands and eyes to heaven,
> exclaimed, with emphasis,) "Glory to God, there is
> one place besides heaven where a slaveholder can
> not go to." 76

In holding slavery to be incompatible with a Christian
life, a circuit rider such as Cravens followed official
Methodist policy of the period. [77] Cravens and his colleagues stressed personal rather than political or economic solutions to the problem of slavery. But even this

---

76. Wakeley, The Bold Frontier Preacher, pp. 98-99.
77. A policy was originally designed to prevent slaveholders from being Methodist ministers. The Wesleys had
even encouraged a boycott of slave made goods by the
late eighteenth century.

138

preaching was inflamatory in the **South of the period**; and
by the mid 1820's Cravens and many of his colleagues had
left the South by force or foresight. [78]

Cravens, who would not give a last communion to those
who did not free their slaves before death, [79] ridiculed the effort of those who tried to make slavery
compatible with Christianity. The incongruity he saw
was the basis for humor. Dr. Thomas Bond reported
Cravens' Baltimore sermon of 1800 which described the
Masterbuilder erecting the spiritual edifice:

> He beheld a stone of rare beauty, that he admired
> exceedingly; and said this stone must have a con-
> spicuous place in the front part of the building,
> for it will greatly add to its beauty. He placed
> it upon the wall adding, "That is a most beautiful
> stone," but, to his surprise, it would not fit the
> living stones -- it would not lie down, and a corner
> of it stuck out, making it look very awkward. He
> took his hammer and knocked off a corner of it to
> make it smooth, so it would lie down; but it still
> stuck out, and it would not lie down. He tried it
> again, with no better success. He took his hammer
> and struck the stone a heavy blow, in order to make
> it lie, when to his surprise, the stone broke, and
> out jumped a negro and a whiskey bottle. 80

And once when a slaveholder was coughing in a meeting
where he was to become a member of the Methodist society,
Cravens called out, "Cough away, brother; that's right,
cough up the negroes." [81]

James Axley and Jacob Gruber were other Methodist circuit
riders in the South who employed humor to ridicule the
compatibility of Christianity and slavery. Axley, who
later became a colleague of Peter Cartwright in Illinois,
began his ministry in the upper South and often related
this story in his sermons:

78. Ibid., p. 98.
79. Ibid., p. 89.
80. Ibid., pp. 65-66.
81. Ibid., P. 46.

Ah yes! you sisters here at church look as sweet
and smiling as if you were angels; and one of you
says to me, 'come to dinner,' and I go; and when I
go, you say 'Sit down brother Axley while I go about
the dinner;' and you go to the kitchen, and I hear
something crying out, 'Don't Missus,' and I hear the
sound of slaps, and the poor girl screaming, and
the sister whaling and trouncing Sally in the
kitchen as hard as she can. And when she has performed this office, she comes back looking as sweet
and smiling as a summer's day, as if she had been
saying her prayers. That is what you call Christianity, is it? 82

Gruber rode circuit through Virginia until forced to
leave after being tried in 1818 on unproven charges that
his preaching aroused slaves. [83] Gruber's sarcastic
comments did arouse slaveholders if not the slaves. In
the sermon for which he was indicted, Gruber held up to
ridicule the linking of slave holding and church going.
We may imagine the way in which this sarcastic Pennsylvania German read a sale advertisement out loud:

'For sale, a plantation, a house and lot, horses,
cows, sheep, and hogs. Also a number of negroes,
men, women, and children, some very valuable ones.
Also a pew in such and such a church.' 84

But Gruber went beyond the ridicule of slavery from the
viewpoint of Christian ideals. The nation's political
ideals also served as a background for Gruber's humor.
In reflecting on the opposition to this preaching Gruber
noted, "I have heard of Republican slaveholders; but I
understand no more of what it means than sober drunkards."
85

---

82. William Henry Milburn, The Pioneers, Preachers, and
People, (New York: Derby & Jackson, 1860), p. 372.
83. Strickland, The Life of Jacob Gruber, p. 124. He
was defended by Roger Taney whose 1857 Dred Scott deci-
sion denied that Congress could prevent the spread of
slavery in the territories.

84. Ibid., p. 84. We note this same incongruity as the
basis for humor in a lithograph of the period, The Slave
Sale, Harry T. Peters, "America on Stone Lithography
Collection," Smithsonian Institution.

85. Ibid., p. 253.

140

And in a July 4 sermon on what freedom should mean in
America, Gruber related an incident in which he had met
a procession of three whites driving along several dozen
chained colored men and women about the time that Americans were protesting the English impressment of American
sailors and the English interference with the free movement of American vessels:

> As I passed them I said, 'Hail! Columbia, happy
> land; is this free trade and sailors' rights?' 86

Northern preaching using humor during the period prior
to the Compromise of 1850 focused on the ministers who
either failed to deal with slavery or dared to defend
slavery on biblical grounds. In Baltimore, Baptist
Jacob Knapp entered the pulpit to preach against slavery
and related giving this reproof to ministers who feared
to preach on the subject:

> A number of ministers were in the pulpit when I
> entered; and two of them were skulking down behind
> the desk, lest they should be hurt by any missles
> that might be sent at me. I gave one of them a jog,
> and told him to sit up, for he had not religion
> enough to make him worthy of martyrdom yet. 87

Knapp's Baptist colleague Jabez Swan handled minister's
arguments that slavery was a "divine institution" in the
following manner:

> "You pretend to think that slavery is right. You
> contend that it is a divine institution. Very well;
> for the sake of argument, we grant it. So is hell
> a divine institution, as only too many will find
> out; but we don't propose the extension of either."
> 88

---

86. Ibid., p. 120.
87. Knapp, Autobiography, p. 102. Theodore Parker's
comment on the minister who would 'close his window' to
pray is another example of humorous attack on less than
courageous clergy (cf. chapter one).
88. Denison, The Evangelist, pp. 436-437. The extension
of slavery was necessary if the slave forces were to
keep a balance of power in the senate and so preserve
slavery.

Common was the resort to ridicule in dealing with arguments that the bible provided a sanction for slavery. In the 1840's Reuben Tinker responded:

> The bible is so much the patron of slavery, that the planters of the South withhold it from their slaves. They enact laws which prevent them from learning to read it. They may imprison you if you go there, and fully and faithfully preach it. And yet they pretend that the Bible sanctions slavery! 89

Henry Ward Beecher noted:

> The Bible Society is sending its shiploads of Bibles all over the world -- to Greenland and the Morea, to Arabia and Egypt; but it does not send them to our own people. The colporteur who should leave a Bible in a slave's cabin would go to heaven from the lowest limb of the first tree. It was hell, among the ancients that was guarded by a hundred-headed dog; in this country, it is heaven that has the Cerberus. 90

In a sermon first preached at the formation of a congregation in Broadway Tabernacle in 1840 and widely circulated in 1841, Leonard Bacon propounded the positive doctrines of Paul in a way to ridicule those who argued for a biologically created basis for slavery:

> "God hath made of one blood all nations of men to dwell on all the face of the earth." How strange to an Athenian! One blood! All nations of one blood! We Greeks -Athenians - sprung from the soil - we of one blood with the Jew and the wild Scythian! What! The Ethiopian or Celtic slave that trembles in my presence, of one blood with me! 91

---

89. Tinker, Sermons, pp. 417 and 126. Tinker took a rare shot at slave holders as well: "The master of the plantation has as much as he deserves, and a thousand fold more; and as for religion he has all he wants -- for he wants none of it." Ibid., p. 126.

90. Proctor, Life Thoughts, p. 184.

91. Leonard Bacon, "The Primitive Christians," The American National Preacher, (June, 1841), XV, No. 6, p. 135.

After the Compromise of 1850, pulpit humor shifted some
of its focus to issues   concerning Federal laws; but the
attention to "biblical" apologies for slavery was not
altogether abandoned. Leonard Bacon had his attention
and humor redirected to the biblical arguments as late
as 1860, when an unnamed visiting preacher gave a sermon
in New Haven to argue for slavery. In a sermon entitled
"The Jugglers Detected," we may hear Bacon's sarcastic
presentation of the apologist's views:

> (He) attempts to make men believe that the Bible is
> the warrant, and God the patron of American slavery.
> It is said that slavery of the enforced class in
> the United States is only the fulfillment of an
> ancient prophecy pronounced by Noah upon one of the
> sons of Ham. (Gen. ix.25.) So it might have been
> said in Egypt, by iron-hearted theologians, that
> the slavery of the Israealites there was only the
> fulfillment of a more recent prediction, and the
> more pertinent and explicit one. (Gen. xv.13).
> . . .Beware then of the juggle, when the author of
> that sermon fixes your attention on the fact that a
> certain sort of servitude was tolerated in the Hebrew
> commonwealth, was recognized by the Apostles -- and
> then quietly, and with an air of perfect simplicity,
> assumes that his American slavery in the 19th cen-
> tury of the Christian era -- this slavery with the
> barracoons of Richmond and New Orleans -- this
> slavery which breeds human beings to be sold in
> distant markets, as they breed horses in Vermont,
> and cattle on the prairies -- this slavery with a
> slave trade which has swept more than ten thousand
> wretched victims within the last twelve months, from
> the one State of Virginia, to toil, not for wages,
> but under the coercion of the lash, in the cane-
> brakes and cotton fields of regions farther South
> -- is all right. 92

The assertion that slavery was "all right" evoked the
minister's most sarcastic pulpit humor.

The Law

The National Congressional and Court actions of the

---

92. Leonard Bacon, The Juggler Detected, (New Haven:
Thomas Pease, 1861), pp. 4, 5, and 16.

1850's shifted the attention of pulpit humor from the
ridicule of biblical arguments to a ridicule of legal
arguments for slavery. The Fugitive Slave Act, ("fugitive in more senses than one" according to Reuben Tinker's
sermon [93]), made it a Federal Law for all citizens to
withhold assistance from escaping slaves and report such
runaways to the authorities. We have already seen how
Theodore Parker treated Webster's argument that this
"disagreeable duty" was the obligation of every citizen.
When one fugitive slave was captured in Boston and the
people tried to picket the court house against the marshall who had cooperated in apprehending him, the court
house was cordoned off so that no one could enter to
present the protest. Parker responded in a sermon,
"Behold the people shut out from the courts -- I will
not say of Justice!" [94]

That a statute on the books (e.g. the Fugitive Slave
Law) must be enforced by all officers in the community
was ridiculed by Parker in this way:

> So in Pharaoh's time it was a moral duty to drown
> the babies in the Nile; in Darius' time to pray to
> King Darius, and him only; in Herod's time to mass-
> acre the children of Bethlehem; in Henry the Eighth's
> time to cast your Bible to the flames. Iscariot
> only did a disagreeable duty. [95]

That the will of a majority in a particular place at a
particular time could frame a law which all men could or
should morally follow was ridiculed by reference to
several hypothetical situations including the following:

> Fancy all the ruffians and man-killers assembled in

---

93. Tinker, Sermons, p. 417.
94. Parker, Speeches, II, p. 282.
95. Parker, The Laws of God and the Statutes of Men,
p. 26.

San Francisco, -- it would be a fit place, for there
were twelve hundred murders committed there in less
than four years, -- held a convention of violence,
and sought to organize murder, and declared, "There
is no law higher than the might of the lifted arm,"
-- would they have the moral right to kill, stab,
butcher whomsoever they pleased? 96

The attack on the law was connected to the attack on the
faith that the majority possessed a moral rectitude. We
have explored dimensions of this ridicule of democracy.
The crises of the 1850's were reflected even in some
comments of those usually optimistic when speaking of the
common man's potential for improvement. When "reasonable
argument" had produced a Kansas-Nebraska Bill and bloody
Kansas, Henry Ward Beecher spoke in a way that encouraged
Sharp's rifles (dubbed "Beecher's Bibles") to be sent
to Kansas:

> I am a peace man. I believe in moral suasion. I
> want to see Kansas covered with churches, and tracts
> and Bibles; but just now I know of nothing so likely
> to keep the peace as a good supply of Sharp's
> rifles. It's wonderful the amount of moral suasion
> they have over those Missourians. 'Send the Bible,'
> do you say, to those Border Ruffians? Why, the
> Bible is addressed to the conscience, and they
> haven't any. You might as well read the Bible to
> a herd of buffaloes! 97

That the Union itself was used as an argument for the
extension of slavery finally brought ridicule of that
concept as the nation entered a period of Civil War.
The proposals of Northern peace groups which would have
saved the Union at the expense of further guarantees for
slavery were likened by Beecher to the plucking of
feathers and eyes out of the Union eagle to leave it
nothing but "a mere buzzard. Then will he be worth
preserving? Such an eagle it is that they mean to depict

---

96. Ibid., p. 27.
97. Fowler, The American Pulpit, p. 173.

upon the banner of America!" [98]

The Abolitionists

Pulpit humor directed at abolitionists was prompted by
the abolitionists themselves who attacked other clergy
for not joining in the cause which was for some abolitionists synonymous with Christianity. The equating of
immediate action in a current cause with the demands of
the Christian life evoked the humor which put down such
immediate action as something less than the fulfillment
of Christianity. Horace Bushnell resorted to this humor
most often. As early as 1839, his sermon on the slavery
question ridiculed the effectiveness, bravery, and bold-
ness of those who met in Philadelphia to take a stand
against slavery. . . in the South. [99] And to the aboli-
tionist charge that Bushnell and other ministers were
"dumb dogs" in relation to slavery, he responded:

> If we must be dogs, I think it is well that we are
> dumb dogs, for barking will never put down slavery.
> [100]

Bushnell's response to abolitionists may be seen as a
part of his general attitude toward those who equated
showy social activism and polemics with the ethical
demands of biblical faith.

In a sermon on "Unconscious Influence," Bushnell stressed
the importance of small acts of Christian living which

---

98. Beecher, "The Battle Set in Array," Freedom and War,
p. 101. The sermon was delivered on April 14, 1861,
during the seige of Fort Sumter. This passage is one
example of pulpit humor inspired by humor in lithographs
of the period: cf. "Our National Bird As It Appeared
When Handed to James Buchanan, March 4, 1857 and the
Identical Bird As It Appeared A.D. 1861," M. A. Woolf,
artist; T. W. Strong, publisher; pen lithograph; New
York Public Library. See the cover of this book.

99. Horace Bushnell, Sermon: A Discourse on the Slavery
Question, (Hartford: n.p., 1839), p. 13.

100. Ibid., p. 21.

gradually affected others; and he ridiculed the great
acts which did no permanent good:

> Whether it is a mistake more sad or more ridiculous,
> to make mere stir synonymous with doing good, we
> need not inquire; enough, to be sure that one who
> has taken up such a notion of doing good, is for
> that reason a nuisance to the church. The Christian
> is called a light, not lightning . . . . It is folly
> to endeavor to make ourselves shine before we are
> luminous. If the sun without his beams should talk
> to the planets, and argue with them till the final
> day, it would not make them shine; there must be
> light in the sun itself, and then they will shine
> of course. 101

Such ridiculing of abolitionists and other reformers
does not form a large body of material in pulpit literature of the period; but a few employed humor to diminish
the attractiveness of becoming lightning instead of
lights to the world. [102]

---

101. Horace Bushnell, "Unconscious Influence," Sermons
for the New Life, (New York: Charles Scribner, 1858),
p. 203. (cf. in the same volume, "Living to God in
Small Things.")

102. Cf. The views of Leland and Knapp, Autobiography,
p. 267; and Charles Wadsworth, "The Young Man's Mission,"
Sermons, p. 323. Wadsworth's sermon contains the only
explicit reference to activists as Don Quixotes tilting
at windmills.

CHAPTER IV

THE USE OF HUMOR

IN EXORCISING IDOLATRIES OF WISDOM

Yes; there are plenty of brains in hell. You understand that, don't you? . . . What is culture worth
if it is but the whitewash on a rascal. I would
rather be in heaven learning my A,B,C's than sitting
in hell reading Greek. 1
We have been clamoring for 40 years for a learned
ministry and we have got it today, and the church
is deader than it ever has been in history. Half
of the literary preachers in this town are A.B.'s,
Ph.D.'s, LL.D's and A.S.S.'s. 2

Two anecdotes from Sam Jones' sermons open our consideration of the pulpit humor used to put down the idolatry
of wisdom. [3]   Personified and placed in hell, wisdom
was placed the lowest of all attributes, because it was
held the highest in esteem and expectation. From the
beginning of the period studied, there was a regard for
reason as the closest link to God so that Jonathan Mayhew
could call criticism of reason "blasphemy." In an
increasingly democratic era, reason, which was supposed
to be a potential common to all, had a democratic
appeal; [4]   and by the middle of the period, many in the
temperance movement revealed the high regard for reason
by listing the restoration of **reason as a major purpose
of the movement so as to save the country** through a

1. Sam Jones, "Grace and Salvation," Hot Shots, p. 18.
2. McLoughlin, Modern Revivalism, p. 288.
3. While some of the humor in this chapter was directed
against abstract thoughts that we might classify as
"knowledge", other of the humor was directed against the
internalized dimensions of knowledge that we might call
"wisdom." This chapter title used the word "wisdom"
because this was the word used by Lyman Beecher and others
to sum up one of the things in which men trusted more
than God.
4. Mayhew, Sermons, pp. 40 and 51.

democratic process. And as a culmination of expectation, Horace Mann promised to eliminate all crime if the parents of the country would place their children in the hands of education. [5]

The high regard and exaggerated expectations for reason, logic, analysis, and education may be more obvious in "Infidel" thinking; but certainty in doctrine and its implications by Calvinists was revealed as an inordinate reliance on reason. These exaggerated expectations and certainties formed the target for humor. Methodists, who were the least enamored with some of these expectations as they related to the improvement of the ministry and who were the most inclined to use humor against ministerial education, had doctrines of their own which were the targets of humor. The period's pulpit humor was concentrated not only in attempts to put down the general widespread pretensions of reason, which was shown to be limited and ridiculous in its certainties and quests and in its higher education (which humor linked to a lower, rather than higher moralization) but also in the attempts to put down particular thoughts revered by Atheists, Unitarians, Universalists, Presbyterians, Congregationalists, Methodists, and Baptists.

Putting Down General Pretensions of Reason

The Highest Faculty In Hell

In most instances where 19th century pulpit humor spoke of hell, the highly educated were pictured as populating it. The uncertainty which death presented was used to mock the certainty of knowledge with which the educated often threatened church doctrines. Sam Jones declared:

5. Anti-intellectualism in 19th century religion which Richard Hofstadter criticized should be seen as set against the idolatry of education which (from a preacher's perspective) was a false God incapable of saving man and the nation.

A little colored child three years old in this city
knows just as much about hell as any living
scientist. I suppose some of the dead ones know
more about it. 6

Lorenzo Dow had used the ideas of a chance origin of the
universe to put down those infidels who advanced the
ideas as arguments against heaven and hell and a just
God:

If all things depend on chance, then by chance
there may be a God and a Devil, a Heaven and a
Hell, Saints and Sinners, and by chance the Saints
may get to Heaven, and by chance Sinners may go
to Hell. 7

In some humor there was an implication that prominent
intellectuals were in hell. In a sermon upon Universalism, Edward Taylor announced that the "wicked shall be
turned into hell;" and he then bent forward and looked
down saying, "**Voltaire**, what do you think about it now?"[8]
But similar stories were told with different well educated
men featured by other ministers. [9] And in an undoubtedly fictional account, Robert Ingersoll, a leading
agnostic, was pictured in this scene at the deathbed
of Episcopal Bishop **Phillips Brooks** in 1893. According
to the story, Ingersoll was surprised when admitted at
once to Brooks' bedroom from which all others were
barred:

"I appreciate this very much," said Ingersoll, "But
why do you see me when you deny yourself to all your
friends?"

---

6. Jones, Sermons, (San Francisco: Historical Pub. Co.,
1887), p. 54. One might well study the recurrence of
interest in the "dance of death" in the 19th century as
a part of this reaction to certainty and social pretenses.
The educated were the rising nobility of the 19th century
America as noted earlier by Harriet Beecher Stowe's
Major Broad.
7. Dow, "The Chain of Reason," Dealings, II, p. 7.
8. Haven, Life of Father Taylor, p. 137.
9. (cf. George Whitefield, Fifteen Sermons, p. 45.)

"It's this way," answered the Bishop, "I feel confident of seeing my other friends in the next world, but this may be the last chance to see you." 10

The placing of a leading Infidel in hell was a way to shake the confidence of his followers who might be lulled into a sense of security by arguments these leading lights presented. Speaking of Ingersoll, Sam Jones made explicit this point of the humor:

> And while Bob was lecturing, when he reached the assertion, "There is no hell, and I can prove it to any reasonable man," he got the attention of that crowd, of course. They were interested at this point, and one of them straightened himself up, and staggering to his feet with a hiccup and leer said, "Can you, Bob?" He said, "Yes, I can." "Well," said the fellow, "do it, Bob, and make it mighty strong; for," he says, "I tell you nine tenths of us poor fellows in Milwaukee are depending on how you make that thing." 11

To put down many arguments and interpretations of the educated mind, the question of the individual's eternal personal fate was raised by George Whitefield to make preoccupation with interpretations appear frivolous:

> Do you think these and such like forms of speaking are mere metaphors, words of a bare kind, without any real solid signification? Indeed, it is to be feared, some men would have them interpreted so; but alas! unhappy men! they are not to be envied in their metaphorical interpretation; it will be well, if they do not interpret themselves out of their salvation. 12

The arguments against hell and the disposition to deny hell were further ridiculed in a sermon passage by Baptist Jacob Knapp in which those who denied hell were

---

10. Weisfeld, Pulpit Treasury, p. 36. Ingersoll, a prominent lecturer and son of a Congregational minister, was often the goat of a humorous pulpit story. We noted earlier in chapter one how he was bested by Henry Ward Beecher in a humorous story of doubtful authenticity about the globe. (cf. Sam Jones, Sermons, p. 31).
11. Ibid., p. 55.
12. George Whitefield, "On Regeneration," Works, p. 262.

likened to little chickens who would prefer to stay out
in the open and not be frightened by the mother hen's
warnings to hide among the rocks from a circling eagle:

> But alas! you will not heed the call of alarm. You
> say, "I do not like to hear so much about hell and
> damnation; the ministers are trying to frighten us
> into religion." Why doesn't a chicken reason thus,
> and say to its mother, "I do not like to hear such
> warnings and such alarming preaching as this. Why
> don't you tell us smooth and beautiful things, and
> dwell upon some pleasing themes; and what harm have
> we little chickens done, that there should be any-
> thing to tear us limb from limb? We don't believe
> in such themes as this, by which you are striving
> to frighten us."
> What would you think if you were to hear a hen call-
> ing her brood of chickens along after her, and
> seeking to hide them in a great ledge of rocks, and
> near the base of which there was a cavity running
> twenty or thirty feet into the rock; an eagle is
> sailing along, and turns his piercing eye down on
> the hen, and she spies him and sends out a cry of
> alarm. What would you think, I say, if the chickens
> did not run, but stood still, and complained of
> being frightened? We have a better opinion, say
> they, of our Creator than to think that he has made
> us to be torn to pieces and devoured when we have
> done no harm. And thus, they remain cavilling,
> until the eagle fastens upon them and carries them
> away. 13

Later in the same sermon, Knapp used the spectre of hell
to ridicule a particularly confident Captain who spoke
lightly of such a place:

> As a vessel was about to sail from this port, the
> officers made a farewell supper. As the canvas was
> being spread to the breeze, the captain arose, and
> passing the brandy around the board, called on the
> company to drink to the following utterance: "Now,
> boys, in twenty days, Liverpool or hell." They
> sailed on over the Atlantic for nineteen days. On
> the twentieth day they struck a rock and the vessel
> filled, and on that twentieth day they were -- not
> in Liverpool! 14

---

13. Knapp, Autobiography, p. 294.
14. Ibid., p. 295.

152

We note that Methodists and Baptists, who were antagonistic to the more highly educated clergy and who stressed ways other than education as a means to salvation,
were the main users of pulpit humor placing the educated
in hell; but ministers from other denominations were
concerned to ridicule the pretensions of reason in less
personified forms.

Less Personified Ridicule of Reason

From the beginning of the period studied, pulpit humor
ridiculed the infinite pretensions of man's reason by
pointing out the finite nature of man and his animal
passions which often overwhelmed his reasoning faculty.

The limits of man's reason were recognized by most of
the ministers; but the intensity of the ridicule increased during the period and was greater among those who
relied less on reason to save man. Jonathan Mayhew recognized that "We are, indeed entirely in the dark, with
respect to many things; our knowledge is, at best, but
of small extent. . ." and that the strength of human
passion proved a weakness to reason; [15] but he saw the
admission of such limitations as "no more than to assert
that man is finite, and not an infinite being, a creature and not the creator." [16] Although respecting
reason if using it less often, George Whitefield presented such limitations and passions in a concrete way
which helped the people laugh at the idea of man as a
primarily reasonable creature:

> I have heard of a lady that was so fond of gaming,
> that tho' she had the pangs of death upon her, yet
> when in the midst of her fits, or just coming out of
> one, instead of asking after Jesus, where he was to
> be found, she asked, what is trumps? 17

At the end of the 18th century, Congregationalist Nathan

---

15. Mayhew, Sermons, pp. 10 and 139.
16. Ibid., p. 34.
17. George Whitefield, Eighteen Sermons, p. 86.

Strong expressed orthodox Calvinist insight and derided the revolutionary expectations of those who "ascribed a power to knowledge and to human reason that is not in them, and have overlooked the selfish heart of man, out of which every evil work proceeds."[18] And two years later in the face of Jefferson's victory in the national election, he exclaimed, "the noble creature man, as he calls himself, in seeking the perfection of his nature and of social relations, sinks to the deepest imperfection."[19] From a similar if somewhat moderated theological perspective, Yale President Dwight respected the role of reason but ridiculed it because of the ends which it was expected to accomplish.[20] In some passages likening men to grasshoppers who never escape the bonds of earth however high they jump,[21] Dwight also put man down in other imagery:

> Who would suspect that beings, who left so lofty a crest, were worms, just ushered into existence creeping through their little day of life. 22

We have noted earlier the biblical root of such imagery; and in describing the Lutheran understanding of salvation in a book commissioned as the official history of North Carolina Lutherans, Lutheran Gottleib Shober recalled that Luther long before warned men:

> Despair of your wisdom and reason, for by that you will never arrive at it, but with such audacity precipitate yourself and others with Satan from Heaven to Hell. 23

18. Nathan Strong, A Sermon Preached on the State Fast, (Hartford: Hudson & Goodwin, 1798), p. 12.
19. Strong, A Thanksgiving Sermon,(Hartford: Hudson and Goodwin, 1800), p. 5
20. Dwight, Theology Explained, II, p. 6.
21. Dwight,Sermons, II, p. 245.
22. Ibid., p. 65.
23. Gottleib Shober, A Comprehensive Account, p. 180. Shober was quoting from "Of Holy Writ."

Further removed from academic efforts, Lorenzo Dow
likened the power of human reason to even smaller dimensions with a greater incongruity and humor: "skeptics,
woodtics, politics, with heretics and bed-ticks, and
many other ticks, are shaking this nation to pieces." [24]
And Henry Pattillo, who blended his Presbyterianism with
an ecumenical cooperation with Methodists, referred to
man in a similar size: "reasoning mites." [25] Seeing
man as narrow at the top and broad at the base Dow called
into question the self control of reason: "I can no
more prevent my thoughts than I can prevent the birds
from flying over my head; but I can prevent them from
making nests in my hair." [26]

As the 19th century "progressed," the limited nature of
reason was still cited by some; but the fallen nature of
reason received more attention. George Bethune expressed
the earlier sentiment that the problems resulted from
those with "insect vision" who would not accept the limit
that "to know God as he has made himself known, is to
know that he is infinitely beyond the compass of our
knowledge." [27] And in Bethune's understanding:

> It becomes a profane religion against the supremacy
> of the divine Mind, when we refuse to receive the
> truth of the divine teachings, because we cannot
> comprehend all things in our puny grasp, and heap
> Pelion upon Ossa, that we may scale the heavens to
> seat our reason upon the throne of the Almighty. 28

And Henry Ward Beecher still optimistically traced many
problems to a misapplication of the reasoning faculty

---

24. Dow, "Analetic History," Dealings, p. 336.
25. Henry Pattillo, Sermons, p. 168.
26. Dow, "Chain," Dealings, pp. 17 and 27.
27. George Bethune, "True Glory," Orations, p. 40; and
"Faith Our Best Reason," Sermons, p. 124.
28. Bethune, Orations, p. 43.

or an unwillingness to accept one's limits. Beecher saw
an impoverishing reliance on reason in those who studied
the book of Revelation with a mathematical literalism
and tried to find "a Bonaparte in some he-goat":

> Those precise, unimaginative, barren minds, who
> overlook all this, and study Revelation as they would
> a mathematical problem -- why, they might as well
> measure one of Michael Angelo's pictures by the
> square inch, and say it was better than Raphael's,
> because two feet larger; they might as well weigh
> their mother's love with a pair of steelyards!" 29

Earlier, Hiram Stimson ridiculed Millerites and their
like as minutemen approaching the Bible mathematically
to predict the end of the world. 30 And Beecher criticized anyone who sought to reduce all of life to one
neat whole system:

> No one of these men rises up from his chair and
> says, "We only know a little here and there of the
> great moral realm. We know things fragmentarily.
> We know only in part." So said Paul; but then Paul
> would have had hard times in many modern churches!
> 31

But in this later era when successive efforts to educate
man to his limits as well as his potentials had produced
little reduction of evil, the fallen nature of reason
was more explored with pulpit humor. Bushnell saw the
problems resulting when man attempted to go beyond his
limitations:

> Ignorance trying to comprehend what is inscrutable,
> and out of patience, that it can not make the high
> things of God come down to its own petty measures,
> is the definition of all atheism. 32

---

29. Fowler, The American Pulpit, p. 176.
30. H.K. Stimson, From the Stage Coach to the Pulpit,
p. 182.
31. Henry Ward Beecher, "The Hereafter," Sermons, 8th
Series, p. 2.
32. Horace Bushnell, "Light on the Cloud," Sermons for
the New Life, p. 161.

But Bushnell also saw that the reasoning capacity itself
was in a state of ruin which made the attempts at self-
salvation all the more ridiculous:

> Sometimes it is given as the true problem, how to
> reform the shape and reconstruct the style of their
> heads, and even this it is expected they will cer-
> tainly be able to do! Alas that we are taken or
> can be, with so great folly. . . .Man is a ruin,
> going after development, and progress, and philan-
> thropy, and social culture, and by this fire-fly
> glimmer, to make a day of glory! And this is the
> doctrine that proposes shortly to restore society,
> to settle the passion, regenerate the affection,
> re-glorify the thought, fill the imagination of a
> desiring and disjointed world!
> As soon will the desolations of Karnac gather up
> their fragments and reconstruct the proportions out
> of which they have fallen. 33

Dwight L. Moody criticized Infidels on a similar ground:
"They forget that when man fell in Eden his reason fell
with him." 34 And Henry Ward Beecher ridiculed the idea
that the mind was as reasonable as some argued:

> A man might as well fill a tree full of nightingales,
> and, standing on the ground, attempt to control
> their notes and to hold them chained together, as to
> attempt to control by his volitions the multiplied
> thoughts and feelings of his own soul. Some persons
> hearing this will say, "A man can regulate his mind
> as easily as his house." Certainly, if he has
> nothing more in his mind than is in his house; but
> faculties ought not to be furniture. 35

The recognition of reason's limits and corruptions was
a basis for the humor directed against the minds who
sought answers to all questions; but a more serious
failing of reason was seen in the fact that those who
knew all of the doctrines failed to do as they should.

---

33. Bushnell, "Dignity of Human Nature Shown from its
Ruins," Sermons For the New Life, pp. 65-66.

34. Dwight L. Moody, The Great Redemption, p. 60.

35. Proctor, Life Thoughts, pp. 65-66.

Questions Ridiculed

A part of the recognition of reason's limits was a
realization that arguments neither made nor unmade infidels; or in Presbyterian Robert Henderson's words:

> It is not argument that makes infidels. An alien-
> ation of heart from God, a secret and strong dislike
> to the great doctrines and precepts of the Bible,
> make a hundred deists, where fair reason and argument
> make one. 36

To respond seriously to the questions would further attach
the attention to a quest that would bring the person no
closer to God. The humorous response may have turned
the person away from infinite numbers of questions and
left him time to answer God.

A gentler humor handled the questioner during the 18th
century and a harsher humor met the questioner in the
19th century. In a sermon, George Whitefield reported
this interchange with a woman who wanted him to take
sides on the question of using the sacrament as a means
or an end of regeneration:

> A good woman came to me some years ago, just as I
> had done preaching - some people love to be imper-
> tinent - what do you think, says she, of Cotton
> Mather and another minister? One said I ought to
> receive the sacrament before my experience was given
> in; the other said not, and I believe the angels
> were glad to carry them both to heaven. I said,
> good woman, I believe they have not talked about it
> since, for they will no more talk of these things. 37

A similarly gentle response was given by Congregationalist
Jotham Sewall to a questioner at the end of the 18th

---

36. Robert Henderson, A Series of Sermons, p. 336.
37. Whitefield, Eighteen Sermons, P. 238. Solomon Stod-
dard had extended the half-way covenant by admitting to
communion the baptised but unconverted -- an extension
with which Cotton Mather disagreed.

158

century:

> A somewhat pert young convert, who believed in fall-
> ing from grace, once asked him if a Christian should
> fall from sin, and die in that state, what would
> become of him. He gravely replied, that if God had
> let Enoch fall when he got him half-way to heaven, he
> supposed it would have hurt him very much; -showing
> him, too, how very easy it is to make suppositions,
> and how absurd it may be to build upon them. 38

Timothy Dwight had seriously questioned the value of
introducing certain questions which served more to per-
plex than enlighten the mind. [39] And in the 19th century
his student, Lyman Beecher, treated sharply one
questioner:

> A young man said to him, "What can I do if I am not
> elected?" "When you begin to care about being saved,
> come to me and I will tell you; but while you don't
> care a snap about it, very likely God doesn't." 40

If the man was not elected, according to Calvinist theology, there was nothing he could do about it except to
accept his lot as gracefully as he could in the absence
of grace; and Lyman Beecher was hardly one to be interested in discussing something with no prospect of stimu-
lating corrective action. Some of those who saw
positive action and ecumenical cooperation of the early
19th century sidetracked by doctrinal disputes devalued
disputes. Timothy Flint whose Mississippi missionary
activities had begun in the era of Congregational and
Presbyterian cooperation, had little regard for the
discussions that undermined that cooperation: "Disputa-
tion and discussion, under the mistaken idea of enlight-
ening the understanding, tends to banish the small

---

38. Jotham Sewall, A Memoir of Rev. Jotham Sewall,(Boston:
Tappan and Whittemore, 1853), p. 393.

39. Dwight, Theology, IV, p. 71.

40. Beecher, Autobiography, II, p. 572.

remains of religion among us." [41] And Flint began to
see merit in a Catholic community that discouraged
endless questioning. [42] Missionary Reuben Tinker shared
this distaste for endless questioning in his sermon on
"The Resurrection":

> More objections might be stated, if not answered,
> for there is almost no end to the difficulties which
> occur to inquiring minds when they try, by the line
> of their reason, to measure the infinitude of God.
> We cannot explain it. We need not answer half the
> questions that may be proposed. [43]

That questioning led to nothing or little saving action
was explicitly stressed later in the century. Dwight
Moody ridiculed modern questioning which would have
immobilized Joshua, the preeminent man of action:

> He just did what the Lord told him to do. If he had
> stood, like a good many people, and said, "I don't
> know how I am going to get these people over.
> Hadn't you better wait, Lord, until the next day?
> How am I going to get these million people over this
> angry flood? Hadn't we better wait until the waters
> go down?" . . .But forty years before they would
> have said, when they got opposite Jericho, "What's
> he going to do? How are we going to get over?
> We've got to have a bridge or a pontoon. And even
> if we get over they will see us and defeat us. They
> will slay us here on the banks of Jordon. Guess
> we had better turn round and go back." [44]

And an implicit attack on Calvinist thinking may be seen
in Moody's sermon "On Regeneration":

> We could speak all the time about the origin of
> sins; how it came into the world, but that is not
> going to help us. If I see a man tumble into the
> river and going to drown, it would do no good for

---

41. Timothy Flint, _Recollections of the Last Ten Years_,
(Boston: Cummings, Hilliard & Co., 1826), p. 117.

42. _Ibid._,

43. Tinker, _Sermons_, p. 251.

44. Dwight L. Moody, "Life and Character of Joshua," _To
All People_, pp. 269-270.

me to sit down and bow my head and indulge in deep
thought and reasoning how he came to get in there.
The great question would then be how he was to be
got out. 45

Also showing a 19th century impatience with too much
thought and too little action was San Francisco Presbyterian Charles Wadsworth, who ridiculed questioning in a
similar way by supposing that a child was in a window of
a burning building and his father outside commanded the
child to jump into his arms:

> And now what does this boy do? Does he pause with
> idle questionings about the nature of fire in
> general, or the origin of fire in particular, or the
> reason why his father would save him in this way,
> as indeed with any foolish questions at all? Oh,
> no; the boy does one thing only. He obeys simply
> his father. He drops into those outstretched arms.
> . . .The poor soul goes about with its anxious
> questionings, about the metaphysics of belief and
> the philosophy of the atonement -- analyzing the
> water of life, when it ought to be drinking it;
> speculating about the make of the manna, when it
> ought to be eating it! 46

Henry Ward Beecher joined in the ridicule of those who
were preoccupied with questions and who ended by doing
nothing of substance:

> I know it is said that men have had an existence
> before; and when I consider the slenderness of most
> men, I cannot but think that if they existed before,
> and they accumulated anything, it must have been
> in a world where infinitesimals were common. 47

And Beecher extended his criticism of questioning to
those within the faith who entangled themselves in asking

---

45. Moody, Glad Tidings, pp. 99-100.

46. Charles Wadsworth, "The Child Teacher," Sermons,
pp. 208-209.

47. Beecher, "Present Use of Immortality," Plymouth
Pulpit, (March-September, 1875), p. 111. The sermon
was delivered on October 11, 1874.

all the questions except the important one of their
fruitfulness:

> They sit down and try to recall all their thoughts,
> and feelings, and actions during the day, and then
> they question themselves, "Do you enjoy reading the
> Bible?" Yes, on the whole, they like reading the
> Bible. "Are you fond of religious conversation?"
> Yes, if they can have their choice of people, they
> think they are fond of religious conversation. A
> vine would never be so stupid as to examine itself
> thus; but suppose it should, and should call out,
> "Roots, do you enjoy being down there in the soil?"
> "Yes, we enjoy being down here in the soil." "Stem
> do you like to be out here in summer?" "Leaves, are
> you fond of the sun and air?" And, satisfied, it
> says, "I am an excellent vine." But the gardener,
> standing near, exclaims, "The useless thing! I
> paid ten dollars for the cutting, and I have pruned
> and cultivated it, and for years looked for the
> black Hamburg grapes it was to bear, but it has
> yielded only leaves." He does not care that the
> roots love the soil, and the stem the summer. 48

Higher Education and Lower Moralization

The lack of moral action by the highly educated and the
presence of such action in those lacking such formal
training, was the basis for pulpit humor ridiculing
higher education. The criticism contained in most pulpit
humor leveled at institutional learning was that formal
education of ministers led to pretentious preaching
whose result was far from the saving of souls. Part of
this attack on ministerial education by Methodist ministers was an implicit attack on Calvinism -- an attack
whose explicit side we will explore in a subsequent
section. One must be careful to note that the criticism
was rarely voiced against higher education for those
other than ministers; indeed, many of the ministers were
involved in raising funds for colleges throughout the

---

48. Proctor, Life Thoughts, p. 269.

162

country. [49]

George Whitefield humorusly put down those who would
readily talk in Christian language but not act in
Christian ways:

> Ever since I was a boy, I remember to have heard a
> story of a poor beggar who asked a clergyman to
> give him his alms, which being refused, he said,
> will you please, sir, to give me your blessing;
> says, he, God bless you. O, replied the beggar,
> you would not give me that if it was worth any-
> thing. 50

---

49. For example Peter Cartwright helped establish Mac-
Murray and McKendree Colleges in Illinois; and while a
state assemblyman he introduced the first bill to establish a state university in Illinois. Miyakawa, Protestants
and Pioneers, p. 93. But out of the pulpit, Timothy
Flint ridiculed many of the institutions which called
themselves colleges (cf. Flint, Recollections, pp. 185-
187. "I have been amused in reading puffing advertisings
in the newspapers. A little subscription school, in
which half the pupils are abecedarians, is a college.
One is a Lancastrian school, or a school of "instruction
mutuelle." There is a Pestelozzi establishment, with
its appropriate emblazoning. There is the agricultural
school, the missionary school, the grammar box, the new
way to make a wit of a dunce in six lessons, and all the
mechanical ways of innoculating children with learning,
that they may not endure the pain of getting it in the
old and natural way. I would not have you smile
exclusively at the people of the West. This ridiculous
species of swindling is making as much progress in your
country as here . . .The masters, -- professors, I
should say, -- proposed to teach most of the languages,
and all the sciences. Hebrew they would communicate in
twelve lessons; Latin and Greek, with a proportionate
promptness. These men, who were to teach all this
themselves, had read Erasmus with a translation, and
knew the Greek alphabet, and their public discourses,
-- for they were ministers, -- sometimes dealt very
abusively with the "King's English.")

50. George Whitefield, "Soul Prosperity," Eighteen
Sermons, p. 54.

Jonathan Mayhew, who similarly valued knowledge as it
served some good purpose, derided knowledge that could
not alter the course of events (an implicit criticism
of Calvinist knowledge on a predestined system):

> For what end does the mariner study the art of
> navigation? Not surely, for this only or chiefly,
> that he may please and amuse himself with the theory
> of it; but rather, that he may be able to steer his
> course aright through the ocean, and arrive safe at
> length at the port for which he is bound. Without
> applying his knowledge in this way, all the advan-
> tage it will be to him, is that of being shipwrecked
> with his eyes open, while others run upon ruin
> blinded, and purely through ignorance. 51

And Mayhew further ridiculed those men of inaction who
were preoccupied with detailing and believing doctrines:

> They know their duty so exactly, and believe it so
> firmly, that they imagine they may well be excused
> from doing it. 52

In her novels, we may note this same humorous strategy
in Harriet Beecher Stowe's characterizations of ultra
Orthodox Calvinists, some of whose foresitters Mayhew
undoubtedly had in mind. About the time Stowe was
writing her characterizations, Sam Jones applied a similar criticism to many believers in all denominations
who were so inactive that he could "put forty of them in
a sardine box, and they will have plenty of breathing
room. 53 And "accomplishments" of those noted for
wisdom in other cultures were humorously handled as in
this passage from Reuben Tinker's sermon delivered at a
time when America was priding itself on its new archi-
tectural wonders:

---

51. Mayhew, Sermons, p. 92.
52. Ibid., p. 156.
53. Sam Jones, Sermons Wise and Witty, p. 27.

> The wisdom of Egypt has left us a few pyramids --
> piles of stone and earth, less than a volcano can
> make in one night. . . .54

Pointing out the absence of formal schooling for pious
biblical figures, John Leland humorously played on the
disparity between education and morality and the fool-
ishness of those who assumed schooling was the foundation
of piety:

> But I am as hard put to it, to find anything like
> it in the New Testament, as I am to find out who
> Cain's wife was, or where . . .Cain got his first
> hammer to work with. That righteous Abel possessed
> this true piety, is certain; and who can imagine
> that schools, academies, and colleges, were in
> existence in the days of Abel. Yet, according to
> the text, they must have been the foundation whence
> the stream of piety flowed to the first martyr. 55

Another Baptist, Jacob Knapp, used a similar strategy to
ridicule the importance of the honorary ministerial
degrees: "Who ever heard of Rev. Mr. Paul D.D., or of the
Right Rev. Simon Peter, D.D.?" [56] That such degrees
were granted more frequently to those in most other
denominations that had founded or come into control of
the prestigious Eastern colleges added to the bite in
the humor. [57]

---

54. Tinker, "The Gospel The Hope of Salvation," Sermons,
p. 405.
55. John Leland, "A Little Sermon," The Writings, p. 408.
We do not know whether he delivered this "little sermon"
before a congregation. The reference to Cain's wife
recalls a humorous anecdote: "Where did Cain get his
wife?" 'I should like to give this advice!... Don't lose
your soul's salvation looking after other men's wives."
Weisfeld, Pulpit Treasury, p. 13.

56. Knapp, Autobiography, p. 194. Knapp also held that
the devil was much more knowledgable than any man. Ibid.,
pp. 301-302. Charles Finney asserted that angels and
devils embraced the same truths intellectually but were
affected differently by them. Sermons on Important
Subjects, p. 186.

57. (cf. Appendix Two).

As we have noted through chapter one, in professional
training and association ministers from the more highly
educated denominations ridiculed a preacher's intellectual pretenses; and in one ordination charge, Unitarian
David Barnes told a Mr. Deane: "In attempting . . . to
instruct your people, be careful not to preach what they
cannot understand; and especially be careful not to preach
what you do not understand." [58]   But in sermons to the
people, it was Methodist ministers who most often attacked
the intellectual pretenses of preachers -- although they
made clear that the pretentious preachers were Presbyterians or others whose highly educated minds and polish-
ed doctrines did no one any good. Educated clergymen's
contempt for the uneducated Methodists was the occasion
for some of the humor. Cartwright recounted this
exchange:

> I recollect once to have come across one of these
> Latin or Greek scholars, a regular graduate in
> theology. In order to bring me into contempt in a
> public company he addressed me in Greek. In my
> younger days I had learned considerable of German.
> I listened to him, as if I understood it all, and
> then replied in Dutch. This he knew nothing about,
> neither did he understand Hebrew. He concluded
> that I had answered him in Hebrew, and immediately
> caved in, and stated to the company that I was the
> first educated Methodist preacher he ever saw. I
> do not wish to undervalue education, but really I
> have seen so many of these educated preachers who
> forcibly reminded me of lettuce growing under shade
> of a peach tree, or like a gosling that had got the
> straddlers by wading in the dew 59

58. Letter, James Kendall to Wm. Sprague, December 16,
1848, Sprague, Annals, VIII, p. 34.
59. Strickland, ed., Autobiography of Peter Cartwright,
p. 80. In a frontier setting, Cartwright could portray
the educated clergy as incongruously out of place and
ill suited to meet frontier needs: "Suppose the thousands
of early settlers and scores of early Methodist preachers
by some Providential intervention, had blundered on a
Biblical institute, or a theological factory, where they
dress up little pedantic things they call preachers;
suppose ye would have known them from a ram's horn?
Surely not." Ibid., p. 486.

Jacob Gruber related a similar encounter with a Catholic
priest who ridiculed him for not understanding the
different Latin terms for the mass:

> The priest told me it was owing to my ignorance. I
> did not understand the original language; could not
> tell the name of a horse in Latin. I told him I
> acknowledged my ignorance, and asked for information.
> I wished to know whether horse and mass were near
> alike in Latin. 60

But self defense and defenses of denomination were not
all that prompted the attack on the learned clergy. In
Methodist eyes, predestination which the old light
Presbyterians propounded was antagonistic to encouraging
conversions at revivals. And the combination of an
educated clergy with a doctrine which he viewed as
undermining action gave the force to Cartwright's humor:

> This doctrine is only kept alive by a few silly
> mortals who have long purses and are influenced by
> the prejudice of education. I call them silly, for
> such they would truly be, should they pay a doctor
> for saying to them: "Sirs, if you are to live, you
> will live; and if you die, you will die." Equally
> silly, then, are they for paying a college fop, who
> has spent much time learning Latin and Greek, for
> no other purpose than to tell the people in plain
> English, "If you are to be saved, you will be saved
> and if you are to be damned, you will be damned."61

Other Methodists echoed the note about "Hirelin's like
them high-flowered college-larned (Presbyterians) sheep-
skins." 62 The humor was aimed at the Methodist's

---

60. Strickland, The Life of Jacob Gruber, p. 348.
61. This passage from Cartwright's Autobiography was not
necessarily delivered in his sermons; but I agree with
the method of Dr. Wayne Rood, who selected passages from
Cartwright's written works and presented these as a sermon
to convey the tone of the period's preaching. Wayne Rood,
Peter Cartwright, (13 page unpublished manuscript), p.9.
For Cartwright's handling of Calvinism, consult Strickland, Autobiography, p. 191.
62. Thos. D. Clark, The Rampaging Frontier, Manners and
Humors of Pioneer Days in the South & Middle West,(New
York: Bobbs-Merrill Co., 1939), p. 147.

preaching competition both physically present on the
frontier and remembered from experiences in the East.
The humor would be especially enjoyed by any who had
experienced a sense of inferiority in the presence of the
highly educated. No attack suggested that wealthy Presbyterians supported Predestinarian doctrines in order to
maintain a status quo that was financially beneficial to
them; but the humorous attack as illustrated in one
black pulpit story did point out that much ministerial
"education" (especially honorary degrees) testified
more to the wealth of one's congregation than to the
wealth of one's knowledge:

> Ah calls to min' a Mefdis' preachuh what fill de
> pulpit at St. James in Waco. He de bigges' preachuh
> on de Uppuh Brazos. He been teachin' de preachuhs
> in Waco for many a yeah, but hit happe oncet dat he
> 'lected to go to de genul conference in Philadelphia
> and' he gon mo'n a mont'. Dat's a long time for de
> teachuh to stay way somewhar, so while he's gone a
> white preachuh comed 'long and de preachuhs 'gage
> his servuses to teach 'em. De white preachuh meck
> a charge of ten dolluhs an' he gib all de preachuhs
> a D.D.
> Whe Revun Dawson come home from de genul conference,
> de preachuhs don' relish 'im teachin' 'em no mo'.
> Dey 'low de's smaa'tuh 'n he be, 'caze dey got a
> D.D. an' he ain't got nare one. Revun Dawson so
> out done, he don' know what to do wid hisse'f, so
> de nex' Sunday attah he come back he ast his mem-
> buhship to gib 'im ten dolluhs to git 'im a D.D.
> But de membuhship done gib 'm a suit of clothes
> for de genul conference and fifty dolluhs for
> spendin' change; so dey don' raise but five dolluhs
> for 'im in de collection for de D.D. De Revun tell
> 'em he don' relish dat way of doin', but de trustee
> boa'd tell 'im dey don' relish gibin' 'im no mo'
> money lackwise, so dey don' gib 'im anothuh red
> coppuh cent. Dey say, "Elduh you jes' hab to be
> . . . D.' stid of D.D." 63

In a rare attack upon higher education for all in the
late 19th century, black Episcopal preacher Alexander
Crummell revealed another danger in the idolatry of

---

63. Brewer, The Word, pp. 25-26.

168

education among blacks. He exorcised with humor the
parental expectation that every black child should have
higher education -- an expectation that led the children
to think themselves above the work that they had any
chance to do and above others in their race with whom
they needed to closely cooperate if any true progress
was to be made:

> "Not long ago I met an old acquaintance, and while
> talking about the future of her children, I inquired:
> "What are you going to do with -- I will call him
> 'Tom?'" Tom is a little fellow about fourteen years
> old; by no means a genius; more anxious about tops
> and taffy and cigarettes than about his books; never
> likely, so far as I can see, to set the Potomac on
> fire. Her answer was that his father proposed send-
> ing him to college to make him a lawyer. On another
> occasion I was talking to a minister of the Gospel
> about his daughters, and he was anxious to send his
> two girls to Belgium to be educated for society!
> ...Everybody now-a-days is crazy about education.
> Fathers and mothers are anxious that their children
> should shine. However ordinary a boy or girl may
> be, the parents want them to be scholars. The boy
> may be a numbskull, the girl a noodle. The fond
> parent thinks the child a prodigy. . . ." 64

Putting Down Particular Thoughts

In pulpit humor used to put down the favorite doctrines
of different denominations or groups of believers, we do
not find careful detailing of those doctrines. It was
not in the nature of this humor to render precisely the
thought to be ridiculed. To distort the doctrine to make
it appear ridiculous was the point of the humor. To

---

64. Alexander Crummell, "Common Sense in Common Schooling,
Africa and America,(Miami: Mnemosyne Press, 1969), pp.
331 and 335. Crummell delivered this sermon to his St.
Luke's congregation in Washington, D.C. on Sept. 13,
1886. A few years earlier, a similar emphasis on the
practical uselessness of scientific knowledge was stressed by black Baptist John Jasper of Richmond in his humor
filled sermon The Sun Do Move!,(New York: Brentano,1882).

isolate one fragment of the other denomination's doctrine
and import it into the context of one's own thought made
the fragment appear all the more ridiculous. One may ask
in some of the cases whether the one doing the ridiculing
even understood the doctrine which he ridiculed; and the
answer could be that he did not -- or at least that he
did not understand it in the way that the believer of
that doctrine understood it. But the pulpit humor was
often prompted because the other denomination's thought
was felt to pose a threat to one's own structure of
belief; and the humor was designed to deal with that
threat.

Very few of the ministers studied attempted to stand
above denominationalism. And even fewer succeeded in
any attempt to give ecumenical perspective. From those
who tried, we have a little pulpit humor that makes
light of all denominationalism that took itself too
seriously. George Whitefield, who gained access to as
many different denominational pulpits as any man in 18th
century America, remarked in his sermon "The Lord Our
Light":

> You see now, the sun shines on us all; I never
> heard that the sun said, Lord, I will not shine on
> Presbyterians, I will not shine on the Independents,
> I will not shine on the people called Methodists
> . . . or Papists. 65

And 100 years later, Methodist George Cookman, who had
risen above purely denominational standing as senate
chaplain and presidential envoy, devised one of the
cleverest handlings of denominational differences in a
sermon designed to battle bigotry from whatever source.
He asked his listeners to imagine joining in a battle to
end denominational bigotry. In this battle, each
denomination had its contribution to make: the numerous

---

65. George Whitefield, Eighteen Sermons, p. 125.

Methodists, who prided themselves on self effacement,
would be the nameless infantry and roust bigotry out of
the bushes; the Episcopalians, Presbyterians, and
Congregationalists would be still manning the castle of
establishment, but shoot off an occasional cannon ball
at bigotry and the Baptists would be the navy and give old
bigotry a good dunking if not drown out the old fellow. [66]

But such even handed humorous pokes at each denomination's
pride and joy is rarely found in the period's pulpit
literature. Much more typical were flashes of pulpit
humor which were sparked in interdenominational combat.
And a residue of Calvinism attracted the largest configuration of pulpit humor as most denominations and ministers developed themselves over against those established
American clergy who claimed however dubiously that their
doctrines were the direct legitimate descendants from
the Genevan leader of the Reformation or his chief
American disciple, Jonathan Edwards.

Atheism

That we consider atheists as a group of believers against
which pulpit humor was directed should not be surprising
in view of Dr. Dwight's notation in chapter two that

66. George Cookman, Speeches Delivered on Various Occasions,
p. 39. There is no configuration of pulpit humor directed at Episcopalians outside of a few remarks by
Dwight Moody which we have noted in chapter one, and a
few pre-American Revolution remarks by Jonathan Mayhew
which we noted in chapter three. The absence of much
humor against Episcopalians may be understood when one
remembers that after the American Revolution the denomination was not only disestablished in the South, but
decimated throughout the country because its priests and
very liturgy sided with the king. That Episcopalians
posed no proselytising threat to other denominations and
presented no competition for new converts on the frontier or in the Eastern cities also account for the fact
that it was rarely a target for other's pulpit humor.

"non-believers" and "believers" both believed although
the "non-believers" believed in "doubt" or "nothing at
all." And Dwight humorously juxtaposed the incongruous
beliefs of each of many leading philosophers. [67] Much
of the humor against atheists pointed out the ridiculous-
ness of beliefs held by "Non-believers." Jonathan
Mayhew attacked an extreme form of atheism labeled
pyrrhonism for the belief that there is no truth:

> If there is no such thing as truth, why will they
> please themselves for their sagacity in making this
> discovery? Or why will they endeavour to bring
> others over to their opinion, when by their first,
> and, I might add, their only, principle, those others
> are no more in an error than themselves . . .Thus
> (for example) it follows that there is no difference
> at all in men with respect to wisdom and knowledge.
> For in order to constitute such a difference, it is
> not only necessary that there should be a natural
> distinction betwixt truth and falsehood; but also
> that some at least should have faculties for dis-
> covering it . . . Why will they attempt to inves-
> tigate truth? Or why will they plume themselves
> upon their supposed discovery of this notable truth,
> that men are unable to discover truth? 68

In the 1820's, traveling New York Methodist evangelist
Billy Hibbard ridiculed the philosophical accomplishment
and brilliance of atheists in a similar way:

> Does not all knowledge in God or man imply actual
> existence? For instance, no existence is what we
> call nothing, and what cannot possibly exist, we
> call nothing, and to know nothing is no knowledge
> at all. 69

In Brooklyn in 1838, Baptist Jacob Knapp used their
"belief in nothing" to ridicule atheists in a slightly

---

67. Timothy Dwight, Sermons, I, pp. 320-331.

68. Mayhew, Sermons, pp. 10, 24, and 25. Pyrrhonism is a
name applied to an extreme form of doubt or skepticism
associated originally with a Greek "philosopher" Pyrrho
of Elis (c. 365-275 B.C.).

69. Billy Hibbard, Memoirs of B. Hibbard,(New York: Reed
and Piercy, 1843), p. 371.

more personal way:

> In the course of my sermon, I remarked that atheism
> was the little end of nothing whittled to a point.
> Since the atheist denied everything and admitted
> nothing, it was itself the little end of nothing. 70

And earlier in the century Presbyterian Robert Henderson
had carried the attack on atheism to a still more
concrete application:

> Suppose you elect a man of such principles to the
> first office in your free and happy government, and
> administer the oath of office; you swear him on the
> holy evangelists of Almighty God, that he will well
> and truly, and with good faith, administer the
> government. Is there any sense in what you have
> done? Will not an enlightened, well informed boy of
> ten years old smile at it as a perfect farce, and
> that of the most empty description? He swears on
> the holy evangelists to do his duty, and then turns
> round and tells you that the evangelists are a mere
> fable of the worst contrived, and most bungling
> kind. Now, in all fairness and good conscience,
> might you not just as well have sworn him on Aesop's
> Fables, or last year's almanac. 71

But the infrequent use of pulpit humor against atheists
outside of educated circles in Dr. Dwight's New Haven
and Mayhew's Boston may suggest that atheism was felt to
pose little real threat to organized religion in most of
America. And with the exception of the humor which we
have seen directed against Robert Ingersoll in the Gilded
Age, pulpit humor concerned with atheism ceased after the
1830's. 72

Unitarianism and Universalism

From the perspective of more orthodox denominations,

---

70. Knapp, Autobiography, p. 90.

71. Robert Henderson, A Series of Sermons, p. 305.

72. While the aftermath of the French Revolution disen-
chanted some with atheism, the depression begun in 1837
was seen as undermining atheism in its more popular
forms, (cf. Tinker, Sermons, pp. 398-399).

"Unitarianism" and "Universalism" covered a multitude of sins and were within a group of all enemies classed "Infidels." In chapter two, we have already explored Timothy Dwight's early attack on Dr. Priestly for modes of biblical interpretation; but by later periods such interpreting of texts was evident in many other denominations. Similarly most other grounds for ridiculing Unitarians and Universalists were soon seen inside other denominations. No one doctrine figured as centrally to Unitarian and Universalist thought as particular doctrines did in other denominations;[73] and so the humor was somewhat fragmented as were the Unitarians and Universalists themselves. If any one shape is to be discerned in the humor directed at Unitarians and Universalists it may be seen emerging around the academic approach that marked this highly educated group.

A little pulpit humor was directed at the major Universalist idea that all will be saved. In the second quarter of the 19th century, Baptist Jabez Swan argued:

73. While one may say that the unity of God is the one central doctrine in Unitarianism and that universal salvation is central to Universalism, these churches have been essentially undoctrinal in their approaches. During the period of our study, the Unitarian church was by far the stronger of the two churches which merged formally with more equal numbers of churches and members in 1961. Although the American Unitarian Association did not come into official being in Boston until 1825, and William Ellery Channing may be seen as the formative Unitarian leader in the early 19th century, many 18th century ministers such as Jonathan Mayhew have been classed as Congregational Unitarians and forerunners of the Unitarian thought. We have noted already how Mayhew's doctrine of man was nearly an Orthodox Christian one compared to that of Theodore Parker, a radical Unitarian of the 1840's and 1850's; but considering Mayhew only on the grounds of his attitude toward the Trinity, he was classed "Unitarian." Similarly, such mid 19th century Unitarians as Theodore Parker and Ralph Waldo Emerson could no doubt find more they had in common opposing than they had in common believing.

> I have often said, if Universalism is true, the
> clause of the sermon on the mount which reads, 'Wide
> is the gate, and broad is the way, that leads to
> destruction, and many there be which go in thereat;
> while strait is the gate, and narrow is the way, that
> leadeth unto life, and few there be that find it,'
> ought to be translated, Wide is the gate, and broad
> is the way that leads to heaven, and all will go
> there; while strait is the gate, and narrow is the
> way, that leadeth to destruction, and no one can
> find it. Abner Kneeland, in his translation of the
> New Testament, failed of giving the passage this
> rendering. 74

In a prayer in 1829 at Bromfield Street church, Boston's
Edward Taylor put down the idea more succinctly after a
young minister with Universalist sentiments had become
flustered in the delivery of his trial sermon:

> "O Lord! the way is so broad that he got lost
> in it." 75

While Timothy Dwight did ridicule several of Dr. Priestly's theological terms, [76] no one idea in Unitarianism
attracted so much pulpit humor. But the academic brilliance of Unitarians did attract attention. Edward
Taylor again succinctly expressed the point of attack in[77]
calling Theodore Parker and other Unitarians, 'geniasses."
And comments against biblical criticisms were often
implicit attacks on Unitarians whose dominance of Divinity at Harvard in the 19th century made them the more
conspicuous representatives of academic approaches to
religion. But before Unitarians were an identifiable
group, Mather Byles had criticized academic commentary
as the placing of the text on the rack, and had described
critics as "men who have a wonderful knack to illustrate

---

74. Denison, ed., The Life and Labors, p. 234.
75. Haven, The Life of Father Taylor, p. 273.
76. (cf. chapter two).
77. Haven, The Life of Father Taylor, p. 241. (cf Ibid.,
p. 337 on Ralph Waldo Emerson).

away the meaning of the clearest texts, and explain them
into nonsense." [78] And Horace Bushnell noted in relation
to Revelation 2.4, that the torturing of texts was
common in other groups as well:

> There are some texts of scripture that suffer a much
> harder lot than any of the martyrs, because their
> martyrdom is perpetual; and this I think is one of
> the number. [79]

Edward Taylor, whose presence in Boston and openness to
having Harvard's Unitarian students preach from his
pulpit (if they were willing to listen to his criticism)
may account for his perceptive and frequent direction of
humor toward Unitarians, again summed up the point of
attack:

> A Unitarian preacher having descanted on the ever-
> lingering misery of sinful memory after repentance,
> he compared him to a beetle bug rolling over the
> sand his ball of dirt. [80]

Having little doctrinal target against which to develop
humor in his opposition to Unitarians, Jabez Swan simply
dismissed them as the Fire Insurance Company because all
of their members were certain to go to Hell. [81]

Almost all the pulpit humor aimed at Unitarians and

78. Mather Byles, The Character of the Perfect and
Upright Man,(Boston: S. Gerrish, 1729), p. 11.

79. Horace Bushnell, "The True Problem of Christian
Experience," Sermons for the New Life, p. 243. The
passage from Revelation could be construed as fall from
grace, a proposition Calvinists would deny, but many
Methodists affirm.

80. Haven, The Life of Father Taylor, p. xlvi. As noted
in chapter one, some of the non-Calvinists who attacked
Unitarianism saw Unitarianism and Calvinism as what may
be called symbiotic.

81. Denison, ed., The Life and Labors, pp. 99 and 149.

Universalists came from ministers in the northeast where
Unitarians and Universalists were active. That these
groups posed little competition to frontier preachers
may explain the lack of humor against them in frontier
preaching. The one recorded instance of pulpit humor
against Unitarians on the frontier was prompted by the
activities of a traveling Unitarian evangelist. [82]

Calvinism

When one Drew Seminary student preached a sermon attacking
Calvinism toward the end of the 19th century, he was in
turn attacked by Dr. Robert W. Rogers who claimed that he
was flaying at dead doctrines; but Professor Samuel
Upham remarked:

> I liked the sermon of Brother Berry. My father
> would sit up nights to hate Calvinism! Did Dr.
> Rogers say Calvinism is dead? So much the better,
> for I believe in punishment after death. [83]

Many of the attacks on Calvinist ideas occurred in places
and at times when one could doubt whether there were many
defenders of Calvinism left among the living, much less
among those present to hear the particular sermons. But
much of the humor was designed to help release the ministers' own people from the bondage of earlier experience
with Calvinism; for the Calvinism was pictured in pulpit
humor as preoccupied with developing a theology which
kept the people down and led either to no action beneficial to themselves and others, or to a divisive spirit
that resulted in endless wrangling. While the "Old Light"
Presbyterians, the Congregationalists, the "hardshell"
Baptists, and even the Episcopalians were ostensibly
classified as Calvinist in their heritage, we notice that
the pulpit humor attacking Calvinism was present inside
these groups and denominations as much as outside them,

---

82. Strickland, ed., The Life of Jacob Gruber, p. 320.
83. Joy, ed., The Teachers of Drew, p. 95.

although most of the anti-Calvinist humor inside these groups was used to put off, rather than put down, the consideration of the doctrines.

Henry Ward Beecher observed, "As I recollect it, the God of the Westminster Catechism ought not to be called Jehovah, but Analysis." [84] And Baptist Jacob Knapp attacked hyper-Calvinism for spreading "the palsy of inaction" [85] which Lorenzo Dow christened "Galvinism." [86] The analysis that spread this palsy of inaction from the attackers'point of view may be briefly summarized in the following way. God's sovereignty was elevated above any other of his qualities. With God as all powerful, the conditions of man (whether he went to hell or heaven) was in God's contol and not man's control. To assert man's free will diminished God's sovereignty; and so, as the theology was elaborated, man's free will was eliminated. With God as all knowing, those who went to heaven or hell would have been foreordained to do so by God's will. Man did not definitely know which destiny was his; but his role could not be to alter his destiny but rather to enjoy or desire that which God intended. In the extreme form of Ultra-Calvinism developed by Samuel Hopkins and Nathaniel Emmons, who claimed to be disciples of Jonathan Edwards, this benevolence was developed into a form of disinterested benevolence where all lesser desires came close to being dismissed for this one pure love to desire what God desired; and in this belief, one should even take joy in the punishment of the damned because it was God's will that they be damned. Combined to this doctrine of God and salvation, was a doctrine of man which stressed his constitutional depravity. This depravity made man

---

84. Henry Ward Beecher, "Growth in the Knowledge of God," The Sermons, first series, p. 94.

85. Knapp, Autobiography, p. 73.

86. Dow, Dealings, p. 108.

incapable of escaping sin until death and made any salvation a matter of pure grace from God. While this is an
incomplete and generalized view of American Calvinism,
and late 18th century American Ultra-Calvinism in particular, it will suffice to help one appreciate the point of
the following pulpit humor. From the standpoint of those
urging people to repent or to convert to Christianity,
the effect of this Calvinism was to keep the people from
taking action and to keep the Calvinist ministers as
concerned with seeing that some went to hell as they were
that some went to heaven. Jabez Swan described such
Calvinists reckoning "themselves as elected of God to
sit like watch dogs at the strait gate, to prevent the
non-elect from dodging through." [87]

Edward Taylor summed up his view of this theology's
effect: "For Calvinists to invite sinners to repentance
is like inviting the gravestones home to dinner with
you." [88] Charles Finney used humor to ridicule the incon-
sistency of those ministers who urge the people to immediate repentance, but then added a stricture that man
was helpless to act himself and must await God's action
to save him:

> One day he happily forgot his accustomed inconsis-
> tency; and after pressing sinners to immediate
> repentance, sat down without the usual addition
> that they could not. 89

To his astonishment, one woman immediately repented; and
she noted, "I should have done it before had you not told
me that I could not." [90] Finney then extended the ridicule by reciting the poem "You Can and You Can't" to put

---

87. Denison, ed., The Life and Labors, pp. 428-429.
88. Haven, The Life of Father Taylor, p. 309.
89. Charles G. Finney, Sermons on Important Subjects,
p. 90.
90. Ibid.

down the spirit he labeled as "cannotism" which kept
people in a constant state of "in-betweenity." [91] And
Finney further mocked this doctrine of total depravity
and lack of free will:

> Suppose the greatest anti-Jackson man in this city,
> who has said and done the most of any man in the
> United States, to prevent his election, should be
> reduced to poverty, and had no means of support, for
> himself and family. Now suppose, when the news of
> his extremity should reach the president, he should
> appoint him to a post of high honour and emolument,
> would not this change his heart? Would he complain
> that he could not become the president's friend,
> until the Holy Ghost had changed his heart? 92

In a lecture to his Lane Seminary students in Cincinnati,
Lyman Beecher who had much earlier opposed Finney's
brand of revivalism, but had later welcomed Finney to his
Boston pulpit, used some humor in arguing that God had
constituted appetites rather than natural depravity:

> It is by this theory as if God had placed a man in
> a boat with a crowbar for an oar, and, then sent a
> storm on him! Is the man to be blamed if in such
> a case he is drowned? 93

And Beecher's son, Henry preached in a similar way to
ridicule the notion that man had no free choice:

> It is a queer account of choice; as if upon the summit
> of a glacier a child on his sled starts with power
> to go down, but no power to stop going down! Great
> choice, that! 94

---

91. Ibid., pp. 89-90. The poem is presented in chapter
one. While Lyman Beecher was reported as seeing a state
of "permanent hypochondria" resulting from meditation on
several Calvinist works, Harriet Beecher Stowe rendered
most effectively this state in her novels.

92. Finney, "Total Depravity," Sermons on Important
Subjects, p. 134.

93. Beecher, Autobiography, II, p. 573.

94. Henry Ward Beecher, "Adam and Christ," Kirk, ed.,
Beecher as Humorist, p. 110.

180

And still later in the century Sam Jones ridiculed the
idea of depravity that kept people from repentance:

> That reminds me of a poor fellow that is absolutely
> starved to death. A friend walks up to him, takes
> him by the hand and leads him up in five steps to a
> heavily-loaded table, with every luxury on it. He
> says, "Friend, are you hungry?" "Never was more
> hungry in my life." He says, "There is a table
> loaded with every luxury; walk up and eat." "No."
> "Why?" "Because my hands ain't fit." "Here is
> soap and water and towel. Wash your hands." "No."
> "Why?" "Because they ain't fit to be washed." And
> there he stands, starving to death, with plenty
> within his reach, because he ain't fit to eat and
> because his hands ain't fit to be washed. 95

The other side of predestination was that the elect could
not fall from grace by any action of their own. Jacob
Gruber called this doctrine "the in heaven and key lost"
doctrine. 96 And Lorenzo Dow, whose chief competition
in the South were Calvinist Baptists, attacked the perseverance of the saints in this extended fashion:

> Here is Major Smith, who becomes converted. He
> joins the Church and is safe as a codfish, pickled,
> packed and in port. Of course his calling and elec-
> tion are sure. He can't let 'em slip. He can't fall
> from grace -- not he! Don't be too certain of that,
> my brethren! Don't be too sure of that, Major! "I
> say nothing ag'in the character of Major Smith, mind
> you. He is a very fair sort of man as the world
> goes. Nevertheless they do say that he was in the
> habit of taking, now and then, a glass or two more
> than was good for him. He was fond of a warm gin
> toddy, especially of a cold day, for he was subject
> to wind in the stomach; and then in order to settle
> his toddy he would take a glass of flip, and then to
> settle his flip, he'd take a glass of toddy, ag'in.
> These he usually took in the afternoon and in
> Northrup's Tavern.
> "But as I say, one day Major Smith was converted,
> and taken into the church, and so he must reform.
> He must give up toddy and flip at Northrup's Tavern,
> and he has given them all up, for he is perfectly

---

95. Sam P. Jones, Sermons,(San Francisco: Historical
Publishing Co., 1887), p. 452.

96. Strickland, ed., The Life of Jacob Gruber, p. 363.

sincere, mind you. Well, some six weeks later on
the afternoon of a cold blustering day in December,
he happens to be passing by Northrup's Tavern. Just
at a time, as the devil will have it -- for the
devil is always looking out for a chance -- his old
friend and bottle companion, Nate Seymour, comes to
the door, and sees the Major. Well, the latter rides
up and they shake hands, and talk over the news and
finally Nate says, 'Won't you come in a minute,
Major?' "Now as I tell you it's a cold winter's day
and the Major says he'll just get down and warm his
fingers. He won't drink anything of course, but he
thinks it best not to break all at once with his old
friends, for they may say he's proud. Perhaps he'll
have a chance to say a word in season to someone.
So he goes in, and as it happens, Nate just then
puts the red hot poker into a mug of flip. How it
bubbles and simmers and foams. What a nice odor it
does send forth into the room. And just then the
landlord grates in a little nutmeg. What a pleasant
sound is that to poor, shivering human nature, on a
cold day in December!
"Well, Nate takes it and hands it to the Major. The
Major says to himself, 'I'll just put it to my lips
so as not to seem frumptious and unreasonable, but
I won't drink any.' So he takes it, and it feels
mighty warm and nice to his cold fingers. He looks
at it; its fumes rise to his nostrils; he remembers
the joys of other days; he puts it to his lips!
"Well, and what then? Oh nothing, my brethren, only
I tell you, that elect or no elect, that is a very
slippery moment for the Major!" [97]

Another configuration of pulpit humor around Calvinist
doctrines emerges from those who wished to put off
consideration of those doctrines without necessarily
denying them altogether. To remove from the center of
attention the idea of predestination, George Whitefield
approvingly quoted Dr. Watts' sentiment, "We should go to
the grammar school of faith and repentance before we go
to the university of predestination." [98] And to remove

97. Charles Coleman Sellers, Lorenzo Dow, The Bearer of
the Word,(New York: Minton,Balch & Co., 1928), pp. 138-140.
98. George Whitefield, "The Beloved of God," Eighteen
Sermons, p. 98. Whitefield's Calvinism was a ground for
his disagreement with John Wesley's Arminian developments.
But Whitefield avoided doctrinal arguments when possible.

predestination as a stumbling block in his ecumenical
association with Methodists, Presbyterian Henry Pattillo
observed:

> To ask then, whether you are elected, is to begin
> your building at the top of the house, without
> laying the foundation. Your proper question is,
> what shall I do to be saved? 99

On other issues of doctrine, humor helped the preacher
affirm a truth without implying a doctrine and more than
he wished to say. Henry Ward Beecher upheld the idea
of man's evil nature without becoming entangled with the
doctrine of depravity:

> Do you suppose I study musty old books when I want
> to preach? No, I study you. When I want to know
> more about the doctrine of depravity, I study you;
> and I have abundant illustrations on every side. 100

Using humor Dwight Lyman Moody affirmed Divine sovereignty
and grace in salvation without directly denying freedom
of the will:

> As a Scotchman once said, it took two to bring him
> to God; it took the Lord and himself: A friend
> asked him what he did and he said he fought God,
> but the Lord did all the rest till he gave in. 101

And Presbyterian Robert Henderson avoided a direct affir-
mation or rejection of the doctrine of disinterested
benevolence in the following way which allowed him to
stress the dark side of man:

> Yet how many of mankind are thus volunteering in the
> cause of darkness and serving the devil most disin-

---

99. Henry Patillo, Sermons, pp. 173-174.

100. Henry Ward Beecher, "Sphere of Christian Minister,"
Kirk, ed., Beecher as Humorist, p. 74.

101. Dwight L. Moody, "The Holy Spirit," To all People,
p. 4.

terestedly? This is committing wickedness for its own sake, which is certainly disinterested wickedness. 102

The disputes which Calvinist doctrines caused within and among the denominations were another configuration around which pulpit humor was attracted. Jonathan Mayhew used such humor to point out the shortcomings of the Orthodox Calvinists themselves who argued so uncharitably for their doctrines:

> There are none, perhaps, who have more reason to be suspicious of themselves than your hot, religious zealots; the great sticklers for what they call Orthodoxy -- whether justly or unjustly, it now matters not. You will sometimes see men, wrangling in such an unchristian manner about the form of godliness as to make it but too evident that they deny the power thereof. You will find some who pride themselves in being of what they call the true Church, showing by their whole conversation that they are of the synagogue of Satan. Some contend, and foam, and curse their brethren, for the sake of the Athanasian Trinity, till 'tis evident they do not love and fear the one living and true God as they ought to do. Others you will see raging about their peculiar notions of original sin, so as to prove themselves guilty of actural transgression; about election, till they prove themselves reprobates; about particular redemption, till they show that they themselves are not redeemed from a vain conversation. You will hear others quarrelling about imputed righteousness with such fury and bitterness as to show that they are destitute of personal; about special grace, so as to show that they have not even common; about faith, while they make shipwreck of a good conscience; and about the final perseverance of the saints; and that, if they had ever any goodness or grace, they are now fallen from it. 103

Mayhew, who had been spurned by the Orthodox in Boston, pointed out how they lacked charity and imitated more the scribes and Pharisees than the early Christians. [104] He

---

102. Henderson, A Series of Sermons, II, p. 151.

103. Sprague, Annals, VIII, p. 28.

104. Mayhew, Sermons, pp. 115 and 117.

184

called the Samaritan "a man who had less orthodoxy and
more charity." [105] Although their spurning of Mayhew
was a mild form of persecution by the mid-18th century,
the established Orthodox had persecuted others in earlier
periods of New England history, and so were open to
Mayhew's further characterization of them as far removed
from the way of early Christians:

> Whence comes the doctrine that true orthodox Chris-
> tians have a right to persecute heretics and unbe-
> lievers? (i.e. to be more wicked and immoral than
> heretics and unbelievers?) The scripture, indeed
> (and experience very often) teaches us, that those
> who will live godly in Christ Jesus, must suffer
> persecution; but not that they must persecute
> others. 106

And Mayhew noted that such methods argued against the
truth of the doctrine espoused in such a way:

> A blow with a club may fracture a man's skull; but I
> suppose he will not think and reason the more clearly
> for that; though he may possibly believe the more
> orthodoxly, according to the opinions of some. And
> upon this account it must be confessed that those
> who make use of these methods to propagate their
> sentiments, act very prudently: for their doctrines
> are generally such as are much more readily embraced
> by a man after his brains are knocked out, than while
> he continues in his senses, and of a sound mind. 107

By 1840, Congregationalist Leonard Bacon, who was basically sympathetic to Calvinism, saw the discussion over
fate versus free will as out of place when it became the
center of attention for Christians who had better work
to do:

> Such questions do indeed make a great figure in the
> theology of many modern Christians; but how remote
> is all this metaphysical jangling from the grand

---

105. Ibid., p. 115.
106. Ibid., p. 69.
107. Ibid., pp. 65-66.

principles of the doctrine of Christ. 108

And in calling such wrangling "theological gladiatorship,"
Bacon indicated the inappropriateness of such further
discussions among Christians. [109] Henry Ward Beecher,
who was also well aware of the fruitlessness of heresy
trials and orthodox actions which stressed doctrinal
differences and disrupted the harmony of the church, used
humor to encourage the people to take theology less
seriously:

> There stands a controversial dog at almost every
> turn; and when you approach men on the subject of
> theology, this watch dog shows his teeth. Men call
> it "conscience;" but a dog is a dog. 110

The attack on theology, whether Calvinist or any other,
was also directed at the presumption involved in man
speaking so certainly and so matter of factly about God
and his way of working in the world. We have already
explored the doctrine of man which stressed his limits
to know. Beecher used this basically Calvinist view of
man to ridicule the detailed nature of Calvinist doctrines and the certainty with which they were held:

> Men speak of the divine will as though it were so
> clear and plain that it could be put into the cat-
> echism or into books with chapters and verses. Men
> can almost count the shingles on the roof and the
> nails which hold the different parts together, with
> perfect familiarity! And yet, after all, we are
> but children. 111

And to those who acted as if their own creeds were God's
certain truth rather than man's limited perception of
truth about God, Beecher made explicit their assumption,

---

108. Leonard Bacon, "The Primitive Christians," The
American National Preacher,(June, 1841), XV, No. 6,p.130.
109. Leonard Bacon, The Relation of Faith to Missions,
(Boston: T. R. Marvin, 1852), p. 7.
110. Henry Ward Beecher, Sermons, Eighth Series, p. 295.
111. Henry Ward Beecher, "God's Will," Plymouth Pulpit,
(March-September, 1875), p. 85.

and so held it up to ridicule: "One would think, from the questions which they ask, that the Holy Ghost was the editor of catechisms."[112]

Methodism

The Methodist doctrine of perfection attracted little pulpit humor. The excitement and enthusiasm that accompanied many Methodist meetings attracted the pulpit humor from non-Methodists and Methodists alike. The non-Methodists' pulpit humor was critical of the enthusiasm for using up energy without issuing in action helpful to society. The Methodist pulpit humor was aimed so that no one person's emotional experience would be seen as the only method of conversion which others must emulate or consider themselves unfit for the kingdom. Methodists supplied as much pulpit humor to put down arguments against perfection as was supplied by others against perfection; and traveling revivalists in other denominations added to the Methodist humor which ridiculed the attack on excitement and enthusiasm which was common in many revivals outside as well as inside the Methodist Church.

In the same year that Methodist founder John Wesley was ordained a deacon in England, Mather Byles delivered a sermon likening "the deluded mortals that boast a perfection" to "the proud Pharisee . . .(who) stood and caressed himself." [113] Thus, we see that all attacks on perfection were not necessarily aimed at the particular Methodist position. In answer to questions from his Yale senior class, Timothy Dwight acknowledged that man could make many improvements; but his Calvinist doctrine of man juxtaposed to the expectations of man's perfection produced some humor:

---

112. Henry Ward Beecher, "The Claims of the Spirit," Plymouth Pulpit, IV, p. 528.
113. Mather Byles, The Character of the Perfect, p. 4.

"It will be as far from perfectibility which fools
talk of as the mite from a man, and an oyster from
a whale." 114

The discussions of perfectibility of man with which Dwight
dealt were not only stimulated by Methodist evangelists
(with whom Dwight at Yale had little contact) but by
Unitarians who were also Arminian in theology and much
more visible as a competing force in New England. And a
half century later we do not know from the context whether
in the following remark Henry Ward Beecher had in mind
Methodists, who were more of a force in his day than they
had been in Dwight's, or others in the social evolution
crazed culture:

> Oh, Poor Paul! If he had lived in our day, we would
> have sent him to folks who would have shown him how
> he might be perfect. But as it was, he was conscious
> of the inharmony which existed between the mind and
> the flesh - between himself and the world. 115

While the pulpit humor against perfection was not necessarily directed against Methodism, there is no mistaking
the target of Methodist humor defending the possibilities
of perfection. Referring to Calvinist doctrine that man
could not live without sin, Billy Hibbard commented: "I
have often seen them labor to prove that Christians could
not live without sin; they did not say how much sin would
keep a man alive. . . ." 116

Henry Ward Beecher's humor on religious excitement and
enthusiasm played on the absence of helpful action after
such a great expense of energy in emotionalism:

---

114. Theodore Dwight, Jr., President Dwight's Decisions
of Questions Discussed by the Senior Class in Yale College in 1813 & 1814,(New York: Jon. Leavitt, 1833), p. 332.
115. Henry Ward Beecher, Plymouth Pulpit,(March through
September, 1875), p. 159. The sermon was delivered
October 25, 1874.
116. Hibbard, Memoirs, p. 347 (cf. Ibid., pp. 354-355.).

> I have seen persons who have so exhausted themselves
> by religious emotions, that they have no strength
> left for religious duties. 117

And Beecher likened the overly emotional to the aspen
leaf: "They quiver, but do not change -- forever moving,
and forever stationary." [118] Beecher's Methodist contemporary, Sam Jones, criticized "heart religion" for a
similar reason: "It is generally locked in the heart and
never seen upon the surface." [119] But Jones saw another
sort of inaction that a particular pattern of excitement
cast over those who never experienced the particular
feelings:

> A fellow running on feeling reminds me of a man who
> had just returned from Nashville. A neighbor called
> to see him and asked: "Did you have a nice trip?"
> "Yes," was the reply, "we made quick time. We had a
> pleasant trip, but when only about ten miles this
> side of Nashville, I turned deathly sick and had to
> raise the window of the car." "And you were sick?"
> the neighbor said. "I was, and I was deadly sick
> for about ten minutes." Well, the next week this
> neighbor finds that he has got to go to Nashville.
> Every station he passes is right. He is on the
> Louisville and Nashville cars. It is an L & N
> conductor. The engineer is an L & N engineer, and
> the engine is an L & N engine. And there he is and
> he gets within ten miles of this side of Nashville.
> The conductor passed through the car, and he said:
> "Captain, hold on and put me off this train." "What
> is the matter?" asked the conductor. "I want to go
> to Nashville." "You are going there at the rate of
> forty miles an hour." "No, we are not." "What
> makes you think we are not?" "I have a friend who
> went to Nashville last week, and he was taken sick
> ten miles before he got there, and I know -- I am
> certain we are not on the right road, or I would be
> taken sick here." 120

We may see the same grounds underlying the attack on
emotionalism as we saw underlying the attack on intel-

---

117. H. W. Beecher, "Conduct: The Index of Feeling,"
Kirk, ed., Beecher As Humorist, p. 14.
118. Beecher, The Sermons, First Series, p. 289.
119. Jones, "Grace & Salvation," Sermons, (San Francisco:
Historical Publishing Co., 1887), p. 48.
120. Ibid., p. 450.

lectualism. The preoccupation with either emotionalism
or intellectualism diverted the individual from personal
conversion and subsequent service to others. The humor
aimed to put down the idolization of any one method to
experience or one theological formulation to describe
God's way of working with man in the world.

Early pulpit humor used to defend excitement at meetings
drew upon biblical examples to ridicule those who objected
to such excitement. Later humor cited the excitement
with which politics, money making, and amusements were
approached by those who then objected to excitement in
religion. Another strategy employed to defend excitement
was an attack on the heartlessness or coldness of those
who eschewed excitement. Almost all of those employing
these varieties of humor to defend excitement in religious
meetings were engaged in conducting revivals -- in the
majority of cases among Methodists, but also among
Baptists, Presbyterians, and others.

George Whitefield called the objectors to enthusiasm
"scribes and Pharisees" who would have advised Paul to
avoid roads to Damascus in the future. [121] And Whitefield noted that "Isaiah would be reckoned a dreadful
enthusiast if now alive." [122] Presbyterian Henry Pattillo,
whose ecumenical cooperation with Methodists we have noted
earlier, defended enthusiasm in worship by describing a
modern man's probable response to Paul's enthusiastic
statements of faith:

> (He) would interrupt the Apostle's song; strike his
> harp from his hand, break the golden strings, clip
> the wings of his faith, and bring this towering
> eagle to the ground, by suggesting such raptures
> are dangerous 123

121. Whitefield, Works, V-VI, p. 362; and Whitefield,
Fifteen Sermons, pp. 115, 117, and 118.
122. Whitefield, Eighteen Sermons, p. 61.
123. Pattillo, Sermons, pp. 146-147.

190

And early in the second quarter of the 19th century, Baptist Jacob Knapp compared the detractors of excitement to a biblical character with whom they would least choose to be associated:

> When the woman came to anoint him against his burial, and broke the box of precious ointment and poured it on his head, a heartless Judas charged her of waste, of undue excitement. 124

Knapp also employed humor more common in later sermons to ridicule those who objected to excitement in church but who engaged excitedly in other activities such as politics:

> Notice the interest manifested in politics. Our country is divided into two standing political parties, and sometimes a third party comes up. Each party has its regular sets of candidates and, as election year draws near the anxiety increases; and yet, as a matter of fact, there may be little or no choice in the candidates. Both may be good men, or more likely neither of them fit for the station. But the whole country is moved: a mighty moral earthquake convulses the whole land. Men, women, and children are all excited, from the shores of the Atlantic to the shores of the Pacific. Millions of money are paid out to publish and disseminate partisan documents. Hundreds of thousands of dollars are staked on the results of the election. Log cabins and liberty poles are erected, and flags are flung to every breeze. Farmers, mechanics, merchants, doctors, lawyers, and sometimes ministers, all join in one universal chorus. And when the contest is ended, and one party has come out victorious, a mighty shout is heard throughout the whole United States of America; the telegraph wires are all electrified; balls and parties are multiplied, and the booming cannon roars along through the valleys, and comes thundering over all the mountains. Millions more of money are expended in parades and festivals; but all this is well in the eyes of the world. Formalists, hypocrites, and worldlings have nothing to say against excitement or animal feeling. But let there be a contest between the friends and the enemies of Jesus about the coming of Jesus into every heart, and through all the world, and the dethroning of Satan; and let them manifest half the zeal, expend half the money, make half the sacrifices,

---

124. Knapp, _Autobiography_, p. 280.

to accomplish this end, and all these unbelievers
will cry out, "Enthusiasm!" "Wild-fire!" "Animal
feeling!" "Thou art beside thyself; Much religion
doth make thee mad." 125

Charles Finney's sermons in the late 1830's used a
similar strategy citing not only political excitement [126]
but also excitement over amusements:

> Witness the conduct of impenitent sinners, on the
> subject of religion. If any efforts are made to
> promote the interests of the kingdom of God, to
> honour and glorify him, they are offended. They get
> up an opposition. They not unfrequently ridicule
> their meetings; speak evil of those that are engaged
> in them; denounce their zeal as enthusiasm and mad-
> ness, and something for which they deserve the
> execration of all their neighbours. People may get
> together and dance all night, and impenitent sinners
> do not think it objectionable. The theatre may be
> opened every night, at great expense, and the actors
> and multitudes of others, may be engaged all day in
> preparing for the entertainment of the evening; and
> thus the devil may get up a protracted meeting, and
> continue it for years, and they see no harm in it;
> no enthusiasm in all this. Ladies may go, and stay
> till midnight, every evening. Poor people may go,
> and spend their time and money, and waste their
> health and lives, and ruin their souls; why is there
> no harm in all this? But let Christians do anything
> like this, and exercise one-tenth part of this zeal
> in promoting the honour of God, and the salvation of
> souls; why, it would be talked of from Dan to Beer-
> sheeba. Sinners may go to a ball, or party, and
> stay nearly all night; but excessively indecorous
> it is for ladies to go out to evening meetings, and
> to pray till 10 o'clock at night. Abominable! 127

Later in the century, Dwight Moody also used this strategy citing excitement over politicians [128] and amusements:

> Some saloons keep open all night, and men get so
> excited that they knock one another down, and kill

---

125. Ibid., p. 277.

126. Finney, Sermons On Important Subjects, p. 128.

127. Ibid., pp. 127-128.

128. Dwight L. Moody, "Christian Enthusiasm," To All
People, p. 24.

one another, and yet we must not have revivals because there is "undue excitement." There is more
excitement in the billiard halls and the gambling
dens, brothels and drinking saloons, in one week
than there is in the whole church of God in a
year. 129

Excitement in meetings was defended also by attacking the
lack of excitement in others' endeavours. In the early
19th century Methodist William Cravens answered an earlier
speech by a General Blackburn who criticized shouting
Methodists and noted that "still water always runs deep."
Cravens responded:

General, did you ever see still waters run at all?
And who are the inhabitants of still water? Snakes,
toads, turtles, tadpoles, etc. This is their birth-
place, their home. Still water is very impure,
stagnant, unlike the sparkling spring, or the clear
running brook. 130

And Knapp reduced to the absurd the position of those
who eschewed all excitement:

Suppose a man is sinking a well. After getting forty
feet below the surface of the ground the sides cave
in, and he is buried beneath the fallen earth; but,
by means of some timbers, air enough reaches him to
keep the breath of life in him for a time, and by
putting your ear at the mouth of the cave you can
just faintly hear him cry, "Help! Save! For God's
sake, save!" But while some hasten on with spades
and shovels, some throwing the dirt one way and some
another, all working on without regard to rules of
propriety, in the handling of their shovels, suppose
a set of lookers-on should gather around, stand
aloof, and find fault, saying, "This man throws his
dirt very carelessly; that man ought not to take off
his coat, he will get cold; it is now after nine
o'clock, and they ought to go home; 'too much
excitement;'" what would you think of these cool-
blooded croakers? 131

---

129. D. L. Moody, Moody's Latest Sermons,(Chicago: The
Bible Institute, 1900), p. 111.

130. J. B. Wakeley, The Bold Frontier Preacher, p. 48.

131. Knapp, Autobiography, p. 279.

The coolness of those who avoided excitement in their worship was a common point of pulpit humor. Such men's prayers would "freeze us all to death;" [132] and of their sermons, "it would take as many such to convert a soul as snowballs to heat an oven." [133]

Baptist

While much of the pulpit humor against Calvinist theology and Methodist excitement applied to Baptists, the configuration of humor explicitly directed at them was around their central practice of adult baptism by immersion. The ground for the humor was the Baptist claim that their own particular way for the sacrament or ordinance was the only saving way, and that the New Testament supported their claim. Little humor was used by Baptists in defense of their practice to suggest that non-Baptists were missing something. [134]

The inconsistent literalism of the Baptists' conformity to New Testament precedents for sacraments or ordinances was pointed out in some humor. Speaking of the Lord's Supper, Timothy Dwight noted:

> Baptists are bound on their own principles, to spread a table in the evening, to sit in a reclining posture, and thus to celebrate this sacrament on the evening preceding every Lord's day. All this ought also to be done in a large upper room, contained in a private dwelling. 135

Black Congregational minister Lemuel Haynes, a contemporary of Dwight's, recounted how he treated the Baptist insistence that he allow them to baptize him according to the literal account in the New Testament. He readily assented; but as they were about to lead him down to the

132. Ibid., p. 65.
133. Haven, The Life of Father Taylor, p. xxiii.
134. (cf. Stimson, From the Stage Coach to the Pulpit, pp. 154 and 184.)
135. Timothy Dwight, Theology Explained, IV, p. 356.

water, he objected that they were not being faithful to
scripture. When they inquired in what way their practice
was remiss, he exclaimed that according to a literal
reading of scripture, the only true baptism would be in
the river Jordan and they were leading him into Skunk
Hollow Creek! [136] And Peter Cartwright was credited with
putting down the adult Baptism by recalling that Jesus
likened the little children to those who populate heaven
(and Cartwright recalled also the notion that children
who die at birth go to heaven):

> If there are no children in hell, and all young
> children who die go to heaven is not that church
> which has no children in it more like hell than
> heaven? [137]

Putting Down Drinking

Pulpit humor against intemperance is considered in this
chapter on humor related to wisdom because the temperance
movement revealed the high regard for man's reason. [138]
Throughout the period of this study, alcohol was cited as
a God to whom men idolatrously bowed. The enslavement
which this idol imposed on its subjects was pointed out
with a humor directed at the political and economic
powers who were supported by interest in alcohol. And

---

136. Cooley, Sketches of the Life and Character of the
Rev. Lemuel Haynes, p. 125.

137. Wm. Henry Milburn, The Pioneers, Preachers and
People,(New York: Derby & Jackson, 1860), p. 384.

138. The restoration of man's reasoning faculty was most
commonly given as the reason for temperance. cf. Whitefield, Works, V-VI, p. 308; Lyman Beecher, Six Sermons
on the Nature, Occasions, Signs, Evils, and Remedy of
Intemperance, (New York: American Tract Society, 1843),
pp. 11, 52, and 56. But among reasons Dow gave for
temperance was the quenching of the divine spirit and
the charitable instinct. Dow, "Reflections of Matrimony,"
Dealings, p. 39.

most of the humor was from Methodist ministers. Only a
hint of pulpit humor resulted as the temperance movement
itself became absolutest in insisting upon total absti-
nance, including the elimination of wine from communion.[139]

George Whitefield exclaimed, "Was St. Paul to rise again
from the dead, he might be tempted to think most of us
were turned back to the worship of dumb idols; had set up
temples in honour of Baccheus. . . ."[140] Early in the
19th century, Methodist William Cravens played upon the
copper used in distillery equipment in calling drinking
the "copper-headed god" to which worshippers bow till
they cannot help but grovel.[141] In the early 1850's
William Taylor attacked the despotism of King Alcohol in
San Francisco.[142] Later in the East, Dwight Lyman Moody
deplored the fact that many "worship a rum bottle;"[143]
and Leonard Bacon called even fashionable drinking
"despotic."[144]

The despotism of drink was explored with humor to put
down the powers that profited by the idolatry. In St.
Louis where the temperance movement was opposed by those
who argued that the city government and services could
not be provided without the revenues from saloons, Sam
Jones argued:

I expect a great many professing Christians in this

---

139. Edward Taylor's support of the temperance movement
stopped short of placing grape juice (which he dubbed
"raisin water") on the altar. In his last instructions
to his congregation he advised, "Cast from this church
any man that comes up to the altar with his glue-pot and
his dye'stuff." Haven, The Life of Father Taylor, p. 266.

140. Whitefield, Works, V-VI, p. 304.

141. Wakeley, The Bold Frontier Preacher, p. 76.

142. Wm. Taylor, Seven Years of Street Preaching, p. 150.

143. Moody, The Great Redemption, pp. 342-343.

144. Leonard Bacon, The Four Commemorative Discourses,
p. 32.

town will be astonished when they get to heaven to
find out how God Almighty can run the Celestial City
without a few saloons to help keep up the taxes. 145

The financial power of anti-temperance forces was stressed
and the forces themselves ridiculed in the story of Elder
Jabez Swan reported during one election. Hoping to buy
Swan's silence in the election, the anti-temperance
candidate sent him a twenty-five dollar donation. Swan's
response was, "It is not enough: Judas received thirty
pieces." 146 And the social beneficence of the saloon
keepers was ridiculed by Sam Jones. To reports that a
widow of one local drunk had been supplied with a few
groceries by local saloon keepers, Jones responded:

> "They are generous," you say. Well, they ought to
> be. They will make a pauper out of a husband,
> widows out of wives, and send a man to hell, and
> then this generous whiskey dealer will send his
> widow a sack of flour! Ain't that generous? Ain't
> that nice? 147

The strategy of pulpit humor around drinking was to lead
the people to laugh not at the drunk (except when he might
interrupt a worship service) but rather at those economic
and political powers which perpetuated a system profiting
them but degrading many and keeping attention away from
God.

---

145. Jones, Sermons, (San Francisco: Historical Publishing Co., 1887), p. 119.

146. Denison, ed., The Life and Labors of Jabez Swan,
p. 434.

147. Jones, Sermons: Wise and Witty, p. 16.

CHAPTER V

THE USE OF HUMOR

IN EXORCISING IDOLATRIES OF WEALTH

I saw in the paper the other day where an old
fellow -- a man -- said to another:
"Did you hear about Mr. So and So being dead?" "Yes."
"He is a millionaire, and he willed the last dollar
in the world he had to the bar-keepers." "He did!"
"Yes! Well," he said, "he didn't will it directly
to them, but he just willed it indirectly to them --
he just gave it to his boys, and the bar-keepers
will get it sure." 1

An anecdote from a Sam Jones' sermon toward the close of
the 19th century opens our consideration of the pulpit
humor used to put down the idolatry of wealth. The
attack on wealth was stimulated by pragmatic consider-
ations of the effect wealth had on those who sought and
possessed it, an effect that extended beyond the individual to one's family and church. In the process of accumulating wealth and its trappings of fashionable clothes
and fashionable living, the individual's concern and
attention were seen to narrow not only in terms of con-
centrating larger and larger percentages of one's wealth
on oneself and one's family for essentially needless
trappings when others outside one's family had real needs,
but also in terms of acquiring a calculating mind that
no longer appreciated or manifested the dimensions of life
valued in biblical faith. As in Jones' story of the
fortune being wasted, the person's concern and attention
concentrated in such a way was seen to result in nothing
of lasting value to society, but rather had the effect of
orienting one's children in a similar direction which
reduced moral fiber and produced vegetative organisms.
In other humor the effect was seen in wealthy men's
churches as well. The fruitlessness of those who

1. Sam Jones, "Lying Up Money," Sermons, (San Francisco:
Historical Publishing Co., 1887), p. 257.

197

attended so intently to accumulating wealth as with the
fruitlessness of those who attended so intently to
accumulating knowledge or religious feelings was the
point of attack for pulpit humor.

Ministers irrespective of denomination joined in the
attack with humor. [2] There was greater concentration of
such attacks on wealth in the last half of the 19th century (when there were more prominent new accumulations
of wealth), although there were attacks on wealth throughout the period of this study. [3] And in the pulpit humor,
the work and needs of missionaries at home and abroad
were often contrasted to the wealthy man's accumulation
of riches -- a contrast that was a primary pragmatic
reason for the negative judgment on such accumulation.
We examine first the attack of pulpit humor on a narrowing of attention that was attributed to those who accumulated wealth. We then consider the fruitless or purposeless end which was pictured in much of the pulpit
humor directed against accumulation of wealth. And
finally we examine the pulpit humor used to put down the
effects of wealth within the church where ultimate values
were raised to dwarf and ridicule the value of wealth.

Putting Down the Narrowing Attention to Wealth.

In one of his sermons to young men of Indianapolis in the
early 1840's, Henry Ward Beecher characterized the proper

---

2. One might think that Calvinists would have been more
inclined to greet such accumulation of wealth as a sign
of the sanctification of God's chosen; but Calvinists
were as active as others in this use of humor.

3. What Washington Gladden labeled "The New Idolatry"
at the opening of the 20th century was thus not nearly
as new in America as he averred, cf. Washington
Gladden, The New Idolatry, (New York: McClure, Phillips,
and Company, 1905).

and improper ways to handle riches. "When rationally
used, riches are called a gift of God, an evidence of his
favor, and a great reward." [4] In Henry Ward Beecher's
view and in that of most other ministers studied, it was
a matter of stewardship to use riches and not accumulate
them. The humor was directed against accumulation of
riches that indicated an inordinate attention to riches
-- attention that should have been given to recognition
of God and his service. The making of riches into an
end in itself without reference to God was the idolatry:
"Avarice seeks gold . . . to kiss and hug the darling
stuff to the end of life with the homage of idolatry." [5]
The narrowing of attention to one's gold was seen as often
resulting in the narrowing of attention to one's self 'to
make an idol of one's self for fools to gaze at." [6] And
such an attention to accumulation as an end in itself
produced a blasphemous creed which excluded the poor from
one's concern:

> The creed of the greedy man is brief and consistent;
> and, unlike other creeds, is both subscribed and
> believed. The chief end of man is to glorify GOLD
> and enjoy it forever: life is a time afforded man to
> grow rich in: death, the winding up of speculations:
> heaven, a mart with golden streets: hell, a place
> where shiftless men are punished with everlasting
> poverty. [7]

4. Henry Ward Beecher, "Six Warnings," Lectures to Young
Men On Various Important Subjects,(New York: J.B.Ford
& Co., 1873), p. 52. The first few of these sermons
were delivered in 1843.

5. Ibid., p. 54. Presbyterian Reuben Tinker, whom we
noted in chapter two had characterized the race for
riches as an idolatrous race away from God, grounded his
perceptions on the biblical story of the rich young ruler
"who idolized his wealth and forsook his Saviour."
Tinker, who had served as a missionary in Hawaii, was
pragmatically motivated in his attack on those who accumulated money when the mission movement needed funds to
spread the gospel, Tinker, Sermons, p. 343. Theodore
Parker labeled money as the God of Gold and the most
popular idolatry. Theodore Parker, Speeches, Addresses,
and Occasional Sermons, I, pp. 70 & 270. II,pp. 244-246.

6. Beecher, Lectures, p. 55.

7. Ibid., p. 60.

Attending to One's Own Business

True to his practice of introducing controversial comments
with humor, Beecher opened one sermon of 1869 on "Stewardship in business" with the words to deal with those
who felt ministers should mind their own business and
not interfere with businessmen:

> Complaint is often made on that ground, of ministers,
> that they meddle with things they do not understand.
> I think they do too, when they preach theology. 8

Beecher thus humorously raised the question of what was
the "Sphere of the Christian Minister", and inferred that
spheres of concern were not narrow ones. A businessman's
vision that his business was his own and of no concern
to a minister (or to God) was the narrow focus of attention that Charles Finney employed humor to broaden in a
sermon on "Stewardship:"

> Suppose that a company of merchants in the city
> should employ a number of agents to transact their
> business in India, with an immense capital, and
> suppose these agents should claim the funds as their
> property, and whenever a draft was made upon them,
> should consider it begging, and asking charity at
> their hands, and should call the servant by whom
> the order was sent a beggar; and further, suppose
> they should get together, and form a charitable
> society to pay these drafts, of which they should
> become "life members," by paying each a few dollars
> of their employers' money into a common fund, and
> then hold themselves exonerated from all further
> calls; so that, when an agent was sent with drafts,
> they might direct the treasurer of their society to
> let him have a little, as a matter of almsgiving.
> Would not this be vastly ridiculous? What then do
> you think of yourself, when you talk of supporting
> these charitable institutions, as if God, the owner
> of the universe, was to be considered as soliciting
> charity, and his servants as the agents of an infi-
> nite beggar?. . .Nor is it less ridiculous for them
> to suppose that by paying over the funds in their
> hands for this purpose, they confer a charity upon
> men: for it should all along be borne in mind, that

---

8. H. W. Beecher, Sermons, First Series, p. 310.

the money is not <u>theirs</u>. They are God's stewards, and only pay it over to his order -- in doing this, therefore, <u>they</u> neither confer a charity upon the servants who are sent with the orders; nor upon those for whose benefit the money is to be expended. Again: You see the great wickedness of men's hoarding up property so long as they live, and at death leaving a part of it to the church. <u>What a will!</u> To leave God half of his own property. Suppose a clerk should do so, and make a will, leaving his employer part of his own property! Yet this is called <u>piety</u>. Do you think that Christ will always be a beggar? And yet the church is greatly <u>puffed</u> <u>up</u> with their great charitable donations and legacies to Jesus Christ. 9

The minister's practical experience with raising funds as well as his theological view of the creation as God's was reflected in the humor that would help the people see all of their life as subject to God.

The narrow attention to one's own business was held up to ridicule in the last half of the 19th century because such focus of attention kept the person from seeing the true wealth that lay around him. Dwight Lyman Moody recounted a story in which the businessman was cast in the role of a skeptic who did not support missionaries:

Some men in London, who had returned from India, gave a dinner party. Among others who were invited were a wealthy merchant, who was a skeptic, and a foreign missionary. During the dinner party they brought up the question of native converts, and the English merchant turned up his nose, and said: "I have lived in India for twenty years, but I have heard more about native converts in London than I ever heard in India. I never saw one native convert all the years I was there." The guests looked for a reply from the foreign missionary, but he said nothing until later in the evening, when he turned to this man and said: "Did you ever see any tigers

---

9. Charles G. Finney, "Stewardship," <u>Sermons on Important Subjects</u>, pp. 215-216. Tinker's point of attack was similar in ridiculing those who would go to a "reasonable" extent in their giving with the assumption that the property was theirs and they were entitled to determine what was reasonable for God to ask. Tinker, <u>Sermons</u>, p. 345.

in India?" The merchant's face lit up at once. "Oh
yes," he said, "I have not only seen them, but I
have shot a good many." "That is strange," said
the missionary, "I have never seen a tiger." One
had been looking for tigers and the other for
converts. You generally get what you look for. 10

Sam Jones ridiculed a similar narrow attention that
misses most that life offers:

> Going to church is like going shopping. A sister
> goes into this magnificent dry goods store; there
> are $200,000 worth of goods in it, but she buys her
> paper of pins and goes out. That's all she came
> for -- just a paper of pins. 11

Attending to One's Self

The attention to one's own business entailed a narrowing
of one's attention which when carried to an extreme
ended in attention to one's own body. While the ridicule
of this end is considered in a later section on the
fruitlessness of the idolatry of the material world, the
narrowing of attention to oneself was subject to some
pulpit humor. Beecher, who had described this attention
to oneself in Lectures To Young Men (which we studied at
the opening of this chapter), further ridiculed the
overattention to adorning oneself:

> A coat poorly fitted is the unpardonable sin of his
> creed. He meditates upon cravats, employs a pro-
> found discrimination in selecting a hat or a vest,
> and adopts his conclusions upon the tastefulness of
> a button or a collar with the deliberation of a
> statesman. 12

10. D. L. Moody, Moody's Latest Sermons,(Chicago: The
Bible Institute, 1900), pp. 114-115.
11. Jones, Sermons, p. 44.
12. Beecher, Lectures To Young Men, p. 6. In a somewhat
similar vein, George Whitefield had employed a little
humor against those "who are more afraid of a pimple on
your faces, than of the rottenness of your hearts."
George Whitefield, Eighteen Sermons, p. 56. But a
different emphasis of the ministers may be seen in
Beecher's contrasting of the statesman to the one preoccupied with buttons, and Whitefield's contrasting of
Salvation to the one preoccupied with pimples.

Such an expense of energy upon buttons and collars was
ridiculous in light of the larger issues ignored.

Calculating Approach to Life

Pulpit humor also aimed at the calculating mind that
resulted from attention to accumulating wealth -- a mind
that did not appreciate those qualities of persons and
actions that could not be measured or justified in terms
of worldly success and profit margin. In his sermon
"Watchfulness," Henry Ward Beecher noted, "Men mean to
get to heaven, but they do not mean that it shall cost
them any more virtue than they can possibly help." [13]
On another occasion, Beecher pointed to Pilate as the
preeminent calculating mind who was "calm and cool,"
"keen and sharp;" [14] but Beecher noted that Pilate's
attempt to limit his responsibility was not possible. Of
the killing of Christ, Pilate and others who could have
prevented it do "not take a dividend of it -- each man
is guilty of the whole." [15]

Before the war, Baptist Jacob Knapp used humor to put
down the seeming sensibleness of the business mind:

> We can imagine how some of his old associates spoke
> of him. One said, "I really thought that Paul would
> amount to something." Another remarked, "He might
> have been somebody if he had not got excited about
> these miserable followers of the Nazarene." "Yes,
> said another, "he might have occupied a high place
> among both the Jews and the Romans, and commanded
> a high salary, and been one of the first men of his
> age, but he has completely thrown himself away by
> joining this illiterate set of fishermen. He has
> made a fool of himself. 16

---

13. Beecher, "Watchfulness," Kirk, Beecher As Humorist,
p. 56.
14. Beecher, The Sermons, First Series, p. 66.
15. Ibid., p. 68.
16. Beecher, Plymouth Pulpit, IV, p. 429.

In Knapp's humor, conventional business talk and values appear foolish. Henry Ward Beecher expressed a similar critique of the calculating mind as incapable of being carried away by any passion and likened such spirits to the elder brother of the Prodigal Son. That such souls avoided problems was no credit to them, they were simply "too stingy to get drunk" and too "self-contained" to be carried away doing any good either. [17]

And much earlier in 1830, criticism of mission giving prompted Methodist George Cookman to humorously point out the inconsistent application of some people's economic concern -- an application that in no way restrained their expense on themselves, but would cut off all funds to carry on mission work to others:

> How can we be warranted, say they, in sending so much money out of the country? I must confess I am at times perfectly astounded at the inconsistent reasoning of some men on this very subject. Now, sir, they argue all on one side of the question. We may have English stage players, both male and female, French dancer, Italian opera singers, -- and ten times the amount of our missionary fund will be sacrificed -- and these very men will pay their money, admire, and find no fault. And yet, forsooth, when a few hundred dollars are expended in the outfit of a missionary to carry Heaven's best gift to distant lands, they raise a hue and cry, as though the national credit were endangered. [18]

The focus of one's attention to one's own business produced some persons with wealth who attended lavishly and thoughtlessly to their own "needs", while the needy were neglected for sound economic reasons after "careful" thought.

Putting Down the Fruitlessness of Wealth

The fruitlessness of all the attention to wealth was

---

17. Beecher, Plymouth Pulpit, IV, p. 429.
18. Cookman, Speeches, p. 66. This sermon was delivered on April 19, 1830.

stressed in pulpit humor that pointed out how little of such wealth was ever given to the needy, and how much of the wealth was wasted in useless duplication of possessions. The humor noted how the uselessness of the possessions was reflected in the purposelessness and uselessness of the lives of the possessors who became as inanimate as the objects they adored. And if such purposeless life led to any activity, it was seen as fatal to others.

Accumulating Useless Objects by the "Benevolent"

Both before and after the Civil War, the benevolence of the wealthy was revealed by pulpit humor to be of little consequence compared to what they could and should be doing. Reuben Tinker noted:

> The public prints may applaud the benevolence of one who has endowed a college, a hospital, or a mission, while the servants in his household, and the clerks in his establishment, might be indebted much to the papers for such a new and unlooked-for discovery as benevolence in their master. 19

Henry Ward Beecher similarly noted how the benevolence of the wealthy was peripheral to their lives:

> They are like the oak which stands in the night to gather dew for itself, and then, if the wind in the morning shakes it, is willing to part with a few drops that it really can not hold on to; and they call themselves benevolent! 20

The humor of Tinker and Beecher also shared a vision that concentration of wealth resulted in less being given to the church or any charitable cause. Tinker observed,"The heavier the purse hangs down, the tighter the strings are drawn;" and he contended that the rich gave proportionately less than the poor: that if one thousand people

---

19. Tinker, "The Centurion," Sermons, p. 209.
20. Beecher, "Duty of Using One's Life for Others," The Sermons, First Series, p. 11.

206

were given a thousand dollars each, they would give much more than a wealthy man with one million dollars. [21]
And Tinker also noted:

> Should a rich man give as much in proportion to his means as many an indigent one does, it would be heralded through the land as a most wonderful generosity. A little religion passes for a great deal with a rich man. [22]

Beecher used humor to express a similar insight into the uselessness of concentrated wealth:

> Money, in the hands of one or two men, is like a dung-heap in a barn yard. So long as it lies in a mass it does no good; but if it was only spread out evenly on the land, how everything would grow! [23]

The uselessness to the individual or to anyone else of accumulated possessions was stressed by both Beecher and Sam Jones in the 1870's and 1880's. Jones led the people in laughter at the accomplishment of John Jacob Astor, who had died 37 years before Jones' sermon of 1885, and had left a fortune of $25,000,000 earned largely from real estate transactions in New York City after successful fur trading operations through The American Fur Co., America's first modern business monopoly:

> John Jacob Astor was walking on Broadway one day, and two fellows were walking behind him, and one says: "Jim, would you attend to all old Astor's business for your meals and clothes?" Jim said: "No; I'm no fool." "Well,"says the other, "that's all old Astor gets." He owned 20,000 houses in New York, and he couldn't live in more than one of them to save his life, and I live in that many myself, and I get along as well . . . I'm not bothered with the thing. Money is like walking sticks; one will help you along, but fifty on your back will break you down. Money is like salt water; the more you get,

---

21. Tinker, "The Rich Fool," Sermons, pp. 394-395.21. Tinker, "The Rich Fool," _Sermons_, pp. 394-395.

22. _Ibid._, p. 121.

23. Beecher, "Love of Money," _Sermons_, First Series, p. 177.

the more you want. When you are full, you want it worse than ever. 24

The image of the rich man as a slave to his own wealth and no longer in control of what he did marked Beecher's illustration of "The Deceitfulness of Riches" which also stressed how all the rich man's efforts came to nothing:

> So they roll their possessions, as winter-boys in New England used to roll the snow. In rolling, it increases in magnitude, and it is at last vaster than they can shove. And when they have amassed it, what do they do? They let it stand where it is, and the summer finds it, and melts it all away. It sinks to water again; and the water is sucked up, and goes to make snow once more for other foolish boys to roll into heaps. 25

Becoming Useless Objects

Pulpit humor throughout the period ridiculed the wealthy by likening them to the useless and inanimate objects that they accumulated around them. The centering of one's attention on oneself manifested in fine clothing provided the visible target for much of the humor. Such humor also contained a word of reproach to parents who accumulated the wealth with the result that their children lived an indolent life.

After the Civil War, Presbyterian Charles Wadsworth developed most fully this humorous treatment of the value of wealth in the achievement of man, "the result of that poetic progress whereby a man escapes all human cares, and attains to the serene dignity of a vegetable!" 26 Wadsworth stressed that potential for purpose which was wasted in the attention to the fashions wealth encouraged:

24. Jones, Sermons, Wise and Witty, p. 28.
25. Henry Ward Beecher, "The Deceitfulness of Riches," The Sermons, (8th Series), p. 20. The sermon was delivered on March 10, 1872.
26. Charles Wadsworth, "The Mothers of Sorrow," Sermons, p. 334.

> Certain I am your head has too much brain to be a
> hatter's show-block, and your heart too much brave
> blood to serve as a tailor's lay-figure. You are
> here to become men, not manikins. And if one of
> these poor ephemera of fashion, who eat their fath-
> er's bread and use their sister's perfumes, should
> cast on you a glance of patronizing friendship,
> just tell him you were created an immortal being,
> and not a zoophite -- that you live by work and do
> not vegetate by suction. 27

About the same time Alexander Crummell in Washington,
D. C., was calling such vegetating young people nothing
more than "clothes-bags;" and Crummell more directly
stressed parental responsibility for providing wealth
which allowed the young to continue in their ruinous
course. 28

The pattern of indolent young men who were supported in
their pampered indolence by parents who provided wealth
was more commonly attacked by pulpit humor after the
Civil War; but there is evidence of this pulpit humor in
previous periods. In his Lectures to Young Men, Henry
Ward Beecher had used some humor which underscored the
purposelessness of the man who found performing "Life's
great duty of feeding . . . second only in importance
to sleep." 29 And early in the 19th century this problem
of young men who cared only to dress and not to work was
faced and treated with pulpit humor at Yale College by
Timothy Dwight:

> How miserably do parents err, how deplorably must
> parents be disappointed, who send such children to
> a seminary of learning? How much less expensive,
> how much less mortifying, would it have been to
> dress them at home. 30

And juxtaposing their ultimate end in death to their life

---

27. Ibid., pp. 339-340.
28. Crummell, "Common Sense in Common Schooling,"
Africa and America, pp. 338 and 330-335.
29. Beecher, Lectures to Young Men, p. 2.
30.Dwight, Sermons, II, p. 123.

spent in attention to adorning their own form, Timothy
Dwight employed a macabre humor rare in American pulpit
literature and extended the commentary on the purposelessness of such life even if it be lived by a king:

> But his Body was now gone. His face and limbs, so
> delicately fed and adorned, were turned into a pale
> and lifeless corpse, divested of all its former
> beauty and splendour, and clothed with deformity
> and corruption. The form, which he once idolized,
> was now carried out of the palace which it so long
> and so proudly inhabited, and laid in the solitary
> grave. There it was proved to have been pampered
> only for the feast of worms. 31

Becoming Worse Than Useless Objects

In elaborating on his description of idlers at Yale,
Dwight noted a more dangerous dimension to such char-
acters:

> It is not true that they do nothing. It is only
> true, that they do nothing to any valuable purpose
> . . . They do much; but all which they do is mis-
> chievous to themselves and to others; often, very
> often it is fatal to both. 32

That the idle hours of "gentlemen" were soon filled with
activity ruinous to others was the point of some pulpit
humor. Most of such humor was directed at those in the
West who sought the easy life wealth offered during a
period of westward expansion. In San Francisco in the
1850's, William Taylor spoke sarcastically of one "gallant
young gentleman" who beguiled another man's wife into
taking her husband's fortune under the pretext of returning East to buy provisions for a new business venture:

> When she bade (her husband) adieu, her heart seemed
> almost to be breaking; and she concealed her face in
> her handkerchief to hide the tears she did not shed.

---

31. Ibid., p. 298.
32. Ibid., p. 123.

A gallant young gentleman, a particular friend of
the family, who had been boarding at the house for
a number of months, was missing about the same time;
and the poor husband soon learned that his gallant
boarder and his wife had set up for themselves in
the city of San Francisco. The 'nice young man' as
usual, soon deserted the runaway wife; and she found
-- I was going to say a home, but I will not de-
grade that endearing name with such an association
-- a hiding place in a den of infamy. The poor
husband, crushed and ruined, sunk beneath the
flood. 33

Mr. Mustachio, a stock character in the period's plays,
also made an appearance in the period's sermons as the
wealthy idler who indulged in varying degrees of villainy.
Descriptions of this character allowed the preacher to
attack simultaneously wealth and the manners, fashions,
and evil that it bred. William Taylor told this story
in its fullest form:

Now the smooth, graceful, honorable Mr. Mustachio,
dropping in occasionally to spend an evening, as the
special friend of the family, manifests a great deal
of sympathy for the poor woman. He thinks it a pity
that a lady of so rare excellence should be reduced
to such drudgery, and to cheer her up he presents
her with a few 'gold specimens' and some articles of
jewelry it may be. Then he thinks that, with the
consent of the husband, an occasional 'carriage or
buggy ride' would be very serviceable to her health;
and, as the husband has neither time nor money to
spare, and as the honorable gentleman has plenty of
both, his services, so disinterestedly proffered,
are very cordially and thankfully accepted. All
that is necessary now to restore the good lady to
cheerfulness of spirit and a happy reunion of feeling
with her husband, is to accompany this generous
friend of the family to a few balls, and a round or
two at the theaters. This process, together with
the inspiring influence of wine, does up the business for that family. 34

In such a story, the preacher could discredit many things
(balls, theaters, and wine) as evil by simply associating

33. Taylor, Seven Years of Street Preaching, pp. 319-320.
34. Ibid., p. 317.

them with Mr. Mustachio. In his <u>Sermons to Young Men</u>
in Indianapolis a decade before Taylor's sermons in San
Francisco, Henry Ward Beecher ridiculed the nobility of
a similar character:

> He is a man of honor; not that he keeps his word or
> shrinks from meanness. He defrauds his laundress,
> his tailor, and his landlord. He drinks and smokes
> at other men's expense. He gambles and swears, and
> fights -- when he is too drunk to be afraid: but
> still he is a man of honor, for he has whiskers and
> looks fierce, wears mustachios, and says: <u>Upon my
> honor, sir; Do you doubt my honor, sir</u>? 35

<u>Putting Down the Effect of Wealth Within the Church</u>

In pulpit humor, many of the characteristics of the
wealthy were pictured as carried into some churches that
sought to make the wealthy feel at home in their places
of worship. Such fashionable accommodation of the wealthy
was contrasted to the neglected mission of the church
from which the accommodation detracted. And in the pulpit
humor, the value of wealth was juxtaposed to the ultimate
values of Christianity to which men were encouraged to
attend.

<u>Ridiculing the Pillows of the Church</u>

Sam Jones urged his hearers "to be one of the pillars in
the church -- I don't mean p-i-l-l-o-w-s -- you have a
great many of this sort of pillars in your churches in
this town . . ." 36 The attention to making the church
buildings fashionable and comfortable to attract others
was seen to detract from the mission of the church, and
accommodate those who sat and did nothing. While Gruber
and other Methodists had mocked the "fashionable flum-
mey" of city churches at the beginning of the nineteenth

---

35. Beecher, <u>Lectures to Young Men</u>, p. 5.
36. Sam Jones, <u>Sermons</u>, (San Francisco: Historical Publishing Co., 1887), p. 143

century, [37] much of the pulpit humor directed at such attention to appearances was used during the periods of prosperity later in the century. Another configuration of humor turned on the deficiencies of wealthy members of churches and stressed the important place of the poor in churches.

Sam Jones mocked the fine outward appearances of many churches and Christians by likening them to a train engine that did not run, but to which some pointed with pride:

> "Look at that cab; it's the nicest cab ever sent out of the shop. Look at that bright piston rod; how it glistens in the sunshine. Look at those magnificent driving wheels." [38]

That attention was attracted away from an attitude of worship was the reason given by Henry Ward Beecher for singling out with some humor the handling of the organ at his fashionable Plymouth church:

> It is bad taste to play an organ so as to let folks know what a splendid organ we have got! . . . The business of the organ is not to pierce between every two verses of the hymns something of which people will say, "That is fine as a fiddle!" [39]

But the chief criticism of attention to fine buildings, furnishings and equipment was that such concentrations diverted funds and energies that were needed for the

---

37. Strickland, The Life of Jacob Gruber, p. 93. George Whitefield had used a little humor against those who attended church at the fashionable 11 o'clock hour: "They are not up time enough to their matins; they go and say, we thank God, who has brought us to the beginning of this day, and that when perhaps the clock strikes twelve, and they just up . . ." George Whitefield, "Neglect of Christ, The Killing Sin," Eighteen Sermons, p. 218.

38. Jones, Sermons, p. 99.

39. Beecher, The Sermons, First Series, p. 301.

mission of the church. Before the Civil War, Baptist
Jacob Knapp used humor to turn one church's attention
away from furnishings and to mission. In a church that
was embroiled in plans to fashionably furnish their place
of worship, Knapp expanded on the Old Testament text of
the king's advice to Jacob:

> 'Regard not your stuff; for the good of all the land
> of Egypt is before you.' I said the old king knew
> if they remained tinkering among their old furniture,
> they would never get to Egypt; I also told them my
> doctrine, deduced from the text, was 'Lesser good
> should be sacrificed for the greater, when the good
> of God's kingdom demanded it.' 'Now,' said I, 'your
> condition of things at the church is all stuff. Let
> the whole repairs lie over; let the painting be
> dismissed, and the carpet replaced; and when obli-
> gations to God are met, then fit up the sanctuary.'
> They smiled; and the next day repairs on the house
> ceased, furniture was returned, and when Sabbath
> came we had room for the host to come in, and work
> also. 40

Within the week the people were supporting an extended
meeting and its related revival activities. But concern
with furnishings was a continuing problem. Just before
the close of the 19th century, Emory's Methodist president Warren Akin Candler succinctly summarized the
problem that attention to furnishings posed to the church:
"The early church sold all to give; the modern church
buys more to keep from giving." 41

Financial contributions which the fashionable did make
to churches were minimized in importance by pulpit humor
which pointed out the deficiencies of such persons.
Dwight Moody characterized these persons as "paying
members rather than praying members." 42 Sam Jones put

---

40. Denison, The Evangelist, p. 354.
41. Elam Dempsey, ed., Wit and Wisdom of Warren Akin
Candler, (Nashville: Methodist Episcopal Publishing House,
1922), p. 118. The source for this sermon excerpt was a
student who took down parts of Candler's sermons in the
late 1890's.
42. Moody, The Great Redemption, p. 379.

down the financial gift of such 'believers' by noting
that it was the least these inactive Christians could do:
"There ain't a railroad in heaven or earth that don't
charge extra for a sleeper, and you ought to pay it." [43]
And by reminding congregations that 'the poor' had an
honored place in the church, some preachers mocked the
people's desire for wealth which assured no blessing.
Henry Ward Beecher observed in 1872:

> We all think, "Blessed are the poor;" and yet, if
> there be one blessing which we would prefer not to
> have more than another, it is that of poverty! [44]

During the same year in a fund raising sermon for a
Catholic hospital in Newark, Dominican Thomas Burke used
a humorous exemplum (popular in the medieval period and
earlier) to stress the church's special regard for the
poor and also to dispel the contemporary Protestant
charges that the Catholic Church was rich in material
things:

> When St. Lawrence was in his dungeon awaiting death,
> they told the Roman Governor that he was a deacon of
> the Christian Church, and held all the immense riches
> which it was whispered that they had hidden. They
> lied in that day about the priests of the Church
> just as we hear their lies now, and say that we
> priests are always trying to get the people's money.
> When the governor heard this, he called his prisoner
> and said to him, "Tell me, is it true that this
> Christian Church to which you belong possesses such
> great treasures?" "Perfectly true." "Then," he
> said, "I will give you your life on one condition:
> that you bring all the treasures of that church and
> hand them to me." St. Lawrence went out and gathered
> all the blind and the lame and the wretched and the
> poor and the sick, and brought them all, hundreds of
> them, before the palace gate, so that when the gov-
> ernor came down, anxious to gloat over the stores
> of gold and silver and precious stones which he
> looked for, he saw only this multitude. And when he
> asked St. Lawrence where was this treasure, the

43. Jones, Sermons, p. 96.
44. Beecher, "Bearing One Another's Burdens," The Sermons,
Eighth Series, p. 234.

deacon answered, "Behold! These, O praetor, are the treasures, and the only treasures of the church of Jesus Christ." 45

The story not only revealed that the poor were the wealth of the church, but also made a fool of the man who did not understand this and sought material wealth.

Raising Ultimate Values Against the Value of Wealth

A large configuration of pulpit humor resulted from juxtaposing the images of heaven, Christ and worship to scenes detailing man's quest for and display of wealth. The humor was directed less at the quest for wealth, than at the display of wealth. Such display was ridiculed in terms of both fashionable clothes and fashionable entertainment. In the early 1870's Henry Ward Beecher did use this strategy of humor to put in perspective the growing wealth of the New York financial community. Speaking of some millionaires, he noted that "The Kingdom of Heaven, to them,means the bank." [46] And to a Brooklyn congregation filled with many who commuted to their Wall Street offices each day, Beecher observed that few were bound for heaven "who go up and down Wall Street -- that straight and narrow way (at any rate, few there are that find it, and fewer that get through it to heaven, I fear) . . ." [47] It was left to the listener's imagination to envision where such Wall Street activity did lead.

But more common was a juxtaposition involving the display of wealth. Such humor contrasted the burdens and joys of the cross and resurrection to the frivolous aspirations of those who sought to be fashionable. In a sermon in Toledo at the end of the century, Sam Jones paraphrased a hymn to deal with the weighty concerns of some

45. Thomas Nicholas Burke, "Christian Charity," The Sermons, Lectures, and Addresses,(New York: Peter F. Collier, 1877), pp. 381-382. Ambrose first recorded the story of Lawrence who died in A.D. 258.
46. Beecher, The Sermons, Eighth Series, P. 25.
47. Beecher, Plymouth Pulpit, IV, p. 212.

216

in the congregation:

> Some of you sing,
> "Must Jesus bear the cross alone,
> And all the world go free?
> No, there's a cross for everyone
> And an Easter bonnet for me." 48

And the placing in heaven of such concern with fashion
produced this bit of humor on the vital mission activities chosen by some congregations:

> I once said to a brother who attended one of my
> meetings that his church was but the Lord's crochet-
> ing society. He went away insulted. I also told
> him that if the Lord did not change him somehow, he
> would not be in heaven three days before he would
> have all the angels rigged out in lace. 49

We have noted in the first chapter how Cartwright and
Gruber used humor to put down attention to fashion in
camp meetings. One additional example from Gruber
employed this style of juxtaposition. To deal with the
advent of the "petticoat and habit" which came into
vogue among young Methodist ladies in the 1820's, Gruber
employed this strategy at a camp meeting near Franklin,
Pennsylvania:

> During a prayer meeting some of these fashionables
> were grouped together, singing a hymn which was very
> popular in those days. This hymn, the chorus of
> which was:
> "I want to get to heaven, my long sought rest,"
> they sung with great animations, and their animation
> increased as they saw the presiding elder advance
> and join them. It was discovered after a while that
> he changed the last line of the chorus, and instead
> of singing, "I want to get to heaven, My long sought
> rest," he sang, "I want to get to heaven with my
> long short dress."
> One after another, as they detected the change in
> the chorus, ceased singing until all had stopped,
> and Gruber was left alone. 50

---

48. McLoughlin, Modern Revivalism, p. 320. McLoughlin
located the sermon report in the Toledo Bee.
49. Jones, Sermons, p. 52.
50. Strickland, The Life of Jacob Gruber, p. 79.

Still earlier, Timothy Dwight had juxtaposed the pressing
mission of Christ and his messengers with the leisurely
appraisal of apparel indulged in by some:

> When the messenger of Christ came to him, with the
> tidings of peace, reconciliation, the resurrection
> of life, and eternal glory; would he find leisure,
> or inclination, to scrutinize his dress, his airs,
> and his accomplishments? 51

The implication was that no person preoccupied with such
attention to fashion was fit for the kingdom.

Similar humor juxtaposed the image of Christ, his ministers, and churches to fashionable entertainments. Jones
used this device to put down dancing:

> A Methodist, a Baptist, a Presbyterian, a Catholic
> in a ball room! Their feet, that they have pledged
> should follow in the footsteps of Christ, are there
> cutting the pigeon-wing to music! 52

In an attack on the tendency to turn churches into social
clubs and approve fashionable entertainments such as the
theater, Beecher carried the juxtaposition to an extreme
(or what would have struck his congregation as an
extreme):

> To this millenial scene of church and theatre I
> only suggest a single improvement: that the vestry
> be enlarged to a ring for a circus, when not wanted
> for prayer meetings; that the Sabbath-school room
> should be furnished with card tables, and useful
> texts of scripture might be printed on the cards,
> for intervals of play and worship. 53

The force and humor of such juxtaposition may be lost on
the modern reader who has grown up in churches where it
was common place to have scripture texts on playing cards

51. Dwight, Sermons, II, p. 250. Before Dwight, Jonathan
Mayhew had based a critique of fashion on the biblical
association of the first clothing with man's sin and
shame; but this basing of humor on the biblical text was
rare. Mayhew, Sermons on the Following Subjects, p. 153.
52. Jones, Sermons, pp. 75-76.
53. Beecher, Lectures to Young Men, p. 175.

in the Sunday school room, if not a circus ring in the
vestry. Similarly, to the degree that we have succumbed
to any of the idolatries discussed in these pages, we
may find little about which to laugh in the pulpit
humor. [54] One closing passage from a Charles Finney
sermon juxtaposes prayer and a minister's presence to a
frivolous party. That the humor of this passage will
not be apparent to many today, indicates how far the
church and its ministers have come; but as with Beecher's
description of Wall Street, it is left to the reader's
imagination to envision the destination of the church
and its ministers who have come so far. Speaking of
those who hold fashionable parties, Finney argued with
pointed humor:

> In some instances, I have been told, they find a
> salve for their consciences, in the fact that their
> minister attends their parties. This, of course,
> would give weight to such an example, and if one
> professor made a party and invited their minister,
> others must do the same. The next step they take,
> may be for each to give a ball, and appoint their
> minister a manager! Why not? And perhaps, by and
> by, he will do them the favor to play the fiddle.
> In my estimation, he might quite as well do it, as
> to go and conclude such a party with prayer. 55

---

54. Albert van den Heuval, who served in the 1960's
as secretary of the division of communications for the
World Council of Churches, observed that that at which
we cannot laugh has become for us an idol. He urged
churches to develop "liturgies of ridicule" to put down
potential idols. Albert van den Heuval, Celebration,
(Chicago: Argus Communications, 1970), tape recording
No. 4136, Tape I, side 2.

55. Finney, Lectures on Revivals of Religion, p. 232.
Finney did play a fiddle in worship, a common practice
before the organs were introduced. But playing a fiddle
for the purposes of helping people worship and playing
it for "purposes" of helping people dance away their
hours at fashionable parties were in his estimation two
separate things. Ibid., p. 232.

An Evaluation

This dissertation establishes that there was a widespread use of humor in the American Pulpit among leading preachers from George Whitefield through Henry Ward Beecher, and that this humor was used purposefully to deal with many idolatries which emerged within 18th and 19th century American political, intellectual, and economic developments. For scholars of American humor, this study has significance not only as a body of humorous materials which has hitherto been largely unknown, and is needed to correct the place of religion in assessing the contours of American humor; but also as a body of humor which is related to faith (Christianity) and a particular medium of expression (preaching). This work opens the way for a number of comparative studies: comparisons of how styles and subjects of humor differ when based on different faith or no-faith and how different art forms (prose, poetry, painting, and preaching) admit different expressions of humor and faith.

For scholars of church history and 18th and 19th century studies, this dissertation testifies to a polemic dimension of much American Christian worship (its concern with the political, intellectual, and economic life of the culture) that has previously been obscured by inattention to the humor and sermons of many leading American preachers. While Perry Miller uplifted sermons for primary attention in 17th century and early 18th century studies, too many scholars have neglected sermon literature that figured prominently in shaping the popular American religious mind of the later 18th century and 19th century. This study suggests some of the rewards of attention to sermon literature of the periods.

For those in the church and particularly for those planning worship and preaching, this study suggests the use of humor as one strategy to deal with cultural

idolatries. The pastoral emphasis of many modern ministers may not provide the distance from which the traveling and lecturing 19th century preachers glimpsed
their parishioners' idolatries and exorcised them; and
the interest of many 20th century theologians in humor
as an expression of ambiguous truth and an end in itself
may lead some to see the 18th and 19th century use of
humor as a low one. But the earlier humor in the American
pulpit should remind the modern pastor that his task is
not only to develop the best expression of divine truth,
but also to lay low the idols that stand forth in the
culture and hold man's attention and service away from
God.

In the preface to this study, we noted Reinhold Niebuhr's
thought that laughter is appropriate in the vestibule of
the temple, but not in the holy of holies. Such a thought
is based on a misunderstanding of the purpose and meaning
of Christian worship. Properly understood, Christian
worship is held not in the Jewish way at the end of time
on a Sabbath day of rest, but rather on the first day
of a work week. When Constantine declared Sunday to be
a holiday and no longer the first day of the work week,
much of the tension and symbolism in the day of Christian
worship was lost. The early American Puritans were
further mistaken when they identified the day of their
worship with the Old Testament concept of the Sabbath.
But the 18th and 19th century preachers studied in this
dissertation restored something of the earlier tension,
when they put laughter to work in worship; for when we
see worship not as an end in itself, but rather as a
means to bring God's kingdom on earth, then laughter is
not only welcomed, but needed in the worship center.

APPENDIX ONE

PREACHERS NOTED FOR PULPIT HUMOR

Name	Period of Preaching	Denomination
Alexander, Archibald	1791-1851	Presbyterian
Arnold, Smith	1800-1839	Methodist
Asbury, Daniel	1786-1825	Methodist
Axley, James	1822-1871	Methodist
Bacon, Leonard	1825-1881	Congregational
Balch, Stephen Bloomer	1779-1833	Presbyterian
Barnes, David	1753-1811	Unitarian
Beecher, Henry Ward	1837-1887	Congregational
Beecher, Lyman	1799-1853	Presbyterian
Bethune, George W.	1827-1862	Dutch Reform
Buell, Samuel	1741-1798	Presbyterian
Bumpass, Sidney	1837-1851	Methodist
Burke, Thomas Nicholas	? -1883	Catholic
Bushnell, Horace	1833-1876	Congregational
Byles, Mather	1733-1788	Congregational
Cartwright, Peter	1802-1872	Methodist
Caskey, Thomas W.	? -1896	Methodist
Chase, Abner	1810-1854	Methodist
Clark, Thomas	1764-1793	Associate Reform (Presbyterian)
Coffin, Charles	1799-1853	Presbyterian
Cogswell, James	1744-1807	Congregational
Cookman, George G.	1826-1841	Methodist
Cox, J. T.	ca.1853	Methodist
Cravens, William	1800-1826	Methodist
Crummell, Alexander	? - 1898	Episcopal
Cushman, Elisha	1809-1838	Baptist
Dannelly, James	1818-1855	Methodist
Dow, Lorenzo	1794-1834	Methodist
Durbin, John	1815-1876	Methodist
Dwight, Timothy	1777-1817	Congregational
Eaton, Samuel	1764-1822	Congregational
Farrand, Daniel	1752-1803	Congregational
Finney, Charles	1821-1875	Congregational
Flint, Timothy	1801-1840	Congregational-Presbyterian
French, Jonathan	1772-1809	Congregational
Gibson, Robert	1818-1837	Pres. Reform
Glendy, John	1799-1832	Presbyterian
Going, Jonathan	1811-1844	Baptist
Grafton, Joseph	1784-1836	Baptist
Gruber, Jacob	1800-1850	Methodist

Haynes, Lemuel	1785-1833	Congregational
Henderson, Robert	1788-1834	Presbyterian
Hibbard, Billy	1798-1844	Methodist
Hildreth, Hosea	1811-1835	Unitarian
Hinton, Isaac Taylor	1832-1847	Baptist
Howe, Nathaniel	1790-1837	Congregational
Ireland, John	1861-1918	Catholic
Jasper, John J.	? -1893	Baptist
Johnston, John	1806-1855	Presbyterian
Jones, Sam	1871-1906	Methodist
Kirkland, John Thornton	1793-1840	Unitarian
Knapp, Jacob	1822-1874	Baptist
Lee, Jesse	1782-1816	Methodist
Leland, John	1775-1841	Baptist
Lockley, Elijah B.	ca. 1852	Methodist
Mayhew, Jonathan	1747-1766	Unitarian (Congregational)
McAuley, William	1794-1851	Assoc. Reform (Presbyterian)
Milburn, William	1843-1903	Methodist
Mills, Samuel John	1763-1833	Congregational
Moody, Dwight Lyman	1860-1899	Non-denominational
Moody, Samuel	1698-1747	Congregational
Nisbet, Charles	1785-1804	Presbyterian
Parker, Theodore	1837-1860	Unitarian
Pattillo, Henry	1757-1801	Presbyterian
Pierpont, John	1819-1866	Unitarian
Porter, Ebenezar	1794-1834	Congregational
Porter, Samuel	1789-1825	Presbyterian
Potter, Henry C.	1857-1908	Episcopalian
Roan, John	1744-1775	Presbyterian
Sewall, Jotham	1798-1850	Congregational
Shober, Gottleib	1810-1838	Lutheran
Smalley, John	1757-1820	Congregational
Speece, Conrad	1801-1836	Presbyterian
Stanford, John	1786-1834	Baptist
Stanton, Benj. Franklin	1815-1843	Presbyterian
Stearns, Charles	1781-1826	Unitarian
Stimson, H. K.	1830- ?	Baptist
Storrs, Richard, Jr.	1846-1900	Congregational
Strong, Nathan	1772-1816	Congregational
Swan, Jabez	1822- ?	Baptist
Taylor, Edward	1815-1871	Methodist
Taylor, William	1841-1902	Methodist
Thacher, Thomas	1756-1812	Unitarian
Tinker, Reuben	1830-1854	Presbyterian

Turner, James	1791-1828	Presbyterian
Upham, Samuel	1856-1904	Methodist
Wadsworth, Charles	1842-1882	Presbyterian
Welch, Moses Cook	1754-1824	Congregational
Whitefield, George	1736-1770	Anglican(Methodist)
Worden, Jesse Babcock	1818-1855	Baptist
Wynkoop, Richard	1826-1842	Assoc. Reform (Presbyterian)

"The period of preaching" normally denotes the time from ordination to death (although in some cases the earliest date represents extensive preaching before ordination and the last date represents termination of preaching for reasons other than death).

APPENDIX TWO

HUMOR AND VARIABLES IN SPRAGUE'S

ANNALS OF THE AMERICAN PULPIT, I-IX

Volume	Pages	Men	DDs	Humor in Sermons	(DD)	Humor in lives	Total	%
I. Congregational (1629-1770)	723	208	53	7	(3)	30	37	18*
II. Congregational (1771-1841)	763	144	82	6	(3)	28	34	24
III. Presbyterian (1683-1792)	632	126	62	9	(5)	19	28	22
IV. Presbyterian (1782-1841)	825	129	81	7	(5)	23	30	23
V. Episcopal	815	152	90	0	(0)	25	25	16
VI. Baptist	854	172	33	7	(2)	24	31	18
VII. Methodist	841	181	12	8	(0)	28	36	20
VIII. Unitarian	571	81	49	7	(5)	27	34	42
IXa. Lutheran	216	55	15	1	(0)	5	6	10
IXb. American Assoc., Associate Reform, and Reformed Presbyterian	392	76	24	4	(2)	21	25	33
TOTALS		1324		56		230	286	22

* If one considers only those ordained after 1696 (a time period more contiguous with the other groups) then this percentage is much higher: of 124 ordained, 7 exhibit humor in their sermons, and 21 more in their lives for 23%. This adjustment is probably fairer as there are very few of the personal letters (which usually testify to any humor) for persons before 1696.

The one variable having relation to the percentage of humor within a denomination is the number of pages devoted per man (e.g. the number and length of personal letters describing the minister). The more we know about the ministers, the more representative the users of humor appear. The high percentage among Unitarians could be explained by the larger number of pages devoted to each man; and the lower percentage among Lutherans may be due to the absence of many personal letters about them. (The low percentage for Episcopalians may result from the disruption of that church during the Revolution, and the subsequent infrequence of personal letters

about the priests). But other factors should not be
discounted as Unitarians may have had more subjects
to ridicule and fewer restraints. As for other variables
(geography, etc.), it is not possible to assign most of
the ministers to exclusive categories of "frontier"
preaching or "settled" preaching. The ministers themselves (with the exception of many Congregationalists,
Unitarians, and Episcopalians) were very mobile. In any
event, although these statistics are suggestive of the
commonness of humor's use in ministers' lives and sermons,
we should not take any of the figures too seriously.

BIBLIOGRAPHY

Primary Sources

Sermons

Alexander, Archibald, "Means of Growth in Grace," The
American National Preacher, (January, 1828),
No. 8, pp. 122-128.

_____, "The Nature and Means of Growth in Grace," The
American National Preacher, (January, 1828), III,
No. 8, pp. 113-121.

_____, "Objections Obviated, and God Glorified, By the
Success of the Gospel Among the Heathen," The
National Preacher, (October, 1829), IV, No. 5,
pp. 253-268.

_____, Practical Sermons: To Be Read in Families and
Social Meetings, Philadelphia, Presbyterian
Board of Pub., 1850.

Bacon, Leonard, The American Church, New York,
Baker, Goodwin and Co., 1852.

_____, "Duties of Young Christians," The National
Preacher, (June, 1828), III, No. 1, pp. 1-8.

_____, "The Example of Christ," The National Preacher,
(June, 1828), III, No. 1, pp. 9-16.

_____, Four Commemorative Discourses, New Haven, T. J.
Stafford, 1866.

_____, The Jugglers Detected: A Discourse, New Haven,
Thomas H. Pease, 1861.

_____, "The Primitive Christians," The American National
Preacher, (June, 1841), XV, No. 6, pp. 125-141.

_____, The Relation of Faith to Missions, Boston, T. R.
Marvin, 1852.

_____, "What Is It To Become a Christian," The American
National Preacher, (June, 1841), XV, No. 6,
pp. 141-148.

Balch, Stephen Bloomer, Two Sermons, on the
Certain and Final Perseverance of the Saints,
Georgetown, Day and Hancock, 1791.

Barnes, David, Sermons, Boston, Munroe, Frances,
and Parker, 1815.

Beecher, Henry Ward, Evolution and Religion, New York, Fords, Howard, and Hulbert, 1886.

_____, Forty-eight Sermons (preached prior to 1867), 2 vols., London, R. D. Dickinson, 1871.

_____, Henry Ward Beecher's Last Sermons; Preached in Plymouth Church, Brooklyn since Mr. Beecher's return from England, October, 1886, London, James Clarke, 1887.

_____, Lectures to Young Men, Boston, J. R. Jewett, 1846.

_____, Life Thoughts, gathered from the extemporaneous discourses of Henry Ward Beecher by one of his congregation, Boston, Phillips, Sampson, and Co., 1858.

_____, Plymouth Pulpit, Sermons preached in Plymouth Church, Brooklyn, 4 vols., Boston, The Pilgrim Press, 1875.

_____, Plymouth Pulpit, new series, 2 vols., New York, Fords, Howard, and Hulbert, 1875-85.

_____, The Sermons of Henry Ward Beecher, 8 vols., New York, J. B. Ford, 1869-1873.

Beecher, Lyman, "The Gospel the Only Security for Eminent and Abiding National Prosperity," The National Preacher, (March, 1829), III, No. 10, pp. 145-151.

_____, "Preeminent Importance of the Christian Sabbath," The National Preacher, (March, 1829), III, No. 10, pp. 155-160.

_____, "Propriety and Importance of Efforts to Evangelize the Nation," The National Preacher, (March, 1829), III, No. 10, pp. 151-155.

_____, The Reformation Society, Four Sermons, New York, Arno Press, 1972.

_____, Works, 3 vols., Boston, Jewett, 1852-53.

Bethune, George W., Orations and Occasional Discourses, New York, George Putnam, 1850.

_____, Our Liberties: Their Danger and Means of Preserving Them, Philadelphia, Mentz & Rovoudt, 1835.

_____, Sermons, Philadelphia, Mentz & Rovoudt, 1846.

Buell, Samuel, Christ the Grand Subject of Gospel
    Preaching, New York, Parker and Weyman, 1775.

_____, The Excellence and Importance of the Saving
    Knowledge of the Lord Jesus Christ, New York,
    Parker, 1761.

_____, A Sermon, Delivered at the Ordination of the Rev.
    Aaron Woolworth, Elizabethtown, n.p., 1788.

Burke, Thomas Nicholas, Sermons, and Lectures on
    Moral and Historical Subjects, New York, Lynch,
    Cole, and Meehan, 1873.

_____, The Sermons, Lectures, and Addresses, New York,
    Peter F. Collier, 1877.

Bushnell, Horace, "American Politics," The
    American National Preacher, (December, 1840),
    Vol. XIV, No, 12, pp. 189-204.

_____, Christ and His Salvation, New York, Charles
    Scribner, 1864.

_____, Crises of the Church, Hartford, Daniel Burgess
    and Company, 1835.

_____, A Discourse on the Slavery Question, Hartford,
    Case, Tiffany and Company, 1839.

_____, Sermons for the New Life, New York, Charles
    Scribner, 1858.

_____, Sermons on Living Subjects, New York, Charles
    Scribner's Sons, 1901.

_____, The Spirit in Man, New York, Charles Scribner's
    Sons, 1910.

_____, Work and Play; or Literary Varieties, New York,
    Charles Scribner, 1864.

Byles, Mather, The Character of the Perfect and
    Upright Man, Boston, S. Gerrish, 1729.

_____, The Flourish of the Annual Spring Improved in a
    Sermon, Boston, Thos. and John Fleet, 1769.

_____, A Sermon, New Haven, Green, 1760.

_____, A Sermon on the Nature and Importance of Conver-
    sion, Boston, Edes and Gill, 1769.

Cogswell, James, A Sermon Preached Before the
    General Assembly, New London, n.p., 1771.

Cookman, George, Speeches Delivered on Various
    Occasions by George C. Cookman of the Baltimore
    Annual Conference and Chaplain to the Senate of
    the United States, New York, George Lane, 1840.

Crummell, Alexander, Africa and America, Miami,
    Mnemosyne Press, 1969.

_____, The Greatness of Christ and Other Sermons, New
    York, Thomas Whittaker, 1882.

Dow, Lorenzo, The Dealings of God, Man, and the
    Devil as Exemplified in the Life, Experiences
    and Travels of Lorenzo Dow, 2 vols., New York,
    Nafis & Cornish, 1849.

Dwight, Timothy, Sermons, 2 vols., New Haven
    Hezekiah Howe, Durrie, and Peck, 1828.

_____, Theology Explained and Defended in a Series of
    Sermons, 4 vols., New York, Harper & Bros. 1849.

Eaton, Samuel, A Sermon Delivered at the Interment
    of the Hon. Jacob Abbot of Brunswick Maine,
    Brunswick, Joseph Griffin, 1820.

Farrand, Daniel, Redemption From Death: Or Christ
    Triumphed Over the Grave, Hartford, Thomas Green.

Finney, Charles, The Guilt of Sin; evangelical
    messages, Grand Rapids, Kregel, 1965.

_____, Lectures on Revivals of Religion, William
    McLoughlin, ed., Cambridge, Belknap Press of
    Harvard University Press, 1960.

_____, Lectures to Professing Christians, Oberlin, E. J.
    Goodrich, 1880.

_____, Sermons on Gospel Themes, New York, F. H. Revell,
    1876.

_____, Sermons on Important Subjects, New York, John S.
    Taylor, 1836.

_____, Sermons on the Way of Salvation, Oberlin, E. J.
    Goodrich, 1891.

_____, So Great Salvation: evangelistic messages, Grand
    Rapids, Kregel, 1965.

_____, True Saints; revival messages, Grand Rapids,
    Kregel, 1967.

French, Jonathan, A Sermon Preached Before His
    Excellency Samuel Adams, Boston, Adams & Larkin, 1796.

Glendy, John, An Oration on the Death of George
Washington, Staunton, Wise, 1800.

Going, Jonathan, A Discourse Delivered at Worcester,
Worcester, W. Manning, 1825.

Haynes, Lemuel, Universal Salvation, A Very
Ancient Doctrine: With Some Account of the Life
and Character of its Author, Newburyport, W. &
J. Gilman, 1819.

Henderson, Robert, A Series of Sermons on Practical
and Familiar Subjects, 2 vols., Knoxville,
Haiskell and Brown, 1823.

Howe, Nathaniel, A Century Sermon, Andover, Flagg,
and Gould, 1816.

Ireland, John, The Church and Modern Society,
St. Paul, The Pioneer Press, 1905.

Jasper, John, The Sun Do Move!, New York,
Brentano, 1882.

Jones, Samuel Porter, Hot Shots; Sermons and Sayings,
Nashville, S. Western Publishing House, 1895.

_____, Sam Jones' Sermons, 2 vols., Chicago, Rhodes and
McClure, 1896.

_____, Sermons, Philadelphia, Scammel & Co., 1886.

_____, Sermons, San Francisco, Historical Pub. Co.,1887.

_____, Sermons, Wise and Witty, New York, Cheap Pub.
Co., 1885.

_____, Sermons and Sayings, 2 vols., Nashville, Southern
Methodist Pub. House, 1885.

_____, Tabernacle Sermons of Rev. Sam P. Jones, St.
Joseph, The Herald Pub. Co., 1885.

_____, Thunderbolts, Nashville, Jones and Haynes, 1895.

Kirkland, John, A Sermon Delivered Before the
Massachussetts Society for the Suppression of
Intemperance, Boston, J. Eliot, 1814.

_____, A Sermon Preached Before the Ancient and Honor-
able Artillery Company, Boston, Belknap, 1795.

_____, A Sermon Preached at Taunton, Cambridge, Hilliard,
1800.

Knapp, Jacob, Universalism a Counterfeit, Boston, W. E. Newell, 1860.

Leland,John, The Writings of John Leland, L. F. Greene, ed., New York, Arno Press, 1969.

Mayhew, Jonathan, Christian Sobriety; Being Eight Sermons Preached on Titus II.6, Boston, Draper, Edes, Gill and Fleet, 1763.

_____, Popish Idolatry, Boston, Draper, Edes, Gill and Fleet, 1765.

_____, Sermons: Seven Sermons, New York, Arno, 1969.

_____, Sermons on the Following Subjects, Boston, Draper, 1755.

Mills, Samuel John, The Nature and Importance of the Duty of Singing Praise to God Considered, Hartford, Ebenezer Watson, 1775.

Moody, Dwight L., Glad Tidings, New York, E. B. Treat, 1877.

_____, The Gospel Awakening, Chicago, F. H. Revell,1883.

_____, The Great Redemption; or Gospel Light, Chicago, The Century Book Co., 1888.

_____, Great Joy, Chicago, Palmer, Augyr & Co., 1877.

_____, Moody's Great Sermons, Chicago, Laird & Co.,1900.

_____, Moody's Latest Sermons, Providence, The News Co. 1894.

_____, Moody's Latest Sermons, Chicago, Bible Institute, 1900.

_____, New Sermons, Addresses and Prayers, San Francisco, J. T. Farrar, 1877.

_____, Overcoming Life and Other Sermons, Chicago, F. H. Revell, 1896.

_____, Sermons and Addresses, Chicago, Fairbanks, Palmer, and Company, 1884.

_____, Sowing and Reaping, New York, F. H. Revell & Co., 1896.

_____, Ten Days With D. L. Moody, New York, J. S. Ogilvie, 1886.

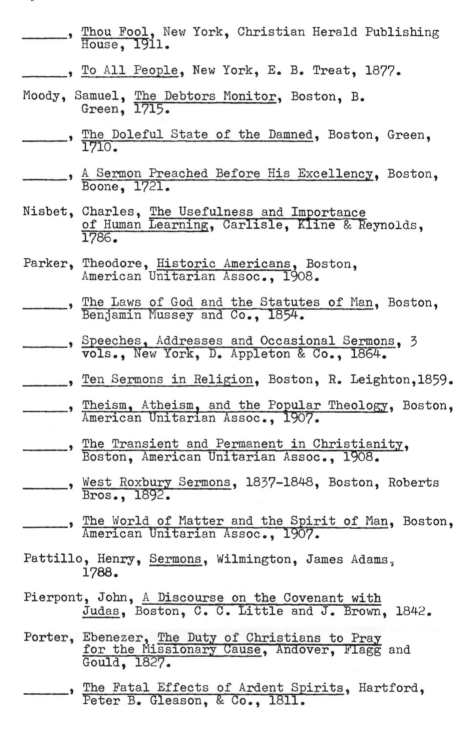

_____, Thou Fool, New York, Christian Herald Publishing House, 1911.

_____, To All People, New York, E. B. Treat, 1877.

Moody, Samuel, The Debtors Monitor, Boston, B. Green, 1715.

_____, The Doleful State of the Damned, Boston, Green, 1710.

_____, A Sermon Preached Before His Excellency, Boston, Boone, 1721.

Nisbet, Charles, The Usefulness and Importance of Human Learning, Carlisle, Kline & Reynolds, 1786.

Parker, Theodore, Historic Americans, Boston, American Unitarian Assoc., 1908.

_____, The Laws of God and the Statutes of Man, Boston, Benjamin Mussey and Co., 1854.

_____, Speeches, Addresses and Occasional Sermons, 3 vols., New York, D. Appleton & Co., 1864.

_____, Ten Sermons in Religion, Boston, R. Leighton, 1859.

_____, Theism, Atheism, and the Popular Theology, Boston, American Unitarian Assoc., 1907.

_____, The Transient and Permanent in Christianity, Boston, American Unitarian Assoc., 1908.

_____, West Roxbury Sermons, 1837-1848, Boston, Roberts Bros., 1892.

_____, The World of Matter and the Spirit of Man, Boston, American Unitarian Assoc., 1907.

Pattillo, Henry, Sermons, Wilmington, James Adams, 1788.

Pierpont, John, A Discourse on the Covenant with Judas, Boston, C. C. Little and J. Brown, 1842.

Porter, Ebenezer, The Duty of Christians to Pray for the Missionary Cause, Andover, Flagg and Gould, 1827.

_____, The Fatal Effects of Ardent Spirits, Hartford, Peter B. Gleason, & Co., 1811.

_____, Lectures on Homiletics and Preaching and on Public Prayer; Together With Sermons and Letters, Andover, Flagg, Gould and Newman, 1834.

Porter, Samuel, A Discourse of the Decrees of God, the Perseverance of the Saints Perfection, Pittsburgh, 1793.

Smalley, John, Sermons, Hartford, Lincoln and Gleason, 1803.

_____, Sermons, Middleton, Hart and Lincoln, 1814.

Speece, Conrad, A Sermon Delivered at Petersville Church, Richmond, Blagrove & Trueheart, 1912.

Stanford, John, A Sermon, New York, T. & J. Swords, 1803.

Stearns, Charles, A Sermon, Boston, Ebenezer T. Andrews, 1792.

Storrs, Richard Salter, Jr., Christianity: its Destined Supremacy on Earth, New York, Almon Merwin, 1851.

_____, Colleges, A Power in Civilization to be Used for Christ, New York, N. A. Larkins, 1856.

_____, "God's Moral System, Superior to the Material," The National Preacher, New York, D. A. Woodworth, 1850, pp. 7-20.

_____, "The Manner of Self-Examination," The American National Preacher, (July, 1847), XXI, No. 7, pp. 149-161.

_____, Orations and Addresses, Boston, The Pilgrim Press, 1901.

Strong, Nathan, A Fast Sermon, Hartford, Peter Gleason and Co., 1812.

_____, The Mutability of Human Life A Sermon, Hartford, Hudson and Co., 1811.

_____, A Sermon Delivered in Presence of His Excellency Samuel Huntington, Hartford, Hudson and Goodwin, 1790.

_____, A Sermon Preached at the Annual Thanksgiving, Hartford, Hudson & Goodwin, 1797.

_____, A Sermon Preached on the State Fast, Hartford, Hudson & Goodwin, 1798.

234

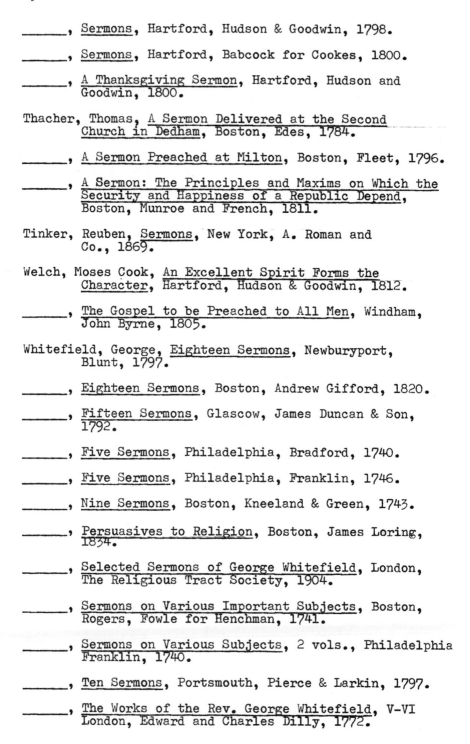

_____, Sermons, Hartford, Hudson & Goodwin, 1798.

_____, Sermons, Hartford, Babcock for Cookes, 1800.

_____, A Thanksgiving Sermon, Hartford, Hudson and Goodwin, 1800.

Thacher, Thomas, A Sermon Delivered at the Second Church in Dedham, Boston, Edes, 1784.

_____, A Sermon Preached at Milton, Boston, Fleet, 1796.

_____, A Sermon: The Principles and Maxims on Which the Security and Happiness of a Republic Depend, Boston, Munroe and French, 1811.

Tinker, Reuben, Sermons, New York, A. Roman and Co., 1869.

Welch, Moses Cook, An Excellent Spirit Forms the Character, Hartford, Hudson & Goodwin, 1812.

_____, The Gospel to be Preached to All Men, Windham, John Byrne, 1805.

Whitefield, George, Eighteen Sermons, Newburyport, Blunt, 1797.

_____, Eighteen Sermons, Boston, Andrew Gifford, 1820.

_____, Fifteen Sermons, Glascow, James Duncan & Son, 1792.

_____, Five Sermons, Philadelphia, Bradford, 1740.

_____, Five Sermons, Philadelphia, Franklin, 1746.

_____, Nine Sermons, Boston, Kneeland & Green, 1743.

_____, Persuasives to Religion, Boston, James Loring, 1834.

_____, Selected Sermons of George Whitefield, London, The Religious Tract Society, 1904.

_____, Sermons on Various Important Subjects, Boston, Rogers, Fowle for Henchman, 1741.

_____, Sermons on Various Subjects, 2 vols., Philadelphia Franklin, 1740.

_____, Ten Sermons, Portsmouth, Pierce & Larkin, 1797.

_____, The Works of the Rev. George Whitefield, V-VI London, Edward and Charles Dilly, 1772.

Autobiographies

Beecher, Henry Ward, Autobiographical Reminiscences of
H. W. Beecher, T. J. Ellinwood, ed., New York,
Frederick Stokes Co., 1898.

Beecher, Lyman, Autobiography, I-II, Charles Beecher, ed.,
New York, Harper & Bros., 1864-1865.

Cartwright, Peter, Autobiography of Peter Cartwright, The
Backwoods Preacher, W. P. Strickland, ed.,
London, Arthur Hill, Virtue & Co., n.d.

_____, Fifty Years As A Presiding Elder, W. S. Hooper,
ed., Cincinnati, Cranston & Stowe, 1871.

Chase, Abner, Recollections of the Past, New York,
Methodist Conference Office, 1846.

Dow, Lorenzo, Biography and Miscellany, Norwich, W.
Faulkner, 1834.

_____, The Dealings of God, Man, and the Devil as
Exemplified in the Life, Experiences and Travels
of Lorenzo Dow, New York, Nafis & Cornish, 1849.

_____, History of Cosmopolite, Philadelphia, J. B.
Smith, 1859.

_____, Quintessence of Lorenzo's Work, Philadelphia,
Jos. Rakestraw, 1815.

Finney, Charles, Memoirs, New York, A. S. Barnes & Co.,
1876.

Flint, Timothy, Recollections of the Last Ten Years,
Boston, Cummings, Hilliard & Co., 1826.

Hibbard, Billy, Memoirs of the Life and Travels of B.
Hibbard, New York, Piercy & Reed, 1843.

Johnston, John, The Autobiography and Ministerial Life of
Rev. John Johnston, DD, James Carnahan, ed., New
York, M. W. Dodd, 1856.

Knapp, Jacob, Autobiography of Elder Jacob Knapp, New
York, Sheldon & Co., 1868.

Lee, Jesse, Memoir of the Rev. Jesse Lee with Extracts
From His Journals, New York, Arno Press and New
York Times, 1969.

Lewis, Henry Taliaferro, Harp of a Thousand Strings With
Waifs of Wit and Pathos, n.p., 1907.

236

Parker, Theodore, Autobiography, Poems, and Prayers, Rufus Leighton, Boston, American Unitarian Assoc., 1907.

Stimson, Hiram, From Stage Coach to the Pulpit, T. W. Greene, ed., St. Louis, R. A. Campbell, 1874.

Swan, Jabez, The Evangelist: or Life and Labors of Rev. Jabez S. Swan, F. Denison, ed., Waterford, W. L. Peckham, 1873.

Taylor, William, California Life Illustrated, New York, Carlton & Porter, 1858.

_____, Seven Years' Street Preaching in San Francisco, W. P. Strickland, ed., New York, Phillips and Hunt, 1856.

_____, Story of My Life, New York, Eaton & Mains, 1896.

Whitefield, George, The Works of the Rev. George Whitefield, I-IV, London, Edward and Charles Dilly, 1772.

Secondary Sources

Biographies

Bacon, Theodore Davenport, Leonard Bacon: A Statesman in the Church, Benj. W. Bacon, ed., New Haven, Yale University Press, 1931.

Burrows, George, Impressions of Dr. Wadsworth as a Preacher, San Francisco, Towne & Bacon, 1863.

Cheney, Mary Busnell, Life and Letters of Horace Bushnell, New York, Harper & Brothers, 1880.

Cooley, Timothy Mather, Sketches of the Life and Character of the Rev. Lemuel Haynes, A. M., New York, Negro University Press, 1969.

Cross, Barbara M., Horace Bushnell: Minister to a Changing America, Chicago, University of Chicago Press, 1958.

Dix, John Ross, Pulpit Portrait, or Pen-pictures of Distinguished American Divines; With Sketches of Congregations and Choirs; and Incidental Notices of Eminent British Preachers, Boston, Tappan and Whittmore, 1854.

Eaton, Arthur, The Famous Mather Byles, Boston, W. A. Butterfield, 1914.

Fitzgerald, O. P., California Sketches, Nashville, Southern Methodist Publishing House, 1880.

Fowler, Henry, The American Pulpit: Sketches, Biographical and Descriptive of Living American Preachers, New York, H. M. Fairchild Co., 1856.

Haven, Gilbert, and Russell, Thomas, Life of Father Taylor, The Sailor Preacher, Boston, The Boston Port and Seaman's Aid Society, 1904.

Hodges, George, Henry Codman Potter, Seventh Bishop of New York, New York, Macmillan Co., 1915.

Howard, Leon, The Connecticut Wits, Chicago, University of Chicago Press, 1943.

Joy, James Richard, The Teachers of Drew 1867-1942, Madison, Drew University, 1942.

n.a., Leonard Bacon: Pastor of the First Church in New Haven, New Haven, Morehouse & Taylor, 1882.

Macartney, Clarence Edward, Six Kings of the American Pulpit, Philadelphia, Westminster Press, 1942.

Matthews, Lyman, Memoir of the Life and Character of Ebenezer Porter, D.D., Boston, Perkins and Marvin, 1837.

Milburn, William Henry, The Lance, Cross and Canoe, New York, N. D. Thompson Pub. Co., 1892.

_____, The Pioneers, Preachers, and People, New York, Derby and Jackson, 1860.

_____, The Rifle, Axe, and Saddle-bags, New York, Derby and Jackson, 1857.

_____, Ten Years of Preacher Life: Chapters from an Autobiography, New York, Derby and Jackson, 1860.

Miller, Samuel, Memoirs of the Rev. Charles Nisbet, D.D. Late President of Dickinson College, Carlisle, New York, Robert Carter, 1840.

Moynihan, James H., The Life of Archbishop John Ireland, New York, Harper & Bros., 1953.

Parkinson, Sarah Woods, Charles Nisbet, First President of Dickinson College, n.p., n.d.

Ridgaway, Henry B., The Life of the Rev. Alfred Cookman;
with Some Account of his Father, The Rev. George
Grimston Cookman, New York, Nelson and Phillips,
1874.

Roche, John A., The Life of John Price Durbin, New York,
Phillips and Hunt, 1889.

Sellers, Charles Coleman, Lorenzo Dow, The Bearer of the
Word, New York, Minton, Balch & Co., 1928.

Sewall, Jotham, A Memoir of Rev. Jotham Sewall, Boston,
Tappan & Whittemore, 1853.

Sprague, William, ed., Annals of the American Pulpit,
I-IX, New York, Robert Carter & Bros., 1857-1869.

Srygley, F. D., Seventy Years in Dixie: Recollections,
Sermons, and Sayings of T. W. Caskey and Others,
Nashville, Gospel Advocate Publishing Co., 1891.

Stowe, Calvin E., "Sketches and Recollections of Dr.
Lyman Beecher," The Congregational Quarterly,
Vol. VI, No. III, (July, 1864).

Strickland, W. P., The Life of Jacob Gruber, New York,
Carlton & Porter, 1860.

Tipple, Ezra Squier, Drew Theological Seminary, 1867-
1917, A Review of the First Half Century, New
York, The Methodist Book Concern, 1917.

Wakeley, J. B., The Bold Frontier Preacher, A Portraiture
of Rev. William Cravens of Virginia, 1766-1826,
Cincinnati, Hitchcock & Walden, 1869.

Brewer, J. Mason, The Word on the Brazos: Negro Preacher
Tales from the Brazos Bottoms of Texas, Austin,
University of Texas Press, 1953.

Kirk, Eleanor, Beecher as a Humorist, Selections from
the published works of Henry Ward Beecher, New
York, Fords, Howard and Hulbert, 1887.

Spalding, Henry D., ed., Encyclopedia of Black Folklore
and Humor, Middle Village, Jonathan David Pub.,
1972.

Weisfeld, Israel Harold, The Pulpit Treasury of Wit and
Humor, New York, Prentice Hall, 1950.

INDEX

As the table of content serves to guide the reader to topics or idolatries at which pulpit humor was directed, this index is reserved to guide the reader to each instance in which a preacher's name occurs within this volume.

About the Author: Doug Adams serves as Associate Professor of Worship and Preaching on the Carl Patton Chair at Pacific School of Religion and as chairperson of the doctoral faculty in "Theology and the Arts" at the Graduate Theological Union, Berkeley, California. He is Smithsonian Fellow in nineteenth century American religion and art and a fellow in the North American Academy of Liturgy.

His previously published books include Celebrate The Revolution: Churches and The Shaping of the State, 1776 and 1976, Dancing Christmas Carols, and Congregational Dancing In Christian Worship. He has edited numerous books including Page Smith's Religious Origins of The American Revolution, Margaret Taylor's A Time To Dance: Symbolic Movement In Worship, and Constance Fisher's Dancing The Old Testament. He is currently working on a new volume to be entitled Meeting House to Camp Meeting: Free Church Worship In America From 1620 Through 1835.

He serves on the editorial board of Modern Liturgy and has authored numerous articles on historical and contemporary ways of worship and preaching that have appeared in that journal as well as in Liturgy, Worship, Share, Colloquy, and New Conversations. He leads workshops and lectures widely across North America and around the world from Jerusalem to Tahiti and Fiji. He has served as pastor in California and is ordained in the United Church of Christ. He received the B.A. from Duke University, the M.A. and M.Div. from Pacific School of Religion, and the Th.D. from The Graduate Theological Union.

Cost $6.95 — Make check payable to **THE SHARING COMPANY**, attach it to this form, and mail to **THE SHARING COMPANY**, P.O. BOX 2224   AUSTIN, TEXAS 78767

name _____

address _____

city _____ state _____ zip _____

enclosed is a check for $ _____ ; please send me _____ copies of Doug Adams' **HUMOR IN THE AMER-ICAN PULPIT FROM GEORGE WHITEFIELD THROUGH H. W. BEECHER** at $6.95 a copy.

PLUS $1 FOR POSTAGE & HANDLING